Probably Up To No Good

A Memoir

To Marti & Sig
I have many happy
memories g time
spent with you both — Hagen
Rosemary

Rosemary Hagen

Table of Contents

Edward, his dog, Vannie, and me a few years before Edward almost killed me!

Trip to Tower

My mother had a cabin in the north woods on Lake Vermilion in Minnesota. She and my dad, who died when I was three, had purchased it from a Boy Scout leader for $900. It was originally built by his fledging Boy Scout Troop. They made a fireplace by cementing rocks to a wooden barrel and then starting a fire in it. After the barrel burned they had a fireplace. We used it almost every night, and although the cabin now is only half there, the fireplace is still proudly standing, ready to go.

The logs were unpeeled, so the carpenter ants really had fun. Every year we came up there were piles of ant sawdust

Edward by the fireplace

by all the walls. We had a friend down the lake who made superior log cabins. He offered again and again to build us a good one which would last forever, but Mom refused. Dad had died, and she had memories of him in the old cabin. Nothing could be changed.

That was OK with me. The ants left me alone and we always had a cat along to eat the mice. And the cabin lasted. The fireplace is still standing, rocks still in place. This cabin had a history and it was responsible for the relationship between me and my brother Edward for a sizable part of our lives.

My brother and I would go up to the lake for two weeks with Mom, and then for a month plus a week with my Auntie Hazel, who got a longer

Our cabin

vacation because she worked for the city of Minneapolis as a librarian. She usually took an additional week off so we could have all of August and Labor Day at the lake. This was quite a sacrifice for her, I realized later when I grew mature enough to think about other people's needs. She gave up her vacation to help her sister raise us.

We were an extended family. Edward, my brother, and I did not always get along with Auntie Hazel. She was single and marched to a different drummer as far as what we could get away with. It was a lot simpler with Mom for both of us.

At the lake, Edward and I went up with my mother the end of June and over the Fourth which gave my mother another holiday weekend with her regular vacation. Hazel then came up for the month of August and the first week in September which gave her Labor Day. She had to pay for the September week, which she did so I didn't have to be alone in the big city. I didn't like that, but I did love the lake, so I never said anything.

The time in July when neither my mother or Hazel was up there was filled by friends or relatives which always included me. I went with the cabin, no matter who went up. A couple of times Edward and Jean Mary, his new wife, came up. Another couple of years my cousin Elizabeth (Uncle Ed's daughter) and her new husband Jay came up. They loved to fish in the canoe and sometimes took me, so that was fun. We would cast with plugs or June bugs and minnows and would we catch walleyes! One year they came with two friends Ernie and Tommie, and Uncle Ed too and we all caught so much fish that Grand View heard about it and asked to buy a bunch of fish so they could finish up a fish dinner they were having for their guests. We all got a big bang out of that.

Auntie Hazel loved the lake and asked a lot of her friends up. Two came regularly. One of those was Cecelia Johnson. Cecelia was a librarian friend of Auntie Hazel's and loved to come up to the lake to visit for a couple of weeks. She was younger than Hazel, I suppose in her late thirties. She was the one who started Hazel clipping pine needles and looking for pretty mosses and wild flowers. Cecelia always brought me great books to read like *My Friend Flicka* or *Lamb's Tales of Shakespeare* and other classics that Auntie Hazel thought were good for me. She was children's librarian for the Seven Corners Library in Minneapolis and knew what kids liked.

Another was a social worker who worked in the same building in which my aunt worked. She was a very nice, quiet, older lady, Florence Davidson who worked with teenagers mostly. Florence was a good egg, and the dog. Skippy adored her and would stand on his hind legs and lap her hands every year when she arrived on the mail boat. Auntie Hazel and I thought it was amazing that the dog remembered Florence year after year I enjoyed both of those ladies and made lifelong friends of them.

One year we were up over the Fourth of July with my mother. Edward was eighteen and I was nine. More than anything he wanted some excitement. That meant fireworks to celebrate the Fourth. My mother, who had a headache, wanted some peace and quiet, so she finally said that Edward could take the row boat with the new 7.5 outboard down to Tower, the town 15 miles at the end of the Vermilion Lake.

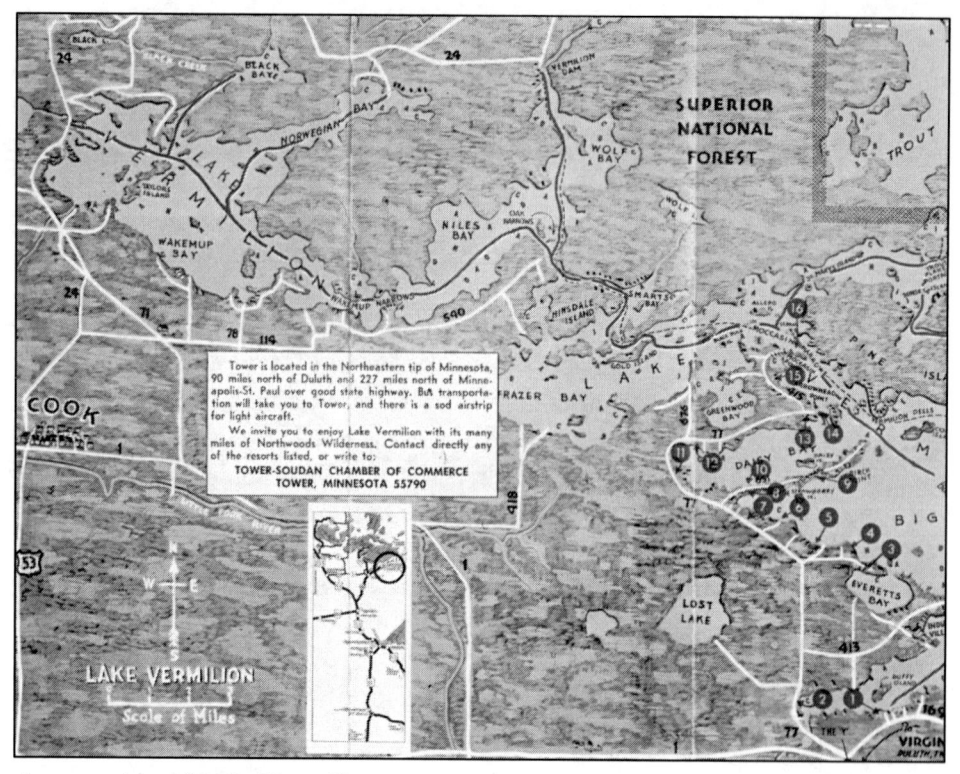

An overview of Lake Vermilion

Of course, I wanted to go along, and for a change he wanted me. I was needed to hold down the bow of the boat because the new motor raised it up too high when it went full speed. The weather was sullen but Edward, with the nonchalance of an 18-year-old, assured Mom that the lake would be as smooth as glass the entire day. This turned out to be a lie, a memorable one. It was the first time I became aware that other people's decisions could kill me.

We didn't bring slickers, and after 15 minutes it began raining and rained all the way. I was sopped by the time we got to Tower, but the wind started up and blew so hard I was dry in about half an hour. Even my tennis shoes were practically dry. Edward bought his fire crackers and wrapped them in heavy paper and put them in a box. They cost so much that we had no money for lunch, and our good friend Mrs. Bruneau we had counted on to feed us had gone to visit her sister in Embarrass, Mn. Yes, that is the name of the town, and it is still there and so is Tower. Both of them with about 500 people each then and about the same size now, I am told.

Edward waited to go home, the wind was so bad. We had to cross a 6 x 8-mile bay with an appropriate name, Big Bay. He was leery of the bay. He

4

had heard tales about Big Bay in a storm and I had too. They were lurid tales with boats sinking and people drowning. I was scared. Of course, being 9 at the time, what I thought or said was unimportant. Edward paid no attention. But I remember this as being the first time he and I talked directly to each other.

There was none of the sneering "I'm your big brother so just listen and shut up, stupid," sort of talk. We spoke quietly to each other. And that was when I really started to get scared. I asked him if we could stay overnight with Mrs. Bruneau. He replied that she wasn't home, and that anyway he didn't want Mom to worry. Well, I could see that. We had no phone at the cabin, and the Franklins, our only neighbors, had no phone either. One of the summer resorts a few miles from us must have had one, but we did not know the owners well, so I suppose that was why Edward didn't want to call them.

He assured me the wind would go down a round five or six, because it always did. "It was a certainty of the weather." So I learned a new word. Certainty. Well, the wind didn't go down It got worse instead, and it was cloudy and dark when we started out. I cannot describe much of that ride. A storm started right away, and the rain came down again, this time with thunder and lightning. All I really remember is bouncing up about a foot off the seat each time the boat hit a wave. In a bad storm like that my weight was not much help.

Edward slowed the boat to take the waves. That caused the bow to go under and the boat to take in water. One time the water was up to my chest I hung on and laughed, it was fun to push through the waves. But after that he increased the speed, and we began the bouncing routine again. It got dark, and there was a lot of lightning. thunder, rain, and wind.

I began to hurt. Really hurt. I cried back to him that I couldn't sit much longer. He yelled to lie down in the front of the boat. I did that, and the pounding on my seat stopped, but started on my hips and elbows. I started to cry but stopped after a while. It didn't seem worthwhile.

I remember seeing the whole wild lake when the lightning flashed, and then us, a dot in the middle of it. Completely helpless. Then, after one flash we saw an island and he steered over to it and put the boat into the calm side. We started to bail it out. But we couldn't get rid of all of the water. Then Edward saw the leak. "I guess we got a crack in the middle," he said. I didn't say a word. I just thought, Would the boat break in two? Would we have to swim in this storm?

I was a good swimmer, but there was no one around. How long would I have to swim? Where would I swim to? Were there any other islands?

"Will we stay here tonight?" I asked

"No, Mom would worry," Edward said. Furthermore, the leak wasn't that bad, and we were almost through Big Bay. We then would stop at Arrowhead Point. He checked the flashlight. He wanted me to work it from the bow so other boats would see it. I refused. I might have to obey him,, but at least I could protect myself. I needed both my hands to hang on if I had to sit at the bow again.

So, growling at me, he took the flash. We shoved off bumping a few rocks as we pushed away. And off we went again. I think this was the first time in my life I ever had to do something I didn't want to do, which I knew was so dangerous I might be killed. The boat cracked up and down, charging up a wave, hitting air and then cracking down. After one horrible crack I thought about the center of the boat and the leak.

I hung on to the sides and tried to take the bouncing on my knees. The middle of the boat was leaking badly. I was in the front, trying to hold it down. Edward was safe in the back with the outboard. I began to picture a terrible thing. What if the boat cracked in two? I would have no power. My half would sink, and he with the motor would drive safely home! I crawled over a seat and headed back to the stern.

"Stay there!" my brother shouted. I kept crawling to the back seat and finally reached him.

"Well, then bail" he growled.

I grabbed our sauce pan and started to bail. In those days, outboard motors had a battery with the motor. Our battery was on the floor of the boat and was about a foot high. The water was an inch from covering it. Even I knew that was bad, and I bailed like mad. But I didn't make much progress. Edward would help a little, but he also had to steer and flash his flashlight every so often in case there was another boat which could help us.

Then we saw a light. He flashed his flashlight. A spotlight caught us. It was the big covered mail launch, which could hold 30 to 50 people. My mother had chartered it to find us. So we were saved.

They got me out first and into the launch. Then Edward and the mail boat captain, Scoop, got our boat tied, and the motor up so there would be no drag while Mom steered the big boat to keep our boat on the lee side. Then Edward came in out of the rain.

I was lying down on a bench seat. I could hardly move. But I will never forget what he said after he had hugged my Mom and taken his wet jacket off.

"We would have made it, you didn't have to come after us!" he said. "I would have stopped at Arrowhead Point." In the angry melee which followed I was exhibit number one. I had to show my bruises to my brother.

And I have to admit, even though I ached all over, I was happy. My brother was finally catching hell. The big shot was really getting it!

Scoop even got upset, breaking the news to Edward that Arrowhead Point had no lights because of the storm, and would be hard, if not impossible to find. Finally, as we left Big Bay and entered Frazier Bay, another huge and dangerous bay, Edward admitted that maybe it had been a big mistake to go to Tower. It had turned out to be a dangerous useless trip because the fireworks got soaked.

And he never could answer my mother's question: Were the fireworks worth risking two lives?

But Mom was the one who took it the hardest. She blamed herself for the rest of her life. What kind of a mother was I? she thought. We'd talk later about it sometimes, and she would turn white and shake her head.

The boat got a piece of tin nailed to its middle and was as good as it ever was. I refused to go any place in the boat with Edward for the rest of the summer. He laughed about that and said he guessed I didn't have faith in him. He was right. I didn't trust him.

But it was more than that. As a 9-year-old, I hated being under his control. I resented his judgment. I resented being little. I resented the whole undertaking. Later, when he behaved like a big shot around me, I would curl my lip and picture the trip to Tower.

"Big shot," I would say. I couldn't forgive him. My brother went to the University of Minnesota and became a big man on campus. He won academic awards, was editor of the humor magazine, and got elected to an honorary fraternity. But to me he was just somebody who didn't know enough to stay out of the rain.

Yes. The trip to Tower was important in my life. I finally got over being nine years old with Edward when I was around 50. We both had left Minnesota and moved back to Minneapolis about the same time. We started to get to know each other, and discovered we had things in common. My biggest discovery was that he really was a nice guy. I said that 20 years later when he died and I was one of the speakers at his memorial. I did not mention the trip to Tower. That adventure was long gone.

Edward being dangerous as usual as I watch with bemusement.

Edward and me pulling a water-skier

Fun on the Water with Edward

At the lake, the only means of transportation we had was boats. We had the old Sea Wolf with a tin patch on the bottom, a souvenir of our trip to Tower, the new Sea Wolf 2 boat purchased from Aronson Boat Livery for $90 which the 7.5 Elto was on, and Edward's canoe, which he and only he used.

He didn't mind if other people used it, he just didn't want me to use it. Later on, when I demonstrated that I could handle a canoe, I got his permission in the Harding way—reluctantly, dramatically, and with a certain amount of conceit. I accepted this gift by pretending I didn't hear him. That was the Harding way.

When I was finally allowed to use the canoe, Hazel and I and my girl friends who came up had a lot of fun with Herculena's kittens. Not Herculena, she did not like the canoe or the water and was miserable the one time we had her in the canoe. But the kittens were curious and fun. We only took one at a time. Usually it showed no fear of water and was very curious about the canoe, sniffing and walking all over it. Then it would climb up on our laps and jump on the sides of the canoe and proceed to walk on the gunnels all around the canoe. The kitten would look at the water...sometimes hiss at it, sometimes growl, but most of the time they just ignored it and finally jumped down and sat in the lap of the person sitting in the bottom.

It was a big green canoe and 18-footer. It was too big and heavy to be portaged. It was a lake canoe. That didn't mean it was that strong. In bad storms if it was left on the dock, the wind took it away. Edward wanted it handy, so he usually kept it on the dock, figuring that he would see a storm coming. He was usually right. Sometimes he was busy and didn't get down to the dock in time.

One time the storm came up suddenly and there was no time to save the canoe. That was the time Auntie Hazel and I saw the wind get under the canoe and take it up in the air. The two of us were watching the storm standing on the bed looking over the top of the canvas curtain which was of course rolled down. The wind lifted the canoe over the other dock and out into the lake where it headed full speed down toward the Franklins' place.

The next day Edward took the outboard and went looking for his canoe. He found it a couple miles down the lake stuck on some logs next to the shore. No damage, luckily, just scraped paint. He sanded that and repainted it. After that in bad weather he was more careful and when a storm was coming move the canoe into the woods where it was safer.

The canoe is a fragile boat, and it could be damaged by being on the dock, or a tree could fall on it in the woods, but that never happened. Mostly accidents to the boats happened because of us humans, although us humans didn't like to admit it.

Sea Wolf 1 and 2 were safe in the dock unless a tornado struck, and that never happened in the time we were at the lake. We finally had to dispose of Sea Wolf 1, it just began rotting before our eyes. That was the red boat which got damaged on the trip to Tower. Once during a storm its tie rope broke and it went cruising down the lake. It was lost for a day before we found caught in the rocks in Hoyt's Island.

We had a ritual in our family, seeing if I could start the outboard. More than anything in the world, I wanted to be able to run the outboard motor alone, go out in the boat alone without someone bossing me.

Every year on the 25th of August, my birthday, from when I was nine until I was about 14, Edward would take me out in the lake in the boat with the outboard and I would try to start it. I had to curl a rope around the flywheel and pull. I would pull and at first the flywheel wouldn't even go around. I was not strong enough. That didn't mean I accepted that fact. Slowly year after year it started responding. But it would never start.

Then Edward got married, and Auntie Hazel and I were up there alone. Someone *had* to start the motor. That was the year she asked Jimmy Hayes and Billy Peterson up for a week or so and they ran the boat. But when they were gone, we would be stuck. I went out with Billy, I think, and pulled like mad and the darn thing started. So that was that. But it was not easy. I had to pull sometimes eight or nine times before it started. Finally, I caught on and we had faster transportation than a rowboat or a canoe.

Edward and I did some crazy things at the lake. Auntie Hazel thought she had her eye on us but she really didn't. When Edward was 19 and 20 we did about whatever he wanted to do. I never had a choice. Sometimes this would burn me up when I was younger, but by that time I was used to it. And Edward, of course, thought his judgment was perfect. Really, it was as stupid as mine.

Auntie Hazel always thought we learned something from these escapades. We both learned the same thing. I know what we learned, because I learned it from Edward. We learned to keep our mouths shut. An adventure that caused an eruption and scolding and raving from Hazel was repeated whenever we felt like it, but never mentioned. Never mentioned became the rule of thumb. Turned out with me that it wasn't safe to mention things to Edward, either. It was all right for him to do dumb things but not me.

As I think back on that now, I remember a phrase my mother used to utter: "Are you growing up or not? Sometimes I can't tell." She would have been really upset if she had heard about the bear. I was fifteen going on three at the time. I was out on the lake in my kayak which I had built. I was maybe half way up the channel to the three cabins when I saw it. A black bear swimming across to the other side. I paddled quickly to overtake it and loosened the rope I used to moor the kayak. I put a loop in it. I would lasso the bear and bring it back to the cabin as a pet. I got closer to it and grabbed the rope. The bear put on a burst of speed and I lost my chance. It didn't want anything to do with me. As I paddled back to the cabin I thought about the bear's reaction. "If he was that nervous around me," I thought "he probably would have not been a good pet." I told my Aunt and my brother about my adventure and they raved and ranted. I don't think they ever told my mother because she never mentioned it. Of course they could have, and she just forgot it. It was the kind of thing it would be wise to forget.

Edward never stopped. He went on until he went to bed. Auntie Hazel told me he was concerned about me.

"Ha!" I said. "That'll be the day!"

"I've got news for you Rosemary," Auntie Hazel smirked. "This is the day."

One of the things we did without telling anyone until my mother saw us do it, was to fool around in the boat. I sat in the bow at the very point of the boat, and Edward would run the motor full force and turn suddenly which would make me fall off. We both thought this was great. Down, down In the water I'd go. Once I even hit bottom. I'd pop up and we'd do it again. We'd do it for an hour or so most of the afternoon. One time he swerved so suddenly that I flipped out close to the boat. It almost hit me and when I was under I had my eyes open to make sure I didn't hit the boat and I saw the propeller zoom by my face. Mom was on the dock that time and she called us in and was really nasty to Edward. He was ashamed—more than usual—and then admitted that the prop almost hit me. For a long time, we didn't do that. When we did it again we were so careful that it wasn't much fun so we gradually stopped.

As I think about myself growing up, I can't get a line on what made me tick. Sometimes I was very adult, much more mature than my brother who was nine years older. Other times I was so thoughtless about my own safety and others that I could be a preschooler at age 15. It was a confusing age. As I dwell on it now, I sometimes don't understand myself any better than I did then. I didn't understand myself at all then.

Edward and I had one more adventure that I still remember. It was a windy day, and it was the same year we almost drowned on the trip to Tower. This time we had returned some guests to Vermilion Dam, which at that time was the nearest place with a road. The wind came up again after we saw our guests off. Edward looked at Niles Bay, then pulled up near the Shafts, who had a cabin on a granite cliff-like hill.

We climbed up and sat in the sun for a couple of hours waiting for the wind to go down. It did not go down, and Edward got restless. He got up and headed down to the boat. He did not answer when I asked if we were headed back despite the wind. But instead of going west, he went south down into Wolf's Bay. This bay was almost opposite our cabin if you walked through about six to eight miles of wood.

We ran into three or four old logging roads which was quite interesting, and some of the time we walked on them. We also found two Copenhagen snuff jars, which were a real antique find. In those days the jars were made out of china and would make nice bedside lamps or flower pots, which is how we used them.

We came out about a quarter of a mile north of the cabin and walked until we were opposite it. Then we yelled and hollered, and Auntie Hazel finally came out and went down to the dock and looked some more and then got into Sea Wolf 1, the red boat, and started rowing over to us.

It was windy, and she had a hard time when she got to the middle of the lake. I wondered if she'd make it, but Edward said she was a tough old cookie and to give her time. She got there, by the three pines, just about where we came out. Edward rowed back. The next day he went down to Grand View and got someone with a boat to take him up to Wolf Bay. I didn't go with them; I was reading my book on taxidermy which had come on the mail boat.

Broken Arm

When I was eight or nine my two playmates, Jimmy Ascher and Davey Hayes and I disobeyed our parents. All of us had been told to stay off the old grape trellis in my back yard. Dad used to raise grapes. He had been dead for about five years, and the structure. which was probably 8 x 20. was just four posts with rickety boards nailed around them and maybe one or two in the middle. But it was there!

So after spending the morning playing tag, riding our bikes, or tossing a ball around, we decided to climb the trellis. Why? Because it was there.

I don't know who got on top first, but the two of us followed. I straddled the board on the side. Dave and Jimmy crawled to the boards in the middle. There were about two boards, as I recall. Neither wide, and both worn from five years of Minnesota sun, rain and snow.

I remember watching Dave and Jim crawl to the boards, which I was afraid to do, when I slipped and fell backwards to the ground and hit my side badly. I tried to stand but wasn't sure I could make it I hurt so much. And then the board that Davey was on broke in two and he fell straight down on his head. Jimmy hung on for a second and then toppled sideways like I did but put out his arm to stop himself. He landed on' the arm and started to scream.

David ran home. I stood there looking at Jimmy watching him cry. No one was home at my house, and Jimmy's mother was shopping on Broadway, a business district three blocks away. Jimmy's arm was flopping. I went over to comfort him and told him to hold the arm, which he already had started to do.

David returned. He said his mother looked him over and was mad at him for disobeying.

"She said I have a hard head!" he said, and that he seemed OK to her. But "blah blah blah" about the trellis. We both stood and looked at Jimmy who was holding his arm close to his body and trying to stop his tears. Just then Mrs. Ascher came down the walk way, put down her packages and asked what had happened.

"Jimmy's hurt," I said. "He fell off the trellis and so did me and Dave. Dave landed on his head, so didn't get hurt, but my side hurts and is going to be black and blue."

Mrs. Ascher got red in the face and grabbed Jimmy.

"Who in hell are you to disobey me?" she yelled. She picked up a stick and started to hit him. It was terrible. Jimmy started to cry and was jumping around trying to get out of the way and his mother was roaring and his arm was flopping. This went on forever it seemed to us.

But she stopped, grabbed him by the neck, and shoved him into the house. That was my first experience with child abuse. Davey was shocked, and tried to make a joke.

"Boy how would you like to have her for a mother! We'd we dead in a week." Eileen, Dave's sister came over. We told her all about it.

"He could have been killed!" she said. "Would she take a stick to him then?" And we started to laugh.

About 10 minutes later his mother and Dorothy, his sister, got him into the car. He was still crying. They took him to the doctor. He came back with the arm in a cast. It was broken all right.

My mother hired a man to tear down the trellis and she gave me a scolding, but it wasn't as bad as it could have been. She was more sorry than mad, and blamed herself for leaving it up. She and Mrs. Hayes got together and talked about it with us. Mrs. Ascher didn't join us. She said Jimmy had a broken arm and there was no need for any further talk about "the damn trellis."

From then on, even after we both married, and hadn't seen each other for years, it was a code word between Dave and me whenever anything unusual happened. I remember during World War II, when Dave was back from basic training, he told me his sergeant reminded him of Mrs. Ascher.

Jim turned out fine. When we were in our 50s Dave and his wife came back to Minneapolis for Dave's brother's funeral and he looked up Jimmy. Jim worked at Ford Motor's truck division in Minneapolis for 25 years and was planning to retire. As Paul and I left the funeral Dave poked me and said "I wonder if Mrs. Ascher is alive. Watch out for her."

His sister, Eileen, heard this and laughed. We all laughed, and I poked my childhood pal.

"How's your head, Dave? Has having a hard head helped?"

Whenever I got mad at Mom when I was growing up, I would think of Mrs. Ascher, and then decide my mom wasn't so bad.

My mom, Leila Witchie Harding

Living with My Mom and Auntie Hazel

Me shortly after my father's death

I had been four years old for three days when my Dad died. All I remember about it was that he was sick. Once I brought a hot water bottle up to him and I unscrewed the lid to be funny. We loved to play jokes on each other. It ruined the bed and Mom was really mad.

My dad died from a mosquito bite which gave him equine encephalitis. He was sick a long time and my mother took care of him. He died in 1928. I wasn't able to spell the disease until I was about 14. In 1928 people had the bodies and funerals in their house, so our house was full of people then.

Everybody patted me on my head and asked my age. When I said I was just four, they would shake their heads and walk away. I didn't care. I didn't know them in the first

Auntie Hazel

place. The funeral made Edward feel very sad. He was 12 and he hid and cried.

I watched him cry for a while and then went to play by myself. In a few days all of the people were gone, and it was just Mom, Edward and Auntie Hazel—who came every day after work—and of course Grandma, who came over all the time.

I wondered where my Dad was and looked for him in the house sometimes and watched for him to come home from work. And I missed him most at the lake because he used to play with me in the water. I remember asking all the time to go swimming because I knew he would appear if we did the things I liked to do with him. Mom made Edward swim with me and he ducked me so much I almost drowned, so I didn't want to swim any more, and I knew then my Dad was gone for sure.

After my Dad died everyone was sad and mad at me. The only one I got along with was Edward's dog, Van. And he only liked me when nobody else was around. Dad wasn't supposed to die. He was only 40 years old. Everyone had a hard time getting over my Dad's death. My mother cried a lot and blamed me for things I did and didn't do.

Auntie Hazel would sympathize and then give me a coffee kiss. I was never sure which I hated the most, being yelled at by my mother or tasting my Auntie Hazel's coffee spit.

They told Edward he was the man of the house. That meant he was in charge. Who was he in charge of? Not my mother and aunt, he didn't dare boss them. So he spent his time pushing me around.

I would yell about it. Mom and Auntie paid no attention, and Edward just got me later. Once he wouldn't get me a drink of water when I asked him, so I went next door and asked for water and the neighbors told Mom. That got back to him and Mom, Aunt Hazel, and later Edward yelled at me. But they fixed a stool so I could get up to the sink to get my own water.

As far as Edward was concerned I was a real pain in the neck. Mom was looking for a job and was really scared she couldn't find one good enough to support her family. My Auntie Hazel bought things the house needed and some of my and Edward's clothes until I was through high school. Then I inherited $3,000 from Grandmother. She had only left me $500 when she died, but the interest built it up to$3,000. I was six when she died. When I got the $3,000 I was able to go to the U and pay all the expenses and have some money left over.

Of course. I lived at home. I got to the U easily enough. I took the streetcar down to Hennepin, walked two blocks and got the Oak Harriet to the U. Took about 30 to 45minutes. I studied on the street car. Then Mom was able to buy a Studebaker coupe and I drove to school and drove her around a lot. Her job wanted her to go to the factories directly to find out from their personnel department how many people they needed and to see the kind of work they did, so she could tell the people who were applying for work.

Umpapa and Auntie Hazel

Auntie Hazel was a big help financially to Mom for quite a while. She took care of Edward and me for five weeks every summer too. And she bought us clothes until we went to college. Getting along with her was different but easy enough if you took the trouble to see the problem her way too, and not just your way.

Uncle John, the ophthalmologist, my Dad's brother, sent Mom $50 a month. At that time $50 was a lot of money. She thanked him for the money at Uncle Harry's funeral and told him he didn't need to send her any more money and that she would never forget his kindness.

Grandma, had remarried a couple of years before to an old guy named George who I called Umpapa. She came over often. She had a black electric car that was noiseless. We kids used to run after it when she was driving. Sometimes Grandma and I had fun together. You could see she was trying to help my mother, but they yelled at each other quite a lot.

We all yelled a lot at each other. We were all scared of Grandma then. She drove that electric car almost every day from Emerson and 22nd to our house at 16th and Dupont, it had big windows and she steered it with a stick. It was black and shiny and COOL!

My Godfather Reginald came around a lot after my dad died. He sold glassware, and one time brought some expensive glasses to the house and dinged on them, and then on ours to show the different noises. I remember that this made Auntie Hazel mad. She said Reginald was trying to sell us some nice glasses we couldn't pay for.

My mother didn't say a thing. I guess my mother thought about marrying Reginald, because then her bills would be paid. I heard her talk about this to Auntie Hazel later on after she got a good job and Reginald was no longer around. He was a stuffed shirt and I didn't like him, and I don't think Edward did either. He always shook hands and walked out of the house when Reginald was around.

After my mother finally got a decent job and calmed down she told us that Grandma had been very helpful, especially when she told Mom that other people lost their husbands too and got through it. Grandma was talking about herself. My Grandpa Edward Witchie, who died before I was born, was her loss and she got over it and married George Sanborn, (Umpapa) who gave me PK gum, and let me sit on his lap. He reminded me of Reginald. My Mom said he was well off.

I remember my Auntie Hazel lived with them and had a nice room next to the hired woman Isabelle, who was very religious. When she went to church, she told everybody she would pray for them. I asked Auntie Hazel why Isabelle thought she needed to pray for her. That got a laugh out of Hazel and she said that personally she didn't believe in prayer, but that Isabelle did and we should respect Isabelle's belief. I never knew what Umpapa believed. He just sat in his chair, looked out the window and never said a word.

After Dad's funeral Edward wouldn't go to a funeral or go see a sick person, and he blamed it on Mom for the rest of his life. He said he should never have been forced to go to my Dad's funeral at 12, which was too young. He had a big fight with my mother about Uncle Harry's funeral. He was 18 then and I was nine, and he didn't think either of us should go. This time my mother insisted and Edward did go to the funeral. He said he didn't want to, but he would go because my mother insisted, but he said she was wrong. He was great at knowing when things were wrong.

At Uncle Harry's funeral I saw Uncle John crying and I started to cry. That started Edward off in the car. He began raving about how young I was and how I shouldn't have had to come to the funeral. My mother told him when he had kids he could deal with them, but it was her job to deal with hers. He was crying then himself and cried "Don't think I won't!"

When Nancy, his oldest daughter was 16 he wouldn't let her go to her Grandfather Stinchfield's funeral; he said it would be too hard on her, so I guess he meant it. When Jean Mary, his first wife died, he told me to pick out the grave stone and get it set up in the cemetery. I did it, and got it put up in the Harding lot. I had the bill sent to him and he paid it, I guess. He never said anything to me about it. He treasured his phobia.

That got me thinking about some of mine. They may seem just as strange to others. I don't like bossy people. I mean I REALLY don't like bossy people, and I have a hard time getting over bossiness. I always remember what my mother did to her guys at the office who wanted her to stand all day and pass out information oral and written. She found a rule which got her out of it. Principals had a hard time bossing me around. For one thing, I couldn't hear.

Another good technique I used was to overreact. Once the principal wanted us to be sure to get the grades in by a certain date, a good three days sooner than usual. This was hard for me, so I went to the office and borrowed the bookkeeper's adding machine so I could average the grades. This slowed her down; lo and behold I was told by my boss that I could have an extra day.

Another time the assistant principal's clerk called me and said that none of my kids could go to the city library one block from the school because it was a field trip and they would have to have permission from the assistant principal. So I sent the whole class of 27 down for a slip. Another phone call. *Rosemary, what are you doing to me?* A class permission slip developed out of that one.

Mom made sure after Uncle Harry died that I learned to deal with death and sickness. She told me sick people had rights, and dead people too. You honor dead people by remembering them and by giving them decent burial places. She told me people should listen to sick people, and then they could really help them. A visit is nice, but if you can help on the visit that is nicer and you should try to help. But remember: If someone is hospitalized, a visit is often pleasant for the sick person, but it should be short, and make sure the sick person wants visitors.

My mother died in her house. She had a slow-moving, rather slow-thinking caretaker named Beatrice who needed some helping. I came over after work to see Mom. One time Auntie Hazel was there to help Beatrice. Hazel was reading a book in the old leather chair that used to be my grandfather's. It was a Sleepy Hollow chair, and Paul and I later gave it to Nancy, Edward's daughter. Anyway, Mom was very sick, could not walk at all any more and could hardly stand, because her leg had been broken and healed poorly. Beatrice had just given her a sponge bath and was holding her arm and flapping a towel at her. Mom's skin was blue and full of goose bumps. I went over and grabbed the towel and began rubbing my mother down. Mom looked at me and smiled.

"Thank God," she said. "Mother is here.".

Auntie Hazel looked up from her book and laughed.

"She's not your mother, dear," she said.

My mother gave her a look: "She's not my dumb sister!"

When I was married to Paul I got pregnant many times. It was before the pill and we didn't always protect ourselves and of course we wanted children. Anyway I kept losing them at 22 weeks. Two did live, only to die after a few days. I lost five babies at 22 weeks. They would not have been fully developed if they had managed to hang in there and they would have had health problems.

According to my OBs I was in the hospital to save the fetus. That was a big laugh. I was really in the process of losing the fetus. Visitors were not terribly welcome. Mom was dead by then. Auntie Hazel would come and be nice and chirp away and worry and I would wish she would go away. Finally I just wouldn't tell her when I was in the hospital. She was too much.

It was a part of our married life we didn't care to share with many others. Family gave us too much sympathy and attention. Friends were easier to be with. Paul told my brother and Jean Mary, and she was helpful about ways to sit and stand when pregnant for I was almost always uncomfortable. Paul told them I wanted to be left alone, and miracles or miracles, they left me alone. Hazel wouldn't though. She knew her duty.

We shut people out because they wouldn't give me air or any chance to be anything except a pregnant woman about to have another dead baby. It certainly wasn't a pleasant time, and remembering it is not pleasant either. The only humorous thing I can remember is one time I had to go to Northwestern Hospital by ambulance, and a funeral car followed us. The ambulance attendant said that they did that quite often.

We decided to go on with our lives and not discuss our failures with everybody. That rule I have followed pretty strictly. The Book Club knew about it, and my immediate family. That was plenty.

My mother was right about visiting sick people. Find out how sick they are and time your visit accordingly. About a year ago I was hospitalized for five days for a pacemaker. It took longer than usual because my blood pressure wouldn't stay down. I was in Sarasota Hospital, 40 miles from Englewood, and I didn't expect any visitors. But Meigs, a Humanist friend who lived in Sarasota, came to see me twice, both times with books. She knew I loved to read, and that I did not like TV. Wonderful! We had good talks and I enjoyed the books. That amazed one nurse. I was reading. The TV wasn't on!

When my mother died, she died in her house. She was sick for some time. I had just lost my baby at six months, because the afterbirth had collapsed. I had lost some blood, so was fairly weak. Jean Mary had just had Freddie, and she was sick with polio after his birth which was a terrible thing they never told me .

After my mother died, selling stuff in the house and clearing it out was done by Auntie Hazel and my husband, Paul. I remember a few things about this time. I remember Auntie Hazel on the top floor of the attic cuddling an old rag doll she had as a little girl and Paul snarling at a man who offered him 15 cents for the ashtray he was using.

Auntie Hazel was a big help at that time. She took over. She had been through so many deaths so she knew what to do. I am afraid her funeral was not so great. She lived longer than my mother. My mother died at 73, Hazel at 86. Most of her friends were gone, and it was a quiet occasion. She is buried at Lakewood with the rest of the Witchies, next to the Hardings, including Jean Mary, Edward's first wife, my mother, Leila Witchie Harding and my dad, Fred Andrews Harding, and then my husband Paul Hagen and an empty place for me next to him.

Fred, Edward's son, owns the burial lot. He said we can all be buried in it. Except Edward didn't want to be buried there, he wanted his ashes to be scattered around his lake place. So that is what he had done. Then Pat, his second wife, sold the place.

Edward also disagreed with the will my mother left. He said she left too much to me. I said that convention said the woman got things like the house silver. So he gave those things to Fred in his will. He insisted throughout his life that we got too much. What we were supposed to do about that beats me. He even got mad when we gave some stuff to his kids. He should be doing that, he said. I was still a pain in the neck to him. (and him to me!)

When Edward was dying he was under the care of Hospice, and he died at his home, which is where he wanted to die. He refused to be on oxygen which they told him might keep him alive about another three months. He had been on oxygen and did not tolerate it well.

Paul and I went to see him the day he died. Pat called us and told us that the doctor had said he would die in a few hours. I had found a pamphlet at an Antique Show about Lake Vermilion in 1925 and how to get there from

Duluth by train. I showed it to Edward and asked if he remembered going to the lake on the train from Duluth. He got so excited he got out of bed and stood talking about how we got to the lake in 1925 and how Vanny the dog had to be in the baggage car and he and his Dad and Mother would go down to visit him. I was a babe in arms at the time and do not remember this at all.

We had a good talk about our adventures at the lake and then Paul and I left. Edward died later on that day. I know Nancy got in from Worthington. Fred was in the hospital; he fell on the job. I called him and said he was all right, so I imagine he got to see his dad. I don't know if Diana could get there in time from Boise, Idaho or not. No one ever said.

Mostly his kids were upset at his will because he left everything to Pat, with any money left after her death to be divided between her kids and his.

Every year on Decoration Day my mother and I and Auntie Hazel picked flowers from the yard and went to Lakewood Cemetery to the Witchie and Harding graves. That was the custom in those days. When I started doing this with them, I received the history of everyone buried there. My dad was buried next to all of the Witchies. That was my grandfather's idea. He gave part of his lot to my father, so our family could be buried next to his.

I got to meet a lot of dead relatives. For instance, Great-uncle John (my grandma's brother) was an officer in the Civil War and he got a special flag by his grave on Decoration Day. I got to like the custom. It taught me to appreciate my ancestors. Edward never went, and Mom never made him. Now the ashes of Jean Mary, Edward's first wife, are buried there and so are Paul's. My ashes will be buried there too with my dad, mother, Jean Mary and Paul, with Auntie Hazel nearby with the Witchies.

I always felt I got shortchanged on Dad's family. I had his diary he wrote when he was in ninth grade, which was mostly about school and his mother and dad traveling to Puerto Rico to see his brother Frank and family. His mother had been sick but was better, but his dad had to be hospitalized when he got back to Hudson, Wisconsin. I read about his father, Frank Harding, from an article Helen Mary wrote for some historical journal.

He was a captain in the engineering corps in the Civil War. He was stationed in Louisiana and was in the battle of New Orleans. Then he was transferred to the engineers and all of the men under him were black. He said that he couldn't have had a better bunch of men. They tore down bridges over rivers and streams in Louisiana, and then built some for the Northerners. Dad's mother was the first baby born in Wisconsin when it joined the Union (or something like that. I am never sure about the Hardings).

Frank Harding, on left, my grandfather

My mother wanted her son and daughter to be independent thinkers and to follow their own drummer. So she only insisted that we do things that she believed were vitally important, otherwise my brother and I were to make up our own minds and to act on what we believed. She was very definite about that. And though she tried to respect our wishes, as did Auntie Hazel, they seldom did. These were two very tough ladies. They wanted us to make our own decisions, but they didn't like it if they were different from theirs and put up quite a fight when they weren't.

I know with me, a lot of this revolved around the fact that when she started working steadily, I was about six. She told the hired girls we got from the nearby farms to care for me that they could tell me what to do, but they could never hit me. She told me that too. And they never did. Then Grace came and became like an older sister and any problems with hired girls vanished.

Grace came from a little town north of St. Cloud which did not have a high school. She was living with a friend of her family. Her mother had died in childbirth, and her father worked as a lumberjack and lumber rep for the area around Bemidji in northwestern Minnesota. It was impossible for Grace to live with him. She had a brother, but he was only a teenager. So

Char

Gracie lived with us, and visited her Dad sometimes in the summer. Never in the winter when there was heavy snow and cold down to 40 below. He traveled half the time too checking on the various camps and the trees.

Anyway, Auntie Hazel heard about Grace from one of the social workers in her building. Mom got in touch with her and Grace started living with us. She graduated from North High and lived with us until she married Curtis Chriss. She got married in our house as us kids outside looked through the windows. I kept in touch with her and visited her in northern Minnesota. She died several years ago, but she has a daughter Charlotte who was also part of the family. Char visits me every year and has traveled with me.

In Peru, Char and I went boating on the Amazon and met a 10-year-old who had a pet python who ate the rats In their maize field. Everyone in the tour group got to hold the python. A beautiful snake! We all have pictures of us holding that green eight-foot snake with big yellow spots.

Char and I were scheduled to go to Costa Rica together but I got bursitis of the hip and my orthopedist just laughed when I asked if I could go to Costa Rico.

"They'll just send you home and it will cost a fortune." he said. So I didn't go.

When Grace came to live with us, her job was to take care of me after school and to keep the house clean and to help Mom with the cooking. She slept in the sun room off the dining room and used the dining room table to study on, and so did the rest of us. Hazel got excited when she saw us all studying and didn't think there was enough room for me. So she bought me a desk. She took me to a furniture store to get it and we spent some time looking at desks. I finally settled on one that had a special drawer for a typewriter. I have to say I didn't use it very much until I got into high school and college and then I used it. After Paul and I got married we both used it, and when we moved to Roseville we had it in the town house basement with the computer.

I think watching Edward, Grace, and me study got to Auntie Hazel and Mom and they began to talk about responsibility and following through on things. Boy did they get excited about responsibility. They almost drove me nuts and Edward too. They were a little easier on Grace, but it is possible that she was pretty responsible, but there was one time with Edward where they both almost wrecked the house. They were horsing around chasing each other, knocking down chairs. Then one of them brought in a hose and turned it on the other and in the middle of that one of them crashed into me and I was holding my Skippy doll and it broke. I started howling and they stopped horsing around.

That was a big deal. My Mom was really mad when she got home and she said she would buy me a new Skippy doll, but I wanted my old one. So they got the old one glued together and for Christmas gave me another. Mom scolded Edward and told Gracie that she was not living up to expectations and everyone was sorry. But it was sure exciting while it lasted.

Another time Edward got excited in chemistry class about an experiment with a flame retardant. He invented his own which he insisted was better than the one in class and would really put out a fire. To prove it he started a fire in the basement. It was just getting going when my mother found out and came down and grabbed a pail of water and doused it out. She was really mad. I never saw her yell so at Edward. He fought back and she told him to drop the subject and forget about his chemical prowess. I learned a new word just standing there. Of course I was pleased; who wouldn't be to see him get it?

Then I started to drive them crazy with my taxidermy correspondence course when I was fifteen or sixteen and skinned cats. A guy down the lake came up and rented a lake house for two years. He was a taxidermist and took orders from some lab in Chicago to skin dead cats which the lab sent him every month. He let me skin some cats and talked to me about taxidermy. He said it really was not a full-time job except for a very few people. Then that winter he lost his ax through the ice and a long metal pole he used to push the ice around. I dove in the water for him and found his metal pole, but even after diving six or seven times I couldn't find the ax, so he told me to give up. That was an interesting summer and Hazel liked that I was working with him and learning responsibility and perseverance.

I once read an article that said arsenic should be used to cure the animal's skin. So I went up the drug store and asked to buy a pound of arsenic. The druggist reported me to Edward, whom he knew, and you can imagine what happened.

Then I actually shot a bird (I still feel guilty about that, I was one crazy kid) skinned it and doused it with the cat's flea powder because they wouldn't sell me arsenic. Then I hung it at the bottom of the basement steps from the water pipes to cure and then I planned to stuff it. Edward went down in the dark to his den in the basement because I had turned the light out wrong, and he bumped right into my bird and he said it scared the bejesus out of him. He never got over it. Kept talking about it for years. He was so scared he ruined the bird; I was never able to stuff it and I didn't feel like shooting another bird, so I dropped taxidermy.

Those were the episodes that got my mother and aunt off on the subject of responsibility. They thought we both needed to learn it, and both of us reacted poorly to their efforts. Yet Edward was a responsible person and so am I.

I remember Edward and the paper route. He hated it. He found the customers were not responsible! People wouldn't pay when he went to collect. He had to deliver papers in rain, heat, or snow even if he was sick and Sunday he wanted to sleep late and he couldn't. That was the day the paper had to be at the doors by six a.m. Sometimes he would miss a house and people would call about it. My mother would try and try to wake him but he wouldn't wake up. So the paper route stopped.

Then I had to take piano lessons because we had inherited my Grandma's piano. I figured that was a stupid reason for me to suffer. But it was really Auntie Hazel. She wanted music to become a part of my life, and she wanted me to learn responsibility and to be able to follow through on what I started. Because of Auntie Hazel I never took any art in school. I had to choose between orchestra and art. This bothered my mother because in college she had a double major English and art. What Hazel didn't understand was that when she chose the thing I was supposed to follow through on, I sometimes had no desire to have anything to do with it.

One day I just went ice skating with my friends on Piano Lesson Day and made sure not to get back home until 6 p.m. when the lesson would be over and the teacher would be gone. Guess what? The piano teacher came, stayed, and when I turned up there was a discussion about my behavior. It was embarrassing for me because the teacher stayed. But Mom didn't care. She never cared when I was embarrassed. She wanted everyone there. I said I didn't want to take piano any more. Auntie Hazel gave me a long talk about the importance of music in the world, and the importance of seeing things through. The teacher looked happy figuring I was going to continue the lessons. I said that I didn't like piano, that I didn't want to learn how to play the piano and it had never been my idea.

My mother listened and agreed with me. Auntie Hazel got kind of mad, but Mom laughed. I recall her kidding Hazel that perhaps she should take piano lessons, she was the one who liked the piano so much. Mom then said that if I really didn't want to take piano lessons, I didn't have to. I was old enough to make up my mind. I was in third grade then. Hazel was mad, but she got over it.

One thing about our family is that we almost always get over our mads. That was my first introduction to older people's wants for me. Geez. What a pain. To have someone watching, watching you all the time. Are you living up to what *they* want? Do *they* follow through on everything? I didn't dare ask that. Next they bought me a violin. That was really crazy. It all had to do with the fact that I thought school was boring and wanted a break!

At Logan School, my school, you could get the whole afternoon off once a month to go see the Minneapolis Symphony Orchestra practice. You could get out of school for half a day! Wow! A bus picked you up at noon and returned you at five and all you had to do the whole afternoon was look at the orchestra and listen and talk to your friends. And it was cheap. It cost just 50 cents for the bus ride. Auntie Hazel paid it. She thought it was great that I was developing an interest in the arts. It was fun on the bus and I enjoyed watching the musicians play and the other kids.

Then Auntie Hazel asked me what instrument I liked best in the orchestra. I had never thought about any of the instruments, but I knew Hazel liked answers, so I said violins, because I sat opposite them and mostly watched the bows go up and down in order. She was really pleased and excited that I like the violins. She never thought it might be because I wanted to get out of school. Auntie Hazel clapped her hands and told my mother they should buy me a violin. I was scared to tell them why I really went to the concerts, so I went along with the violin bit. What else could I do? Of course my mother and Aunt couldn't afford a decent violin. They found one at an antique show for $29.50 and got the man down to $25.00 because Mom said that was all the money she had in her purse. (I still use that technique with sales people).

They got me a teacher, but then Mom said he was expensive and that joining the junior high orchestra would teach me violin. She was right, for we met daily and that meant I played the violin for almost an hour every day. And I never really complained. it was just school, and school was dumb. My violin was off key and the strings kept breaking but I kept on with it until ninth grade.

The orchestra was led by the math teacher, Mrs. Purdy. I didn't fool her. She knew I couldn't play and had me in the next to the last seat in the second violin section. The last seat was Milton Naiditch's and he was always sick.

In the middle of eighth grade I got promoted up next to the front of the second violin section; that was the day I couldn't catch on to what the orchestra was playing—I was off beat. Mrs. Purdy looked at me and stopped the orchestra. She gave a little speech.

"Rosemary," she said, "was the *only* person in this orchestra who was playing the correct beat."

I was a success; Mrs. Purdy said I was finally getting to understand my violin.

But in ninth grade I could take lifesaving, and it met the same time as orchestra. My mother told me it was my choice. Auntie Hazel told me I could take lifesaving at the YWCA downtown, and took me there once after school to swim. There were a bunch of old people swimming. I didn't want to take lifesaving with a bunch of old people, I wanted to take it with my friends.

Then Mrs. Purdy called me out of home room She wanted to know why I was dropping orchestra after I had finally learned how to play my violin. Mrs. Purdy was tall and skinny and wore her hair in a bun on top of her head. I never saw her hit anyone, but she sure looked like she could. She glared at me and drummed her fingers on her desk. I made myself look back and pretended I was talking to Edward. I bit my lip and took a big breath and clenched my fists and said that I thought learning how to save a person's life was more important than playing the violin and that I wanted to take lifesaving class, so if I ever had to save a person's life I would know how.

Mrs. Purdy opened her mouth and then shut it. She waved her hand at me. She finally said that she hoped I saved a lot of lives and let me go back to home room. I told Mom all about it when she got home from work that night and she laughed and said it was my decision and she thought it was a good one. Edward said he would now feel safer in the water, but he shut up when I told him there was no need for sarcasm. He didn't know I knew such a hard word! Auntie Hazel kept asking me if I missed my music. Finally I wouldn't answer her.

Later on, when I married Paul and we got season tickets to the Minneapolis Symphony, Auntie Hazel told Paul that she was so glad we were going to the concerts, that I loved music, but had to give it up because of a conflict in school scheduling. I laughed when he told me that one, and told him that when I played the violin I was depressed for days. Then Jean Mary said she got Nancy a violin because Hazel had told her I had played in the school orchestra. So my violin prowess followed me around the rest of my life. Nancy's daughter took the violin, and Char, Grace's daughter also took the violin. I was annoyed at all this at first, and then I realized that It was their problem, not mine. They all dropped it; none play it now.

My father's family all lived in Hudson, Wisconsin, a suburb of St. Paul about just about an hour's drive from where we lived in Minneapolis. Mom made sure Edward and I got to know my father's family quite well. Edward got to know Uncle Harry's daughters— Helen Mary and Louise Harding— better than me because he was the same age. I got to know Helen Mary a little bit because she lived with us for a few months. But then she and Edward got to like each other, and Mom had a fit. She thought cousins shouldn't marry cousins and phoned Aunt Gertrude in Hudson and Helen Mary had to move. She and Helen Mary never really liked each other after that. Helen Mary once said to me after I was older that there was lot of difference between friendship and marriage, and that my mother had jumped to some false conclusions. My mother never believed they were false, and whenever she talked about Helen Mary she would arch her eyebrows and comment that she never married (she was living with a guy in NYC at the time).

When Helen Mary was in our house she thought I was a brat. I was 10 or 11 and didn't particularly like Edward, so why should I like his girlfriend? It was always about my pets. I had a dog and a cat, Herculena, who had a lot of kittens all the time. Helen Mary was always stepping on them. She didn't like Skippy, my dog, either and neither did Edward. Skippy barked. You had to get used to the sound of his bark—think of something else or to do and then it wouldn't bother you. I tried to tell Edward that and

Skippy

he said the damn dog should adjust to him. It was hard to argue with Edward. He only heard what he wanted.

Auntie Hazel got into our arguments sometimes. She kept telling Edward I was just a kid. He said I should grow up. We argued a lot at dinner, usually about my pets. Often about anything. Mom would get mad and leave the table and Edward would tell me it was my fault and I would tell him it was his fault. I was not terribly good in repartee with Edward. And sometimes Auntie Hazel came from work and yelled at Edward and told him I was a kid, and I would leer at him. And he would growl.

It was bad when Helen Mary was around because she always thought Eddie was just wonderful; she took his side every time. I got to know Helen Mary and Louise and her family when I got older, and we did things together, and I learned to like them both, but I sure didn't think much of Helen Mary—or Higgsy as they called her—then.

Elizabeth, Uncle Ed's daughter, lived in Chicago with her husband Jay. I got to really know them up at the lake because for two or three summers they came up there for two weeks with a couple of friends to go fishing, and my mother made them take me. That was what she did in the summer. If anyone wanted to use the cabin in July when it was empty for a couple of weeks, they had to take me. That was because she didn't want me exposed to the streets of North Minneapolis.

So Elizabeth and Jay brought Uncle Ed too because he loved to fish. Liz and Jay would take me in Edward's canoe and we would cast for walleyes and we caught them! Then I would row Uncle Ed in the red boat and he gave me the history of his courtship of Aunt Gussie, and rave about how Jay should move back to Hudson. I have been close to Elizabeth's family ever since.

When Uncle Ed was dying I went to the hospital and stayed with him when Elizabeth and Gussie couldn't. Even now I am in touch with Luella, one of Elizabeth's daughters and hear from Katherine, another. Louella prefers the name Lu; insists her mother was crazy when she named her

Hanging out with Skippy by the lake

Luella. Paul and I took her and Di and Nancy to the World's Fair in New York in 1967. We stayed with Paul's folks and had a great time.

Luella's son, John, who is a doctor, lives in Valicro, a Tampa Bay suburb., maybe 80 or 90 miles away from my home in Florida. He has been very helpful when I have to be hospitalized or have surgery. He discusses it with me, and does some reassuring, so I won't be so frightened. When I had the melanoma on my face he insisted that I get a doctor who did Mohs surgery, a very careful step by step process which can take days. It took my doctor four days. She cut some skin away, and then sent it in to the lab to be checked for cancer. If the report came back free, she would continue. Otherwise they would x-ray again and start over. It is my fifth year now with no melanoma, so if I am free of it for the entire year, they will claim I am cured. But doctors don't really mean that. They mean that the cancer probably won't return. But. it sure might.

John's daughter, Hannah, is 14 and their son Jacob is in sixth grade, so that makes him around 12. John's wife, Megan, works for a dermatologist as a physician's assistant. The last time they came down Hannah was interested in some of my books, so I gave her *To Kill a Mockingbird* and *The Color Purple* and a book by Jeanette Walls. She is a very pretty girl, fairly quiet. I gave Jake a painting I did of a snake. John also said it was Florida law that I could drive, and that age was not a factor in driving. That burned up Diana, my niece and Peter, Louise's son. I told them that I didn't want either of them around me if they were going to continue to harp on my driving.

It is difficult enough to be old, without constantly being nagged. About the one thing I want at this age is to be productive, content, and interested in just about everything. I don't need to be told I can't do this, I can't do that and that (although they say I will live another 10 years) I also got yelled at about the house not being safe to live in. That was when Edward's kids, not Fred, wanted me out of the house and into assisted living because the time had come I was in my 90s.

"You're going to fall!" one of them yelled at me for half an hour. That was three years ago and I haven't fallen yet. I taught school for 26 years and went through many tantrums with teenagers, but none were as noisy or obnoxious as her yelling about what would happen to me if I didn't do as she said. Loud (because I was deaf) and insistent because I was old (and out of it).

She knew nothing about safe or unsafe houses she just wanted me out. A week later my home was looked over by the nurses who came through Medicare because I had a pacemaker installed. The house was given an A-plus in safety. Of course it would; Paul lived and died in the house with Alzheimer's and he had to have a safe house with his bad back and bad mind. I made sure he had one.

I played tennis for 20 years and my balance is great. My doctor told me I scored 100 on his balance test. Of course people are right when they say I am old. I am in my 90s, but people are different too. They have different wants, appetites, looks, dislikes, abilities. I could go on. I will say this about old age. I have never really encountered prejudice until I became old. People think old people can't be active, and that is where my abilities are. I am deaf; I frequently guess at what people are saying. In fact I just spent $3,000 more than I did for my last hearing aid. This one seems to be better, once I understand it.

What I mean by old age prejudice is the stereotyping. Some people believe old people are just out of it, are incompetent pains in the butt. They stereotype all the time. If you are in your 90s you aren't able to do anything. You are sick. You certainly don't garden, and you shouldn't be living alone because it isn't safe. They do not say why these things are true, but they believe them religiously. This is part of their problem of being unable to discern a fact from an opinion, and it is what I mean by old age prejudice. President Trump can't tell a fact from an opinion, but why copy him?

Tom Forsberg, Wally Cox, Milton Goldstein, Laurel Severson, Lee Swisher, Rosalie Goldstein, and Phyliss Forsberg.

If you are in your 90s *they* believe you should not be in a private home; you should be in assisted living. I have nothing against assisted living. Paul and I lived in an assisted living home for a year in St. Paul. He was sick with Alzheimer's and we were going back to Minnesota for the summer. The stairs in our townhouse got too hard for his back, which was also bad, so we moved into Becketwood, a place that was full of university people and created for independent living. It had a dining room and a gym room and held all kinds of meetings.

Ollie and Inez Severson from the Coon Rapids Book Club were just down the hall from us and that was nice. Paul kept going to the meetings and always getting lost. Ollie and I would hunt for him and finally find him and he would always say, "Where have you been?"

Then Inez died, which really shook up Ollie. He told us that they hadn't planned on that. He was to die first, because he was older. He lived to be 100. His daughter, Laurel, lived nearby and she came over almost every day to see her dad. Laurel is a wonderful person.

My friend, Lee Swisher, from the Coon Rapids Book Club, who also worked with Paul and me on the Anoka County Mental Health Council, was put in Walker Home by her kids. She was in her 90s and she was very mad about it. Laurel called the kids and talked to them and reported back to Lee

My 94ᵗʰ birthday party

and I think got the family back together. While at Walker, Lee wrote two books and was Bean Bag champion. My God! Bean bags! What they do to adults and call it recreation.

I do not want to give up my home. Plenty of people I know hire help and live in their homes until they die. My primary care doctor says that is one way to do it. I cannot face losing all my things I have had for years and cherish—giving them to others when they really don't want them is the same thing as throwing them away.

There is not a mug in the cupboard that doesn't have a memory for me. The sheets are remarkable; they are still good and Paul and I bought them when we bought this place in 1986. I have furniture that we bought together. How much will fit into one room? We have a Norwegian dining room table that is really unique, and we got it by hunting down Norwegian furniture companies in the United States.

And what about all of my activities around here? I would have to get completely reorganized; that is not fun. Where would I paint? How far would it be from the UU church, the Humanists, the Elsie Quirk Library, The Farmer's Market? My doctors are all around here. Just give that up and join 500 people who have been forced to move because they are old?

Sounds like a concentration camp doesn't it? It isn't of course and my friends who are in assisted living seem to like it. They talk about how they don't have to cook, and they have entertainment all the time. I hope it's not bean bags—but who am I to criticize a system? I do not think I would love it and I am happy with the status quo. At my age I just don't want to make the move unless I *really* have to, not because my nutty relatives want me to. I do not live for them. Lord knows they don't live for me. Their father was annoyed at his kids too. Said they were all very tough, rough cookies and did little to try to understand him.

Another strange thing about old age I have discovered. I cannot talk about death to anyone 20 years younger than me. They will not do it. They just say, "You will live forever." Wow! What a horrible thought. Some of my happier moments are realizing I probably won't have to go through the worst parts of global warming or another world war.

I cannot understand people. They apparently think old people cannot think? Decide? Choose? Love? Have sex? Yes, they are experts on all of that. They blather away.

Another thing people with a prejudice against seniors say is that I must be lonely because I live alone, and they would certainly be lonely if they lived alone.

In the first place, that is not true; I live with my cat, Kim Chee. To prove that I still have friends, even though plenty of them are dead, I invited some people I knew to my 94th birthday. I stopped at 81 quests and then realized that this would be a wonderful opportunity for Democrats running for office in Sarasota County. So I invited 10 people running for office—from county commissioner to U.S. House of Representatives. They all came and brought their spouses or campaign chiefs. So I had about 100 people at my party, and we all had a good time.

Loneliness is for 60-year-olds. I am still running my life. I still go to Humanist meeting —I started the group in 2002 when Charlie Miller told me to start a group—that he would not help, but he would come to the meetings. It is still meeting and. this area has a lively group of Humanists, as does the state of Florida. I go to the Venice UU congregation and sometimes to the UU Fellowship in Port Charlotte. I like them both. Paul

Sandy Zelllick, me, Bob LaSallle

and I were members of the Port Charlotte UU. I joined the Venice UU shortly after he died to be with people who did not know him, did not remind me about him, and were still mainly interested in who I was. Then I went back to the Port Charlotte UU because they were working with the Immokalee Farm Workers which I wanted to do.

Now I am back at UUCOV—the Venice UU—because it is easier to get to at my age. I love the people of both groups. I am lucky to have them both around me. I attend plays at the Venice Theatre—my pal, Gloria, and I have season tickets with her niece too, and we also go to the Lemon Bay Theater with Ken Brennan an old UU friend from Minnesota. I attend the Asolo Theater and all the Ringling School of Art openings with my friends Jeanne Ranallo and Rose Sujdak. I have season tickets to the Venice Symphony with Pat Franks and Ken Brennen. We went last year. too. Theater in this area is very good. Many of the plays at the Venice Theater are superiors to Asolo shows. Asolo is the state theater of Florida. It trains people for theater and puts on show with their trainees plus professionals they hire specifically for that play. Last week we saw Music Man and the leads were all hired. It was a good show.

This year I am also going to the ballet with my Jeanne and Rosie. I saw one the other day with the Key Chorale. I have never seen a ballet with a chorus in the back. It was beautiful and unusual. I will always remember it; which I agree is not long at my age! I belong to the Tuesday Art group at the Englewood Art Center and try to go every month to their Art Center show with Gloria, Maria, and Jeanne.

The Hermitage— an art foundation on Manasota Key, has one or two performances a month on the beach. I go there frequently with ,Jeanne; before Paul Spyropoulos's leg got so bad I used to go with him. But we still go to the ART group, both of us, and he is having an exhibit there in January, he told me today. Paul is a real artist. He had a studio in New York City for 20 years and he and Emma, his wife—-one of my best friends, dead now— lived there.

I also work in my garden. It is beautiful this year, even if it is overgrown.

Ken, Char, Pat Beard and Peter and Linda— my cousin Louise's kids have helped a lot. Char, Peter and Linda have come to Florida almost every year. Ken, an old friend from our UU fellowship in Minnesota, comes by frequently often after his Rotary meeting and gives good advice. He is a Master Gardener as is Pat Beard, another friend who stops by and advises me about my plants and takes me out to lunch frequently. I have a pitcher plant I bought at Selby Gardens with Char a year ago. Pat and Ken have been invaluable in their help with that plant. It is flourishing so well that Char was astounded when she came a couple of weeks ago.

I worked for the Democrats in the 2018 election. As usual, this county went Republican. We register by party in Florida. Sixty percent of voters in Sarasota County are Republicans. We still strive to overcome. Many recounts this time and what we found out was that tabulating and recounting get very confusing. I think generally the votes are counted correctly, but I don't think it is an accurate count. The tabulation is usually different each time. Florida is a different state. It has great contrasts. It is extremely advanced, and very backward. It is one of the five states in the nation which refuse to ratify the ERA.

We really need to fix the electoral system. It is outmoded. I think younger people believe it is their job to police the old. I wish they would listen to themselves. As Lu, my cousin says, "People stereotype." I will repeat myself by saying they sure do! They need to study what is a fact, and what is an opinion and not get them so mixed up. It beats me how prejudiced college graduates can be. As the lady next door says, "Kids mean well. They should just listen to themselves and stop being parents"

The fact is I want to live a happy and productive life. I am 94; I can die at any time. I have a primary care doctor, a cardiologist, a dermatologist, a gastroenterologist, a urologist, an orthopedist and a foot doctor who remind me constantly that I am far from whole but doing fine for my age. They are taking care of me physically. The last thing I need are people who live 2,000 miles away determining what I can and can't do! Shades of Auntie Hazel. She was a good egg, but she went way too far sometimes. And I am afraid at age 94, she has returned multiplied.

I remember many good things about Auntie Hazel. I doubt that Edward and I could have managed without her, or my mother either (although she might have debated that). We lived in a big house with a big yard in north Minneapolis. It used to be my Grandpa's house and when he died, my Grandma gave the house to my mother and father as a wedding present. My Aunt Hazel owned part of the house, but I never knew much about that financial arrangement.

My grandfather, Edward Emil Witchie came over from Hindelbank, Switzerland with his parents and brother and sisters. His mother and father died on board the ship coming over, so my grandfather had to be in charge of the rest of the kids. He was 16, and the oldest. The kids were Will, Sophie, Bertha, Lydia and Ida, a baby who could not even walk. They first settled in Michigan and then came to Minneapolis.

My Grandfather wanted to become a homeopathic doctor but changed his mind and taught school for a year or two. Then he read law and became a lawyer. Her had an office on Washington Avenue, about a mile from the house he had built on Dupont Avenue North. Aunt Lydia married a lumberjack from Anoka, Minnesota named Applebee. Her daughters, Inez and Ruby, sometimes lived with my mother.

Aunt Sophie went to San Francisco and lived on a house on a hill and went through a bad earthquake in 1906. Aunt Ida used to come to visit when I was little. I don't know anything else about her. Aunt Bertha visited three or four times when my mother was alive. She was the executive secretary of a plumber's union and she was married three times—always to plumbers. I thought that was unusual and tried to get her to talk about it, but she wouldn't. Didn't see anything unusual in it. She was a nice lady, very kind to me. She really came to see my mother, often about Union things, for my mother knew some Union people in the Twin Cities.

Bertha wanted to get the plumber's unions organized. Uncle Will drank too much and deserted Cousin Katherine and Grace's mother and because of that they never wanted to be around him. But he came back to Minneapolis and lived downtown near the old library. Katherine by that time lived in New York City, but Grace still lived with her husband, Tom, and son Tommy in South Minneapolis. Katherine was a dancer and became a team with her husband Ralph Riggs. They danced in New York and traveled around the states and the world. In London, they danced before the queen. After they retired, Ralph continued as an actor and was in the original production of *Oklahoma* and also toured as the lead in Gilbert and Sullivan's *Mikado*.

My mother lived with Ralph's mother, Rosie Riggs, when Mom was in New York City trying to become an actress. Rosie later came to Minneapolis and lived with us for a year or two until she became ill and had to be hospitalized. She was ill for about two years and then she died. She was a nice person be around. On Thanksgiving and Christmas, I would drive the car to pick up Uncle Will and Aunt Lydia too. She was renting a room in a private house. The brother and sister talked, but not very much.

Aunt Lydia was really a quiet person. That quality didn't pass to Chubbie or Inez, particularly Chubbie. She talked all the time. Inez was really smart and got Phi Beta Kappa in college. Chubbie hated her name Ruby so legally changed her name to Elizabeth even though we still all called her Chubbie. She worked in Minneapolis at intake in General Hospital and one time a man came in the office with a gun and shot it at somebody right behind Chubbie. She was only four-eleven, so she didn't even have to duck. But that experience was very hard on her and she went into a depression.

Before that during World War I she was in Romania with the Red Cross and got a medal. Chubbie was a lot of fun, but she had deep depressions and for a while had to be in a mental institution in St. Peter, Minnesota. When they released her because they decided she wasn't mentally ill, she died.

Edward Emil Witchie. my mother and aunt's father. built what later was my mother's house. As far as his siblings were concerned it was the family homestead, and after he died they all came back to visit Leila and Auntie Hazel. Sophie was very close to Hazel and when she died she willed Hazel some railroad stock. Hazel told me but didn't tell Edward. Jean Mary and Edward wondered where she got the stock, but I figured if Hazel didn't tell them, there was no reason I should.

Grandfather sent both my mother and aunt to the University of Minnesota. He was determined his girls would have an education. He saw what his family went through trying to get work. Mom met my dad at the U of M.

Aunt Lydia believed in education also, like her brother. She insisted that Ruby and Inez go to college. Both went and did well. Aunt Lydia's husband went to Mississippi to work. Then he got sick and Aunt Lydia went to be with him. Her two girls, Inez and Ruby, were going to the U, so my grandfather told Lydia they could live with them until they finished school. Inez finished first, made Phi Beta Kappa and got a good job in Washington

D.C. with the Census Department. Ruby, whom we called Chubbie majored in social work and during World War I she joined the Red Cross.

During World War I, when Chubbie was working in Romania, she got leave and went to Switzerland and looked up the Witchie genealogy. The names of our ancestors were funny, and I recall Cousin Katherine being upset about the sound of some of the names! Hindelbank is a small Swiss town known now for its women's penitentiary. What a struggle the six kids must have had getting settled in the United States all on their own. No one ever told me about it. I guess they didn't like to talk about it.

I learned a little about homeopathic medicine, my grandfather's first career, though. My mother was a true believer in this and as a kid I got the most horrible tasting little pills with wild names, Arnica and Nux Vomica are two I remember. Arnica was rather tasty. They were given to me for practically any illness and as far as I could see had no effect at all. I had a year of sickness in fourth grade; I never did learn fractions well. I had mumps twice, once on one side of my fact and then on both sides. I had German measles and regular measles, I had chicken pox, stomach flu and the regular flu and cold after cold.

I always thought the cause of all of these diseases were the shots I had to get for three months once a month. They were to prevent disease and given by a homeopathic doctor. It was after those that I caught everything. On the other hand, the whole city was infected; school never had more than half attendance that year. However, that was the year we left homeopathy and I began seeing Umpapa's doctor, a regular doctor. He was a nice Norwegian who wore glasses and looked like my violin teacher. He had a roving eye, though, and Hazel was insulted when he came on to her during a physical. He was married with two kids at the time. She switched to another doctor.

According to my mother and aunt, Sophie was Grandpa's right-hand person, and without her the kids would never have been raised. I guess I met her, but the only ones I remember are Will, Lydia, and Bertha. And although I knew Aunt Lydia as a youngster, the others I did not meet until adolescence. I am sorry now that I did not ask more questions—something Paul was always scolding me about.

"You never ask!" he would say—annoyed when I did not know something I should have known. I may not ask enough questions, but I did learn one thing at an early age. I learned how to tell a white lie, or I learned to be sure my decision does not really hurt one person more than the other.

Grandma and Mom once had a big fight over me and it was the first time I had to make a choice between my Grandma and my mother. I was six and

I got scared. I was going to upset Grandma or my Mom, no matter what I said. Grandma was teaching me petit point and Mom had a fit. She hated petit point and told Grandma that no daughter of hers was going to do petit point! Grandma looked surprised and said I was doing very well and seemed to like doing it. Mom then asked me in a real nasty tone if I really liked doing petit point. I looked at the two of them. Grandma was smiling encouragingly and my mother glaring like a dragon.

I thought to myself that I liked doing it, but I don't live with Grandma, I live with my mom. So I said I didn't like petit point, even though I did, and my Mom looked happy. And that was the first time ever lied to grownups. I talked to my Auntie Hazel about lying being necessary sometimes and she acted like she didn't understand me until I caught her lying to her boyfriend, Stan, who brought her another dead pheasant to cook. She said thank you and then swore after he left. I told her that was the kind of lie I was talking about and she said sometimes white lies were necessary and what she said was a white lie.

When I was six or seven my mother got a good job. They paid her less than the men but didn't tell her for a long time. Then Auntie Hazel took me down to downtown Minneapolis to see her working in her new office. I was really relieved that she got a job because she was harping about needing a good-paying job. I really didn't understand what she meant. All I understood was her agony. It became apparent to me that she worked, not only around the house but downtown in an office. And it was a good job, one that could support her family and she liked.

My mother sat behind her desk and smiled at me. She looked different, like somebody important. She had a snazzy dress on and a fancy phone that wasn't upright like ours at home. She was dressed up so different that I was not sure that she really was my mother, but she laughed and then her voice sounded like my mother's, so I figured she had to be her.

Afterwards Auntie Hazel and I went to Ivy's for ice cream. It was what they called a tea room and it meant I had to sit up straight and eat my ice cream like a lady. I always had to sit up straight and be polite when I was with Auntie Hazel. She told me it was her job to show me how to be a lady.

My mother worked for the Minnesota state employment service and was in charge of getting jobs for day workers and women factory workers. My Aunt Hazel was a librarian for the city of Minneapolis. She never married but she could have married Stan. I liked him the best, but she said if she ever married it wouldn't be to someone who did nothing but clean his shotgun every Friday night so he could shoot it all the time.

My aunt was a pacifist, which meant she wanted peace and quiet. But she and my mom argued all the time, and it wasn't peaceful then. Both my mother and my aunt earned salaries lower than men because they were women. My mother crabbed about this a lot. My aunt never said anything much. It was the thing done in those days to pay women less than men. They didn't have the responsibility of men, or the necessity to work that men had, argued the men who determined who got paid what. They also were weaker and because of that men had to help them on the job more. That did get a laugh out of Auntie Hazel, but my mother used it to improve her job.

In her office everyone had to register people once a week for the entire day. This meant you stood behind a counter and handed people who wanted jobs some paper and told them to fill it out and helped them if they were too dumb. She hated doing that; she complained that it affected her bad back. When I said I ddn't know she had a bad back she just gave me a blank look.

What she did at the office was this: She claimed standing all day was heavy work, that she was a woman and couldn't do it. And the men bought it. She was in a good mood for weeks. "Well, that was one of men's myths about women," she said, "I might as well use it." I got an A in class one day because I knew what a myth was—or at least knew it better than any other kid.

The worst part about my mom's job was she had to deal with rich people. She liked poor people better. Mrs. Pillsbury was always calling her for a day worker because one of her maids was sick. She would argue with my mother. There was no set wage for day workers, but my mother told people who called in for one that the going wage was 30 cents an hour. Mrs. Pillsbury insisted on 25 cents and wouldn't pay more. So my mother always announced Mrs. Pillsbury's offer to the ladies who were waiting for a job. She told them not to take it, that Mrs. Pillsbury would give in, but there was always someone who said she needed the money and would take it. That upset my mother, and when we went up to the lake in the summer once we couldn't have any pancakes because all the store had was Pillsbury's pancake flour. I told my mother that Mrs. Pillsbury wouldn't care, and anyway she wouldn't even know. My mother told me to shut up.

When I was in junior high my mother did something no other mother that I know did. She ran for public office. She ran for the Minneapolis library board with her friend, Myrtle Harris. In the middle of the campaign there was a story in the paper with a line all around it saying that my mother's sister was a librarian and that all my mother was going to do on the library board was give my Auntie Hazel a raise. I showed it to mom and she laughed and said, "you damn betcha."

43

She and Myrtle won. And she and Myrtle got the board to vote to give every librarian a raise. Auntie Hazel said she was embarrassed, and Mom told her to give the money to the Minneapolis library book fund. And my aunt got mad, and they were mad for a while, until my aunt called up and apologized.

My mother told me then that I could be anything I wanted to be as long as I was willing to work hard at it. I told her that I wanted to join the army and learn how to fly an airplane and she said, "The army? What have I wrought?"

Mom had a good time on the library board. She went on a convention with Myrtle and they made the board build a new library and get more books for the children. Then civil service started and my mother was a state worker and came under civil service so she had to get off the library board. Was she ever mad!

Mom got her good job from politics. She had always been a Democrat-Farmer Laborite and Dad even ran for alderman once but lost. She got into politics and was elected secretary of the Third Ward Club. Then in a little while she got a job which could support the family. Governor Floyd B Olson gave it to her, and he even called her into his office to tell her; she kept a framed picture of him on the fireplace mantel as long as she lived.

During World War II. the federal government took over the employment service and everyone got the same pay, on a posted salary schedule. My

Ha Ha Island

Aunt Hazel was in charge of the social service branch of the library. It was very quiet there. A whole bunch of social workers were in her building and the idea was that they would use the library. But they really didn't. Hazel stayed there until she retired, then the city moved her branch over to the main library.

Our cabin on Hinsdale Island in Lake Vermilion was located in northern Minnesota's Arrowhead country. It was mostly wild, and full of lakes then, but now is full of tourists and fishing and sailing boats. I grew up at the lake. Started coming there when I was a baby, one year old. I kept on going up there until I was 60. Paul and I had our own island by that time. We bought it from Eddie Woolverton, an old boyfriend of mine, for $600. We later sold it for $50,000 and went down to Florida where, guess what? Woolverton lived 15 minutes down the road.

We had customs which we followed at the lake. One of our favorites was the quiet time at night. There was no place to go. If you wanted to go to a movie, it was a three-mile ride down the lake to the car and then a thirty-mile ride into the town of Cook, population 500. There was one showing of a movie at eight p.m. It was over at 10:30. The movie was usually a very old movie, and not a very good movie either. And then you had to retrace your steps.

Occasionally the lake people would have get-togethers, but these were usually during the day so people wouldn't have to drive on the lake in the dark. There was no TV. There was Edward's radio, which worked well enough. But to tell the truth, it either got South America or the city of Virginia, Minnesota, about 50 miles away as the crow flies. There was nothing on the Virginia radio which interested any of us.

There was no public electricity in any part of Lake Vermilion at that time. Gas or electric lanterns were used. Some people bought generators and had 50-watt lights here and there. Most people used bottled gas. Some just went to bed early.

We sometimes played cards or board games. Monopoly was one of my favorites. But quite often we all read quietly in the cabin with the fire burning in the fireplace. When the fire went down and coals appeared it was time for toasting bread, one of the things we did every night except when it was unusually hot and a fire would be too much for everyone. We had three or four three-foot wiener forks. We would put the bread through the forks and hold it above the coals and toast it. After it was toasted we would go to the table, smear butter and raspberry or strawberry jam on it, grab a cup and fill it with milk and that was our supper. Of course, we all had more than one piece of toast…and more than one cup of milk. And sometimes Hazel made cocoa.

Swimming was one of our favorite past times. Edward always swam to the other side and back of the channel. Our cabin was on Hinsdale Island and the channel separated it from the main land. It was about 100 to150 yards wide. Auntie Hazel and I would swim out to where we could see the three cabins which were up at the end of the channel, when the lake became a bay again.

When we came back, I had to follow one of her rules. Pick up ten rocks from the lake and throw them on the shore. That way, slowly but surely we made a nice swimming area. Later, when I was older, I would swim to the other side of the channel too. And a couple of times I even swam the three-mile round trip to Grand View resort, but a boat followed me. It was not a hard swim for me. I was in good shape. Mostly the sun bothered me. In those days good sun tan lotion didn't exist. I put on olive oil and fried my face.

I remember more unusual things about Auntie Hazel at the lake than about her in Minneapolis. She was part of Edward's and my life. They called her the extended family then. The United States doesn't have that so much anymore because people have moved around and don't have any family near. My two nieces and nephew live 2,000 miles from me. I get really irritated when they "advise" me because they really know nothing about the area or my life because they live so far away.

My mother was two years older and two inches taller than my Aunt at five-two. That was medium sized in those days. Hazel was just five feet. My cousin, Chubbie, was a real shorty at four-eleven. She lived sometimes with us because her mother was Great-aunt Lydia, who was one of my grandfather's sisters, and she thought the house was hers too. It's where she lived as a college student. Lydia had come from Switzerland with my Grandpa, and Chubbie never let us forget it.

She and my mother didn't always get along. Chubbie told me it was because my mother had had a hysterectomy and it made her mean. Chubbie had had one too, and she said it ruined her life, and she would never recover from it. Chubbie came and went in our lives. She was a sad person. She didn't like my cats either. I always had cats and dogs and even a rabbit named Toodles once.

Herculena, my favorite cat, had a lot of kittens all the time. I had named her Hercules when I got it from a guy way down on 6th street. I got Teddy Gaetke to go with me to pick her up. He had to ask his mother, and she said yes because I was two years older. Herculena was a tiny black and white cat who looked hungry. Teddy and I took turns carrying her. I thought she was a him and named her Hercules. But then she had six kittens so I named her

Herculena. My mother called her Poor Dear. She was great at the lake. We never had a mouse.

Chubbie was fun a lot of the time, and I enjoyed having her around especially when she worked nights and was home during the day; she was company. But she thought she was going to be attacked when she was alone in the house, so she would lock all the doors. That meant the cat couldn't get down to the basement to its box. So the cat, it was a tomcat named PISH, went to the bathroom all over the house and once on Chubbie's bed. That made Chubbie and all of us mad. But she still kept the door locked, so the cat did it again and Chubbie got really upset.

Whenever Mom, with the help of Chubbie and Auntie Hazel, cooked dinner they always had a big fight. I don't know why they fought like that. None of them did a great deal of cooking but they all thought they were exceptionally good cooks. I know Jean Mary, Edward's wife, was upset at the first Christmas dinner she came to. You could hear the three of them in the kitchen. They usually argued over the gravy. Then Hazel was on a salt-free diet and Chubbie and my mother would sneak salt in and Hazel would yell.

But the biggest fight was always over the gravy and it never got made right because of the arguing.

"If you do it that way, it will get lumps," my mother would say.

"Why don't you just let me handle it and it will be fine," Chubbie would answer.

Then Auntie Hazel would interrupt.

"Let me in there," she say. "I know what I am doing."

"They're fighting!" Jean Mary said. "How can they get dinner?"

I said to her that it wasn't anything, they had fought over dinners for years.

"It's terrible!" Jean Mary said.

Just then Chubbie stormed out of the kitchen.

"If they will NOT let me help. I won't" she snapped and stormed into the other room where she cornered some poor visitor to tell him or her all about the ongoing failure of the current Christmas dinner. And always, the gravy had to be strained. It had gotten lumpy. Hazel and Leila would argue over whose fault it was and Chubbie would always look down her nose and declare she certainly was glad she wasn't in the kitchen.

I think the whole cat fight gave Jean Mary confidence in her cooking. She had us out one Christmas. No one helped her with the gravy and it did not have to be strained either.

My mother and Chubbie eventually started to fight over the house, which Chubbie thought was hers because her mother was Aunt Lydia and my grandpa's sister, and my mother was just his daughter. My mother asked Chubbie to leave and wrote Inez and said Chub was difficult to live with. Inez never answered. Chubbie got an apartment near the University of Minnesota and took a night course in music appreciation. The cat got back on schedule. Then Chubbie got depressed and felt so lousy she put herself into a state mental hospital at St. Peter, Minnesota.

My mother didn't want to have anything to say or do about Chubbie. Auntie Hazel felt sorry for her and went to see her at St. Peter. Mom went once, and that was all. She said she had tried to help Chubbie and Chubbie had made her life miserable. If she stayed away from her at least one person of the twosome would be happy. A person has a right to be happy, she said. Hazel shook her head and said she would go see Chubbie. I never forgot what my mother said. A person has a right to be happy. Just like they have a right to have a job, my mother said.

Hazel was only five feet tall. She was husky, but not fat. She was different from Mom in so many ways that it was hard to tell they were sisters. Mom was a couple inches taller and more easygoing with us at the lake than Hazel. She usually let us do what we wanted with the admonishment: "I know you have brains and will be careful."

Auntie Hazel had no such trust in us; and she had her own hang ups. For instance, the porch of the cabin had canvas curtains to protect the beds where the women slept. The men had another screened cabin up on the hill in the woods. The canvas curtains *always* had to be rolled down when we were going away for more than two hours. It might rain. Even if the sky was blue and there were no clouds and the sun was shining! I didn't mind unrolling the curtains, but I hated rolling them back up. I had to get behind everything and be very careful or a bunch of stuff on the tables would tip over. My mother always looked at the sky and declare it wasn't going to rain, left the curtains alone and it never did rain.

As I think about those days, and the shibboleths my aunt and mother followed, I realize how much more freedom women have now. My mother refused to drive. She was scared silly at the thought, and society agreed She shouldn't be driving. She was a woman. Most women didn't drive.

She got a Ford with a rumble seat for Edward, and he was the family chauffeur. But except for important things we took the street car or walked. Auntie Hazel was more adventurous or else needed a car, for she bought a Chevy four-door sedan—blue black.

It created quite a stir and all the neighborhood kids ran out to look at it. Hazel bought three or four Chevys, all the same model and color. She drove back and forth to the lake from then on and sometimes in bad weather would drive Mom and me home from Umpapa's. Of course in the nice weather we liked walking.

Auntie Hazel should be alive now, when the car manufacturers adapt to various sizes of people. She was short and small. She had read trouble reaching the gas pedal and the clutch. If she moved the seat all the way up. her knees hit the steering wheel shaft. So she was a jerky driver. Her driving quite often made me car sick. We jerked during shifting especially.

She refused to drive in winter because she skidded once and almost hit another car. She had her car put up on blocks from the end of October to the middle of April. She drove during the time of the stick shift, and she was so small she could barely reach it. She stretched to get to the clutch, and would shift into first with a jerk, second with another and even high with a jerk. The brakes always came on so suddenly that we all fell forward, but it helped if we anticipated her action.so we watched like a hawk.

She was a safe driver, though. Never had an accident. And she went through some weird experiences driving with me. One year my cat, Herculena, had eight kittens in back of the Chevy as we drove from the lake to Minneapolis. I even named one Hazel. I thought she would like that. She argued with me about it and asked why I would think she would like a cat named after her. Then she looked at me seriously.

"Especially the runt of the littler," she said in an offended tone.

"But you are small!" I argued back.

"Not that small," she snorted.

My mother laughed about it and told me that I had learned a lesson. People have egos. I had upset my Aunt Hazel's.

Mom caused a stir in the neighborhood every Sunday afternoon. She and Auntie Hazel and Lucy Hayes—Davey and Eileen's—mother came over to have a drink and *smoke!* Davey and Eileen Hayes and Jimmy and sometimes Dorothy Ascher and I would hide beside the porch bushes and watch the women smoking. My mother said to me sometime later that she wished I wouldn't spy on them.

"It's stupid, impolite and invasion of our privacy," she said. "We can't have a good time with half a dozen kids snooping around." So we stopped doing that. What was the fun if they knew about it?

My mother wasn't much of a drinker. She would serve fruit juice instead—usually tomato juice. She had a bottle of gin for an occasional Tom

Collins and usually a gallon of Jewish wine which she adored. We walked the mile to Mrs. Fischer's house to get the wine.

She and my mother would talk politics and I would play with her dog or watch both dogs after I got Skippy I brought him to Mrs. Fischer's always. Mrs. Fischer lived in the Jewish section of Minneapolis, which was about a mile from our house, maybe a little longer.

My mother loved that sweet wine. She served it when we had my father's relatives over from Hudson, Wisconsin on Thanksgiving and sometimes when she had people in. She even let me have a little of it, and I really shocked my aunt when I told her boyfriend, George, that I had been drinking since I was eight years old.

Because they both worked my aunt and Mom were different from the rest of the neighbors. Their interests were different too. They belonged to The Women's International League For Peace and Freedom and the Foreign Policy Association and went to their meetings. Mom belonged to the Third Ward Democratic Club and helped get candidates elected. She and Hazel went out with men.

Auntie Hazel didn't go to church at all. She said she didn't believe in religion, thought too many wars had been fought over religion, and claimed that her father had never believed in God. That always got my mother mad, and she would snap, "He was my father too! And just because he read Charles Darwin didn't mean he wasn't religious."

Then they went at it with one another. The arguments could last an hour or two. I always went out to play. But I agreed with my Aunt Hazel about one thing, church was a big pain. The only time my mother and I went was on Christmas or Easter

My mother sent me and Edward to the Episcopal Church where my father had been a lay reader. That meant he was big in the church and sometimes even gave a sermon. The church was opposite North Commons Park. It had a stained-glass window with the name "Hasty," my grandmother's name, on it, so we always sat by that window. She had paid for that window when the church was being built.

Edward took communion and joined the church but never went. I took the communion classes but didn't learn the stuff; it seemed strange to me. The rector of the church also made a big mistake. Because of my father, Reverend Buzzelle thought I knew more about God and religion than I did, and I got to be in the advanced class. He talked some about Episcopalian philosophy and about the rights of the poor which was kind of interesting. Then we were supposed to memorize a bunch of prayers.

Later on when my mother and I were in church on some holiday I was mumbling through the Episcopal Creed—skipping words here and there.

With great dignity and in a loud dramatic voice, my mother said in the middle of the church service: "You didn't learn a thing, did you? Not one thing!"

I was embarrassed. Everybody heard her! My mother didn't care. She. wanted to make her point. She didn't care if it embarrassed me or called attention to her. The point was what was important. That was another way she was different from Auntie hazel, who would *never* do anything like that in church. *Never*! But of course she never went to church. But she would never yell at me like that.

At my communion everyone from Hudson came, and my brother who was married by then tried to get out of coming. But Jean Mary, his new wife, wanted to come, so he came and pretended he liked it. That gave me a snicker. Aunt Gussie and Uncle Ed and Uncle Harry and Aunt Gertrude came and made a big fuss over me. Aunt Gertrude told me when I was getting dressed for church that my big toe was apart from the other toes just like all of the Hardings. She did that again when I was getting dressed to marry Paul.

I talked to all of the Hudson relatives except Uncle Harry, who was deaf and just pretended he heard me. He was a very nice guy and smiled a lot. I think of him often now, because I am very deaf and miss a lot of things. What I did to Uncle Harry was mean. I cut him out of the group. I was a dumb, selfish kid, but didn't realize it then, and would have been insulted if anyone had called me selfish. I never even checked to see if he could hear if I raised my voice. He still held down an important job with Hudson Electricity. He must have been able to hear something.

My mother and Aunt Hazel really had different interests. My mother liked people around her and wanted them doing things that were worthwhile. She belonged to many groups and enjoyed doing things with the groups. Mom liked action; she enjoyed going on boat rides, visiting neighbors, going into town, and seeing friends.

Mom liked a crowd at the lake. It was nothing to her to ask 12 or 14 people up for a few days. Of course there was no room for them and they had to camp out in the woods, do the cooking, sleep on the floor, or double up on a camp cot. I remember that most people didn't mind, but that Jean Mary, Edward's wife, thought it was just terrible. She was right, of course. In those days I had to sleep with Mom on an army cot and she snored all night long and refused to stop even when I poked her.

In contrast, Hazel liked to walk in the woods, nap, and read good books (she was, after all, a librarian). She enjoyed sunning herself on the dock, and repairing it when it needed it—and when didn't it? She liked fixing things, and she loved encouraging Edward to fix things. And she complimented him even when he did a lousy job. I would tell him how lousy it was, though. He would just shrug his shoulders.

She enjoyed bossing us around. Auntie Hazel also liked to bird watch and collect mosses and nice-smelling pine needles. She would put the needles in a small pillow case, sew it up, and keep it next to her when she slept. My mother would never do all that, but she enjoyed the smell of the pine pillows and liked the ones Hazel gave her.

Both of them liked to sun themselves on the dock and swim a little. Mom was not into wildlife and slept much deeper than Auntie Hazel. I don't think Mom ever heard the porcupines chewing on the cabin. Or if she did, she just turned over and went back to sleep. I heard them, and so did Auntie Hazel.

My brother slept in the Caboda, a sleeping cabin for men up the hill, so he never heard them either. But he and my mother saw the damage. The darn little animals were chewing on the cabin's support logs and were half way through one. My mother just laughed.

"I doubt they will eat the cabin," she'd say.

Charlie Proctor who owned a summer resort down the lake and was a builder told her she needed to build a new cabin, that our old log cabin was worn out. The carpenter ants and the porcupines were eating it up

My mother used to be an actress. Before she married Dad, she was in New York trying to launch her career. She could get very dramatic when talk turned to rebuilding or changing the cabin. The cabin was an *ikon*, a memory that she would always have of the good times she and my father, Fred, had. *Nothing* was to be done to the cabin. So we enjoyed what we had.

The best thing about the cabin was the fireplace. It was a great fireplace. It burned well and heated the cabin in cold June and September nights. And it was beautiful. We would stick candles on the rough rocks of the fireplace and along with our kerosene Aladdin lamp we had good light at night. Later, when Coleman lanterns and bottled gas came in we had plenty of light. But we still kept the candles because they looked so cool on the rocks of the fireplace.

The cabin was not mouse-proof or bat-proof, but we always had a cat or two and a dog. They took care of the varmints. We used the cabin mostly for cooking, although we had storage with wooden hangars and big dock spikes to hang our clothes. We also had a couple of old storage trunks, and curtains covered the clothes.

A big folding table that was on the porch was for eating, and the Boy Scouts had put up rough shelves which we used to hold our cups and plates. We also had a bed for guests, and for anyone who wanted it, if it got too cold. Usually Skippy slept on it. During the day he and the cat slept on

Auntie Hazel's bed on the porch. At night, he preferred the warmth of indoors. He was a short-haired fox terrier.

Mom and Auntie Hazel ate different things at the lake. Mom liked our refrigeration which was a hole filled with packed dirt and a couple wooden shelves, a wooden floor and a solid wooden door. And things did keep cool with the 75-lb. chunks of ice we bought from Grand View. One thing my mother did not acknowledge, though, was the difference in months. She was up at the lake In June when it was between 55 to 60 degrees. In July and August it got up to 80 fairly often (We never minded the heat up there; there was always a breeze).

Hazel had food favorites that could spoil. She was worried about the ice chunks melting fast or that the temperature in the ice hole was uneven and undependable. Mom always told her to eat fish, but Mom was at the lake at the peak of good fishing. My aunt was at the lake at the peak of poor fishing. We ate very little meat up at the lake because we were dependent on ice to keep it fresh. The meat came from Herman T. Olson's grocery story in Tower and was on the mail boat for two to three hours, and the ice would have melted by the time it reached us. So we had spaghetti with bacon and cheese. Auntie Hazel's favorite meal was kidney beans and rice, which she learned how to cook a special way in Puerto Rico where she spent a year. Another standby was her old dependable chipped beef on toast. Shit on a Shingle, Paul called it. Hazel didn't think that was funny.

Auntie Hazel had a thing about breakfast food. She loved Rice Krispies. I remember as a little girl being taught to listen to the snap, crackle, and pop. I always was given the choice of cereal to order. I could have Rice Krispies, Puffed Rice or Puffed Wheat or oatmeal. I never chose oatmeal because Auntie Hazel liked it and ordered it anyway, so I really only had one choice because I didn't go for the puffed stuff. I could have eaten Edward's corn flakes, but I didn't particularly like Edward, so naturally I didn't like corn flakes.

At the lake, Hazel did all the cooking. She never bothered teaching me or Edward how to cook—she just wanted us to set the table and do the dishes. She even let us out of helping with the dishes if we were really into a good book. She said reading was more important than dishes. At home my mother taught Edward and me to make waffles. That was because we always ate them on Sunday, which was her sleep-in day. She taught us while she lazed in bed upstairs. Either Edward or I would yell up at her: "How much milk?"

She would yell back, "About a quart, but not really a quart!"

"How many eggs? How much flour?" And that way we learned how to cook waffles. When we had the first one ready she would come down in her bright striped satin dressing gown (that's what she called it) and check the first waffle. It was always bad either because we hadn't put enough shortening in the batter, or the waffle iron wasn't ready—it was too cold, or too hot. The waffle iron often needed a sample waffle to ruin. Then it would work.

We never had waffles at the lake because we didn't have electricity. We had pancakes instead, but seldom cooked by Auntie Hazel. She liked cold cereal, canned juice, and coffee for her and milk for me and Edward—coffee if we wanted it. We didn't. We both loved milk.

When Edward married Jean Mary all he could cook was waffles and hot dogs. She didn't teach him how to cook at all. So when she was in the hospital with pneumonia and Edward was home with the two little girls, I got a call from him. The girls were getting tired of waffles and hot dogs. What should he do?

I told him how to defrost a roast but he said he wouldn't dare do that, so I invited them over for dinner. I don't know what they did the rest of the time.

I don't suppose Hazel ever thought of teaching us cooking. She was a good cook, we could have learned from her. I took cooking in eighth grade at Franklin Junior High, so that helped.

We never had fresh meat until we got bottled gas installed at the cabin. Even then we only got it if we went by car to Virginia or Cook. She did not trust the mail boat to refrigerate meat well.

Edward was in charge of all of the heavy work at the cabin, and any man who visited helped. Auntie Hazel believed that women shouldn't do heavy work, it would cause cancer. I would love to see her reaction now to the Women Body Building movement. She didn't want me to do any lifting, and said women were not as strong as men.

"You believe the myth that men have about women," I said to her once, "that they are so weak they have to be helped all the time. And that they shouldn't work because some man is out of a job because a woman is working."

Hazel straightened up to her full five feet.

"What myth is that?" she snapped. "Women need to work just as much as men, and don't you forget it. Women aren't weaker they just aren't as big! And that has nothing to do about qualifying for a job and working."

Edward started to laugh. Auntie Hazel told him that he needed to get more ice at Grand View and that he should take the boat right away and go get some ice.

"And take Rosemary with you!"

After Edward got married, when I was 14 and Auntie Hazel and I would be up at the lake alone, she didn't care if I did the heavy work. I was the only one there who could. I snickered about that. Then sometimes she would ask Jimmy Hayes up and he would do the work, and sometimes Billy Peterson, another pal of Edward's, came up for a couple of weeks. They would get the ice and do the heavy work. I don't know if she paid those guys or not, but they both came up for a few years, and then her true love George Hyde always came for two or three weeks, so she had her male laborers.

We had one hair-raising experience which I will never forget. It was a cool August night. We had a fire and the coals got just right for toast. Auntie Hazel and I toasted our bread on wiener sticks over the fire and were settling down to drink our cocoa and to eat our toast and jam. Edward had not joined us. He was deep in a Doc Savage novel.

I was sitting by the fireplace, and Hazel was in a rocking chair in the middle of the cabin. I was halfway through my toast and raspberry jam when I looked up and saw a bat come in a tiny hole above the door. It zoomed toward the rafters and I watched it casually while I ate. I was chewing my toast and I planned I'd tell Hazel after I swallowed it. But I was too late for that.

She had a cup of cocoa in one hand and her toast in the other. She was bringing the cup up to her mouth when the bat swooped down between her lips and the cup. I had never seen a bat do that. And I have *never* seen anything like Hazel's reaction. She let out a howling shriek, tossed the cup of cocoa up in the air, dropped the toast, jumped up out of the chair, stepped on the toast and started to slide, howling all the time.

Meanwhile, Edward, who had most of the cocoa over him was spitting and spluttering. Then the bat swooped at him. He ducked and looked around for a flashlight and I started to douse all of the lights.

We had had bats before, but none as acrobatic as this bat. We all went out of the dark cabin and left the door wide open. About 10 feet out we stopped. Edward turned on a flashlight (making sure to hold it away from his body). The bat was attracted to the light and flew out of the cabin.

Auntie Hazel was contrite. She apologized to Edward again and again. He was laughing and said he had just about finished his book any way. He grabbed a towel, a bar of soap and went down to the lake to clean up. Auntie Hazel insisted that she would clean up the whole mess and dug right in with a mop And she meant it. We were not allowed to help. Later, the next day she was still on it and both of us told her that it was not often that a bat came between a person's mouth and a cup of cocoa! We told her she could get in Believe it or Not by Ripley, but she didn't think that was funny.

The only time I ever saw her get mad at her true love, George, was when we told him about the bat. Instead of sympathizing with her he went into a long ramble about bats in Texas. Hazel glared at him and said she was going to bed and took her nightgown and purple bathrobe and stomped off to the porch where she slept.

Hazel was worried he would destroy us, I guess. Or she wanted to avoid a killing—either Edward or I were good with a 22 rifle, and we had already shot one porcupine. They could be real pests. Skippy chased them, and never learned! The porcupine would slam his tail against the dog's head and Skippy would be in serious trouble. Luckily, we didn't have to bring him into Cook—a mile boat ride and then a 30-mile ride to Cook. Dr. Franklin, a retired physician had a cabin about a half a mile from us. We could walk down on a path or take the boat. We only took Skip when we couldn't handle the job ourselves which was most of the time. He usually had quills in his mouth, near his eyes and all over his jaw. If there were fewer than a dozen, we would handle it. Someone would hold the dog and someone else would pull the quills. Usually Auntie Hazel did it. If we had to take him down to Franklins, Dr. Franklin and Edward, if he was there, would choke the dog senseless and remove the quills. The ones they didn't get would work themselves out in frightening places like right next to the eye! Edward complained loudly about my dog. He did not particularly like Skippy, and this was proof he was a dumb dog. "He doesn't learn!" Edward would proclaim. I got mad once after he said that and snapped "Just like your dog Van who got killed chasing cars." That really made him mad. And he turned all red. I would never admit Skippy was dumb, but he certainly was persistent. He got into porkies almost every year. I maintained he was trying out different ways to capture a porcupine and Edward told me that I was becoming a comic. Edward offered to shoot any porcupine with his 22, but Hazel was a pacifist and would not hear of it. I think it was the porcupines humming or murmuring while he chewed that got to Hazel., and knowing her I think she didn't want another porcupine shot. One morning she announced that the porcupine needed to be taught a lesson. He had to he stopped in destroying our cabin. Edward wanted to know how she was so sure it was a He. This flustered her. She had to admit she was a feminist. "Even with porcupines," Edward snorted.

The porcupine that liked to eat the cabin was so noisy one night that Hazel couldn't sleep. The next day she vowed to teach Porky a lesson.

Edward offered to shoot it with his .22, but Hazel was a true pacifist. She wouldn't hear of killing Porky. She'd get him another way.

Auntie Hazel prepared a concoction of mustard, red pepper, black pepper, hot sauce, dry mustard, and every other spice she could find in the cabin and made It into a paste. She spread the paste on the log that the porcupine was eating.

"Now we'll see," she chortled. "We'll see if the porcupine likes this special treat." That night around midnight, Porky came. He gnawed for about a minute and then let out a combination grumble and squeak that was so loud we all started laughing. The porcupine tried again in a different spot. But Auntie Hazel had smeared her concoction all over the logs. He couldn't get away from it. He squealed, grumbled and took off down the path. He came again, but never chewed on the cabin.

Hazel was beside herself with triumph. A couple of nights later, Porky struck again, but in a different way. It was a warm night and all of us were sleeping lightly. We heard a scratch on the porch door and we thought it was the cat.

"Who is going to let the kitty in?" Hazel asked sleepily.

I pretended I was asleep, and I guess Cecelia did too or really was asleep. Anyway, Hazel got up with a flourish and dramatically put on her bathrobe and slippers and went to the door.

"Well, Kitty, she said "do you want to come in?"

When she opened the door there was the Porky sitting on the top step. He started to come in

"No, no! Get away from here!" she screamed. She grabbed the pitcher of water from the table and dowsed Porky with it. The animal blinked water out of his eyes, grunted and went down the steps, turned and looked at Hazel and grunted again. She yelled, which scared the animal, and he turned and started waddling down the path by the lake.

Hazel, triumphant that she had scared him, decided to teach him a lesson he would never forget. She grabbed a flashlight and a few chips from the chopping block as she went by and took after him. She hurled the chips at Porky, who would jump a little and run faster. Hazel chased him maybe 25 or 30 yards before she overshot. The chip landed by his nose. He turned, confused and began running back down the path toward her. Boy, did it get noisy.

"Whoop! Whoop!" Auntie Hazel screamed. "He's after me. Save me! Get the door open! Open the door! It's after me!" She tore down the trail with her bathrobe and nightgown up to her thighs, yelling and carrying on. Florence was there by the door and opened it, Hazel almost on top of her.

"Where's the porcupine?" she asked. Hazel stopped short and looked around.

"I don't know," she panted, "he was right there!"

Cecelia said Auntie Hazel yelled like a banshee.

"What is a banshee, and tell me what it looks like, will you please, Cecelia?" Auntie Hazel asked with great dignity. We had a good laugh, even Hazel panting in her purple bathrobe. As we got into bed, Herculena the cat showed up and wanted in. "Who wants to let the cat in?" Hazel asked. "It's not going to be me!"

So I let my cat in.

That was the end of the porcupines that year. We did not see any ever again. Florence never got over that night, and had a good time telling everyone in the Citizen's Aide Building about Auntie Hazel's porcupine experience. One time when I was down at Auntie Hazel's library a complete stranger said to me, "Oh, I've heard all about you and your aunt from Florence. It sounds really wild up at your lake." Auntie Hazel was standing beside me and said nothing.

.

We always had a good time when Cecelia was around. She had a great sense of humor and got into many funny situations. One year, after Edward married Jean Mary, the three of us were up at the lake. The weather was unusually nice that year and we could go swimming early in the morning around six or seven. We were a half a mile from out nearest neighbors, the Franklins, and they were around the bend anyway, so many times we did not bother to put on a swimming suit when we went in the water.

One morning around seven Cecelia woke up and decided to take a dip in the lake. She went down to the lake in her nightgown, took it off, and jumped in. She was swimming peacefully when the mail boat came chugging into sight. This did not bother her. It came by every morning on its way to Tower, 15 miles down the lake, where it picked up the mail and delivered it to the lake people later on in the day. It went all the way up to Vermilion Dam, which was a 20-mile trip from Tower, and stayed there all night. That morning, though, was different. The mail boat turned into our dock. Scoop, the mail man, had forgotten to deliver a package.

Cecelia, naked in the water, was trapped. She swam to the dock, ducked under it and hid in the water up to her nose. The boat stopped, Scoop climbed out and put the package down

"Good morning!" he called out. Hazel had stumbled out of the cabin in her purple robe and waved at him. After the boat was long gone, Cecelia came out from under the dock, climbed on the top of it, grabbed a towel and ran up to the cabin.

"I didn't hear you, Cecelia," I laughed. "What did you say when Scoop said, 'Good morning?'" She turned brick red.

"He wasn't talking to me!" she said.

Auntie Hazel and I teased her and laughed about that for the rest of her life. Years later, when I was married to Paul and we were headed overseas on our joint sabbatical, we were in Washington DC staying with Cecelia who was working then as a librarian in the Department of State Library. I mentioned the episode at the lake.

"He wasn't talking to me!" she laughed. She was fun to be with.

One summer Cecelia agreed to go to the lake with me in the absence of Auntie Hazel or Mom, who were busy. Everybody's worry was that Cecelia and I couldn't manage without a strong man with us to chop the wood and get the 100 lb. blocks of ice from Grand View Resort a mile down the lake.

Cecelia was probably in her late 40s then. She was about five-seven and very energetic. She loved to be doing things. She just laughed at the fear of men's work thing.

"I grew up with five brothers and they never, ever waited on me," she chortled. We got help with the ice at Grand View from Charlie, the handyman who took a liking to Cecelia. At the cabin we dragged it up to the root house on a rug

I ran the outboard down the lake (I could start it by then). I liked to chop wood, but there was enough dead wood around to burn anyway. So Cecelia and I had a great time. I was sorry to see her go after two weeks. But she never went for good. She came up for a couple of weeks from then on when Auntie Hazel was there.

Hazel returned the next year, and so did my brother. He was into radios then and built himself a small cabin out of unpeeled poplar logs where he could work on his shortwave radios in peace. He would come racing up excitedly sometimes when he got South America. Mostly he got the Iron Range stations about 50 miles from us. He got them by climbing up on the roof and attaching a wire on the chimney and then to our flag pole. That way he could get South America any time he wanted, and Virginia and Hibbing, Minnesota too. I was impressed, and so was Auntie Hazel.

Mom and I went every Sunday to see Umpapa and Auntie Hazel. In the late afternoon, we would walk the six blocks up from our house. We would go on the streetcar street, Emerson, in the winter, so if a streetcar came we would hop on it. We always tried hard to get one coming back, because we listened to the Ford Symphony Hour from nine to 10, and never got started home until 10:15. That was too late for women to walk.

We would see the streetcar coming and either I or Auntie Hazel would dash out to stop it and Mom would follow. Mom didn't like to hurry. I never saw my mother walk fast anyplace, no matter what. That was her thing, walking slow.

If the streetcar didn't come and we got tired of waiting on Umpapa's porch, we walked; and in the winter when it was 20 below my mother would say it was damn cold, and Umpapa would sometimes call a cab and give my Mom cab money. We missed Edward, who would come and pick us up when he was home. But he was in college and busy there and living at his fraternity on the money my Grandma left him for college, and I was too young to drive.

People wonder why Auntie Hazel never married. I don't know why either. I do know she did not think marriage was the answer to a happy life, and she did not need to get married because of money or any other reason, for that matter.

She had many man friends; Hazel invited some of them up to the lake. "I get to see them in another situation!" she would tell us. Stan Ryberg was the guy I liked the best, because he liked the woods. He was in charge of the Minnesota Boy Scouts—or some such job and had an office in the same building as my aunt's library.

He was an energetic guy who fixed things, chopped wood, and did many things for us around the cabin. He came up for about three years, but then it ended. He could not give up his love for guns, and this turned Hazel off. One time I saw three horned owls in our swamp down the hill and hurried back to tell everyone. Stan got out his rifle and went and shot them as keepsakes. Hazel told him that they were keepsakes when they were alive, and that she didn't want them in the cabin when they were dead.

Stan and I cut the feet off and we put them on the side of the wall. The next day she and Stan had a long talk about war. She said she was a pacifist. She didn't like Stan after the owls and that argument they had about pacifism. The next year Stan married someone who, "wasn't a pacifist, I imagine," Hazel said when I asked. I asked her if we should take the owl's feel off the wall and she said to leave them be. We should remember they never harmed us. We killed them.

And then Charles came up in white slacks and a blazer and Hazel told him to help by chopping some wood. That eliminated Charles.

Hazel's true love was a dinky little guy named George from Texas. He came every year with a huge box of liquor, stayed two weeks and was fairly drunk some of the time. Hazel drank very little, but she adored George. They were a cute couple. They were the same size and fit together. They would sit out at the end of the dock at night and talk. And then he and

Edward would sit on the porch by the door and sip whiskey most of the night and talk. Hazel would be with them for a bit, but would get tired and announce that it was time for everyone to go to bed. George would laugh at her and then Edward would, too, and they would sip whiskey. My bed was around the corner, and I would hear them droning on most of the night.

My mother thought he got Edward drinking. Edward was just going on twenty. Hazel tried to get George to stop, but he laughed at her.

"The boy's got to learn to hold his whiskey," George would say and then would then pour them both a drink. Edward soon began asking which kind of whiskey was the best, and why gin was better than vodka. The next thing I knew my mother made a trip to the lake, which she almost never did when Auntie Hazel was there.

She brought a man she was seeing at the time and whom she almost married. His name was Louis, and I just loved him. He had studied magic and taught me all kinds of magic tricks, so many that I put on a magic show at my junior high. Louis liked the lake and could identify all kinds of plants and trees and birds and taught us all a lot.

He and my mother came at the end of George's visit and were only able to stay a long weekend because they both worked. Louis and George got along great. They both smoked cigars and loved to brag about their past. The first night George asked Louis to join him and Edward. Louis, who was a very mild man, suddenly raised his voice.

"Yes, I like a good drink and I like to reminisce. But not with a young kid sitting around listening and getting the wrong impression." He looked at Edward. "So you are not welcome."

Edward got mad and started to argue.

George interrupted.

"He's right, Ed", he said "you should go up to bed. We'll do something together another time" And Edward stomped off.

The next morning Louis took Hazel on a walk in the woods to identify berries, and my mother talked to George for some time at the end of the dock. After a while they came back to the cabin, and talked about Mexico. That night, Louis and Mom played Monopoly with me and Edward read. Hazel and George went out on the dock and came back just as Mom landed on my Boardwalk. After we put away the Monopoly, George started to talk.

This was his last visit to Minnesota because he was leaving the United States and accepting an offer to work in Mexico. He had asked my Aunt Hazel to join him, and he put his arm around her. She said she was going to think about it.

Mom and Louis left the next morning. Edward and I took them in the boat up to Vermilion Dam where they had left Louis' car. I was given some money by George to get Louis a half dozen cigars and that caused some talk in the store. Lloyd Shively, who owned the Resort at Vermilion Dam wanted to know if was planning on smoking them all in one day, and all of the people around the bar and store started laughing. But I got the dumb cigars.

Then Louis got funny and said that six cigars probably weren't enough for a long car trip. Then I got funny too, and just stood there and didn't say a thing, although I did have about a dollar in change, which would buy another cigar, but which George said I could keep. So that was that.

The next day George left on the mail boat, which would take him to Tower, where he would rent a car and head to Mexico, I guess. Hazel never went to Mexico, and never talked about George, and neither did my mother. It was if he had never even existed.

George had given Auntie Hazel an old serape which he had said was antique and woven by a famous Mexican Indian weaver. Hazel washed it in cold water and kept it on the bed at the end of the porch at the lake. It was red and green with a little yellow. It brightened up that end and was very pretty. The dog and cat often slept on it during the day. When Hazel stopped going to the cabin after my mother died, and Edward and I got married, and the cabin began to need too many repairs, she kept the serape on the couch in her apartment.

My mother never married Louis, and he just stopped coming around. I asked her why and she took a while answering. She finally said that Louis wanted a hausfrau, and she was not a hausfrau. Jean Mary, Edward's wife said to me once that Edward thought Louis was a real jerk. I told her I liked Louis, but Edward didn't, and I let it go.

I still think about it and wonder how things would have been if they had married. Edward was gone. I was in high school headed for college and then I would be married and gone. Mom could have lived with Louis the rest of her life. Seemed like a no decision to me, but after I married Paul understood my mother. Marriage is love and equality. It does not mean that either partner becomes a different person to please the other partner. What you see is what you get. Each partner has a right to follow her/his own drummer.

Because my mother had a pension, and had an income, she was not in the position of many women her age and in her time. She did not have to marry in order to live and so she refused to live on Louis' terms. She wanted equality, and Louis had no understanding of what equality between the sexes was.

Auntie Hazel moved into an apartment when Umpapa died and had only a few friends. She would play canasta. She was unwell the later part of her life. She had diverticulitis and had to be on a strict diet and that didn't help, so the doctor finally amputated her lower bowel. At the lake, from when I was about 12 on she would take pain pills and rest. The doctor said the lake was great for her, but most of the time she just slept.

We had outings to Cook and Virginia for supplies. Cecelia and Florence would come up and there would be some action. I read a lot during those years. My mother stayed the same. She had high blood pressure which eventually killed her. Edward and I inherited that. She died at 73, much sooner than Hazel, who was 85 when she died. Edward died at 78. Helen Mary lost her eyesight and died in her early 80s and Louise had a different form of dementia and died around the same age. Elizabeth lived until she was 92, but her mind went.

Right now I am I am the matriarch and am still in my right mind in a crazy world, state, and country.

Senior Year

Auntie Hazel taught school for a year in Puerto Rico. She had gone to Puerto Rico with Mom and Dad to visit Uncle Frank, my dad's brother, and his family. They lived there permanently. Uncle Frank was an officer in the United States Army stationed in Puerto Rico.

They couldn't find a teacher for their little school, and they convinced Hazel that she should take the job and see a new country. Hazel didn't like

Puerto Rico. She showed me a bunch of pictures of it and said it was very interesting but rather lonely, and she hated teaching.

My mother once shook her head about Puerto Rico and Hazel. She said that Hazel expected it to be the way it was when Mom and Dad were with her, and that Frank Harding and his family would include her in all their activities. In other words, a permanent vacation. When they left, things quieted down and the Hardings went into their regular routine and forgot about Hazel.

It was a small school of 10 to 12 children. She was the only teacher and it was out in the countryside. There was transportation to the army post, but seldom to San Juan, the nearest big city which was a long way away.

Years later, my cousin, Laura Adelaide, at a family reunion she held in Madison, Wisconsin, reminisced with me. She asked if I ever knew Hazel Witchie. I told her she was my mother's sister. Laura Adelaide told me that Hazel slapped her face in Puerto Rico, that she was her teacher for a year in a small school near her home. She had done something that had made Hazel mad. Laura Adelaide would not tell me what it was. just walked away when I started to question her.

To me, what was interesting was that Laura Adelaide was in her 80s and she still remembered the incident and was still mad about it. That may explain why Mom and Hazel were stony faced when I told them both one night that I was going to be a teacher. I was a little surprised at their reaction, which was silence, but I had other things to worry me at the time than what they felt about teaching.

At the time I had been working my way to freedom from my aunt and mother. I did not want them telling me what to do with my life. I also did not want to cause a rift in the relationships I had with both of them. It was a touchy time. It was hard for me to give up being a baby, and hard for both of them to allow me to grow up and make good and lousy decisions.

I know Hazel thought my decision to teach was a bad decision; my mother was more neutral about it, but of course was influenced by Hazel's experience.

My brother had just married and that had been a traumatic time for both women. Jean Mary had a good many things against her. First, she was Catholic. In the 1940's religion was very important, and there was prejudice against Catholics, Jews, and just about every religion which wasn't the one being practiced.

65

In addition, Mom and my aunt had gone to high school with Jean Mary's father, Roscoe, and neither woman liked him. It was not a casual thing either—they knew him well and did *not* like him.

The other thing was that Edward had recently been dumped by a girl he wanted to marry. Phyllis was a nice girl who apparently couldn't make up her mind between Edward and some guy who was graduating with an engineering degree. Edward was a journalism graduate. She finally took the engineer because she felt that he offered her a better income, and apparently told Edward this. That went over like a lead balloon with everyone. It affected Mom's reaction to Jean Mary and Hazel's too. They were not sure that Edward wasn't on a rebound—that he was just mad at Phyllis.

Edward insisted that Phyllis had nothing to do with Jean Mary, and the Catholic business got settled and things quieted down, and they married. Auntie Hazel said she thought Roscoe had matured a. little. But it was a rocky time for Jean Mary, and I wouldn't have wanted to be her. It was just before World War II started. It was hard to get a job in a newspaper which is what Edward wanted. He finally got a job in Minneapolis selling printing presses. I guess he actually sold one or two.

The thing that impressed me the most about Edward at this time in his life was that he started to do a little house work. He and I were not much on housework. Then the war started and Edward was drafted in the Signal Corps was to be sent to the South Pacific. This never happened because they lost his orders for about two months and Jean Mary and Edward sat around the house. Finally, instead of going overseas he got sent to Aberdeen Proving Grounds in Maryland and did research on rocket development until they discharged him. Jean Mary went with him and they were able to live off post and life was as good as it could be in those times.

I was just entering college then. I had no idea I was going to be a school teacher. I wanted to become a veterinarian and enrolled in the pre-vet course. Although my heart was there, I had not prepared myself well enough in math or the sciences for this field. Not only did I find it difficult going, I found that I really didn't like it.

So I transferred to an area I liked and understood speech, theater and English. I did well in this field. Dr. Whiting of the University Theater told me that opportunities in the field were limited to stage, movies, or teaching. He recommended teaching. I agreed with him. I had been enrolled in speech-English for over a year and taken several theater courses. My skill was in directing plays. I was no future stage or movie actress.

My other field was radio. I could have entered that if I wanted to. But I thought teaching offered more security, so I decided to become a teacher. It

Paul during his time as an Army sergeant.

proved to be a good vocation for me. Drove me crazy at times, but I succeeded and became a good teacher.

Shortly after I decided to become a teacher, I met Paul. He was a veteran returning to finish his senior year. His draft board insisted on sending him to war even though he had just started his last year at the University. Most Minnesotans were allowed to finish their senior year. This was not true in Connecticut, where Paul was from. They gave no breaks to anyone.

At the time I was a member of Minnesota Masquers, the theater group. They wanted to have a fundraiser and wanted someone to direct a play. They were not particular about what play. We dinged around about this for a meeting or so and I finally said I would be glad to direct a play. I can't remember how we decided it was to be a melodrama. I am not sure whether I decided that or the group did. Probably I did, because one of the things we were taught by Dr.Whiting was that the director chose the play.

I chose a play called *Love Rides the Rails* and scheduled tryouts. The man who was going to do the lights, Marvin Hannibal, and his pal Dick Spear sat in on the casting and gave me some encouragement. Not help. They never told me what to do, they just pointed out choices, and approved whatever choice I made. We had two choices for the heroine: Mary Lou, a good friend, wanted the heroine played like a dingbat. Pam, another good friend, wanted it in the classical melodrama style. Marvin and Dick were very noncommittal here. They told me that both girls would be fine in their parts. What I would have to do is decide what kind of interpretation I wanted the heroine to have.

Scenes from
"Love Rides
the Rails"

Marvin, me, Maggie, and Paul

I chose Pam. Both of these two were good friends of ours, but Mary Lou never let me forget that she would have done the heroine in a really funny way. We found a wonderful hero, a very serious boy, strikingly good looking, who was a naval cadet in a special University program. He had some experience in acting and was such a sincere, open person that he was almost being typecast. We wanted a villain but could not find one. I found a kid from the music department who had a good, loud voice but had no experience. I cast him as the assistant villain and began casting minor parts.

Marvin and Dick went to look for a villain. They returned with the word that Hagen was back from the wars, and that he would be fine.

"Hagen?" I asked, "who's he?"

Marvin hugged me

Paul in character

"Don't worry," he said, "he'll show up."

And they both vanished to work on other plays. Dick and Marvin posted another notice on the board. "Needed: Villain for melodrama and other people for minor parts." And Paul Hagen showed up to try out for the villain.

By that time I had decided I would turn the show into a musical melodrama. Pam was taking voice lessons, and Lew, the hero could sing and so could several of the bit players. The assistant villain was a voice major in the music department who had a lovely baritone. Paul tried out for me and he was wonderful. His villain would have heart and feelings for others but could not help doing crooked, awful things. I cast him in the part and told him he would have to sing two songs. He looked upset.

"I can't sing" he said.

"Nonsense," I said, "everybody can sing a little. You are the villain. You can sing off key."

Paul looked forlorn: "I sing monotone."

I looked at him. "Sing." I said. "Sing *God Bless America*."

So he sang. He was right. It was terrible. Then a thought came—the assistant villain could sing Paul's songs for him. That would work. Paul and John, his assistant villain had a plan. John would sing off stage and Paul would mouth the words. So the show was cast.

A woman named Grace Krause, a Masquer member who no one really knew showed up to help build the set and she did so well she took over—built the rollers, designed the canvases which were our backdrops and put together a marvelous roller full of local University dinky town merchant's names.

The show was very successful. It ran Thursday through Sunday in the Green Room at the University Theater. This held about 50 to 60 people and I decided to put tables up so that singers and chorus girls could walk around the audience. We had to extend the show for another three weeks, so it ran for 10 weeks. I got to know Paul very well. We went through a lot of problems together.

Although I had the help of the Masquers, there were plenty of things I needed help with which I did not get. Selling tickets was one of them. People who called in, called my number and got me and I made the reservations, the changes and any additions or cancellations. I also ended up selling pop and Coca Cola. During the war, sugar was rationed. It was very hard to get Coca Cola. We had to do with root beer, ginger ale, orange crush—and people complained. They wanted Coca Cola, or beer. They were not allowed to have beer. Paul came to the rescue. He had a cousin who was vice president of the local Coca Cola company. He called his office and we made an appointment to see him. He was a skinny guy about 45 or 50 and very serious. I thought for a minute or so he was related to our hero, he was so serious.

"I can give you my personal allotment of Coca Cola for the month. And, I don't pay for it—so you can have it free." So we got a case for nothing. I gave him two tickets. He gave them back. It was too much trouble to get a sitter. We left. Paul was disgusted.

"He didn't do much," he said He could have given us more than a case."

"Be happy with what you've got!" I said as we went to pick up the case. The Coke was very popular and everyone at the U Theater wanted to know where we got it. I told them to ask Paul.

After most of the shows we all went down to the East Hennepin Cafe to have a beer and a hamburger, and by the time the play finally closed, Paul and were in love. And our families were scrambling to see the play. Paul's mother flew in from Connecticut. Ann, and Doug and Alice came to the play after all. My mother, not to be undone, asked Auntie Hazel and the Gavins—Grace and Tom Gavin and their children, Betty and Elmo and Tommy. And my mother wanted the tables put together so that she could talk to everyone conveniently. Marilyn Dean told me about this.

"She can't do that!" I said. Marilyn went back to tell her this and shortly returned.

"She is moving the tables herself!" Marilyn said. "You'd better get out there."

I went out. and met an implacable force. I gave up. Let her have her way. After all, the show was to start in five minutes. I went back and told the chorus girls who went into the audience to sing that they would have to do it on the edges of the audience instead of the middle because we had a party taking up all of the space. Paul guffawed, Marilyn giggled and I finally smiled. But it must have affected me, because I still remember what my mother did.

The show finally ended after a 10-week run. Finals were coming and our senior year was coming to an end. Then the Army wanted us to do the play for them at their downtown center and Old Log Theater, a community theater at Lake Minnetonka, asked me if we could do it as their opening play because their regular director was still in the army.

Everyone was beside themselves with excitement except me. I certainly did not want to spend days and hours recasting parts for people who had other summer commitments, making arrangements to move the scenery, paying the U theater for their costumes, and probably their scenery. It was the end of the year and I had finals and other classes besides theater to finish. and the Old Log was a business. They should be paying all of us.

Lake Vermilion looked very inviting. My mother, of course, took this another way. As a former stage-struck actress trying to break into Broadway 50 years earlier she could not fathom why I was not interested in Old Log. To her it meant only one thing. I was in love with Eddie Woolverton, a family friend who'd turn up repeatedly in my life—but not as my husband! So my mother suggested that politely, without any trauma to him, we should get rid of Paul.

She had met Eddie's parents, gotten along with them and genuinely liked Eddie. She assumed that Eddie was my true love. He was just a good friend of mine at the lake whose parents were visiting, so I asked them over with a couple of other friends for a party one night. Mom liked Eddie. She wanted me to marry someone who would be able to fix things. Mom had asked Paul to do some repairs and he failed miserably. I remember my mother saying to me later that he was a good comedian as a repair person. She also wanted me to find a husband who would be a good provider. She could tell, she said, that Eddie would succeed in life. She got that right. He became a millionaire. He played the gold market.

Then Old Log notified me about the melodrama. No melodrama. The company's director had been discharged from the army and he was back in the saddle. So I went up to the lake, and Paul went home to New Haven, Connecticut. Our romance was put on hiatus and I enjoyed the north woods.

Paul and me during happy college days.

We had both graduated, so we had our resume's out. I enjoyed my time at the lake with my mother. She liked boat rides around the lake and we had a good time visiting neighbors.

Then Eddie struck. He asked me to go on a weeklong canoe trip with him and a pal and his girlfriend. A week, I thought. And what do we do on a canoe trip for a week besides paddle? I told him I would think about it. I did not mention it to my mother. But Eddie did.

"Do it." she implored. I was shocked. As a matter of fact I am over 90 now and I am still shocked at her. Here was my mother, who guarded our lives as if we were newly discovered uranium, telling me to go off into canoe country with Eddie. Then she threw out yet another reason why she preferred Eddie over Paul. Paul was bald. He had lost his hair at age 20. In fact, all of the Hagen men were bald except Emil.

Mom thought Paul was also much older because he was bald. I straightened that out He was five years older than I was. Eddie was six years older. She didn't use that argument any more. Again I was amazed. Here was a woman who taught me prejudice was wrong, I mentioned that too.

"Will he be successful?" she responded.

I walked away from her. I got a letter from Paul the next day or so. He had applied to graduate school and had a job as a teaching assistant at the University. My mother and my aunt did not like graduate school. Neither did Mrs. Jones, who was an old pal of theirs. I ignored all three of them and became engaged to Paul and let my mother handle Eddie. She was the one who was interested in him anyway.

We got married in Mom's house because my mother was romantic It was a crowded crazy wedding. My maid of honor, Joyce, was getting married in two days, so she was there in spirit only. My other attendant, Mary, was annoyed at Paul's best man, Joe, because he hadn't asked her out.

Paul's Uncle Durrell, who was very shy with women, unmarried in his late 60s, asked a friend of Mom's out. Bette had been married four times. Nothing came of it.

Edward and Jean Mary could not make the wedding. So on our way to Connecticut we went to Washington D.C. to see them. All I remember about the visit is seeing Cousin Inez in Washington and Ed and Jean Mary in Maryland.

"Watch out for Mr. Plimpton, he's sitting over there," Jean Mary said to me one night at a party during our visit. She started to say more but was interrupted. On my way across the room to sit down, I tripped on Mr. Plimpton's wooden leg and spilled my drink. Jean Mary shook her head.

As fate would have it, we ran into Eddie again and again. When my mother's cabin deteriorated so badly it needed total replacement, Paul and I bought three-acre island three miles down the lake for $600. And from whom did we buy it? Edwin Woolverton. And did he give us a good buy? We thought he did. Was it because I was a good friend? It might have been. It also might have been that he thought he had made enough profit from it—he bought it for $3. No wonder he became a millionaire.

When we wanted to sell the island 20 years later, we used Eddie's daughter, Vicki Woolverton, as our agent. By that time Eddie had retired to Florida, which is what we did too. Interestingly enough it turned out he retired to Placida, Florida, which is 15 miles from our retirement home in Englewood.

He visited us a couple of times. He could only stay a half an hour because he was allergic to dogs and cats. We had both.

"See?" Paul said. "It would never have worked."

"You think I would not give up a dog for Eddie?" I asked.

Paul made a face. "Maybe a dog. Never a cat!"

Paul died 17 years ago. Eddie is still going strong. I went down to his 100th birthday party with a manatee I painted for him. I couldn't find him

Happy together

anyplace, so I went home. He called me a couple of hours later. They had celebrated at the club house. I should have come up. The fact that I did not know where the club house was did not bother him at all. The last time I saw him, he showed me how to buy gold. Haven't done it yet.

Eddie has been a good friend. We have known each other since I was seventeen. At age 100 he told me he thought I always held it against him because he didn't have a college education. For crying out loud!

He then asked me if he could tell me about his sex life.

Radio Drama

Rosemary Harding   final script
Radio drama
Into the swamp
Betty: college senior...a searcher...knows something's wrong but isn't sure until the end
Dick: college senior...mature
Kath: former stage star...theatrical as anything...broad a's
Adams: old man...mean and crotchety
Hole: middle aged and angry.
Jim: average person harried by finals
Bim: frightfully busy and in a hurry constantly
Churchill: Winston Churchill
Byrnes: Jimmy Byrnes
Russian: accent
Cot: old but polite
Stiggs: positive, authentic
Sound: Falling of body through air and thumping on ground...comic effect if possible.
Swamp noises
Splash of water
Zooming of body into air and into tree
Ripping of canvas
Snap of snare
Thump of camp cot onto ground
Music: Very simple

Betty: It's peaceful in the swamp. It's dark and you can't see your hand in front of your face. And I like the people. Especially my cousin, Katherine. She's been in the swamp ever since I was 10 and won't come out because she says she can't find the path. There's a regular blazed trail that she could take out anytime she wanted to, but she won't take that one...says that she doesn't like the way it goes...so she keeps hunting for some other one. You'd think she'd finally give up. But anyway, whenever I feel blue or disgusted with life or when I hate people or men or just anything and everything. I go down into the swamp to see Katherine...and you'd be surprised how much she cheers me up. Or maybe it isn't her...maybe it's the rest of the people down there or maybe it's just the swamp...I'm not sure.

    Anyway, today I knew I was headed for the swamp because I had another class from Stiggs, who is perhaps the most moronic of all morons teaching I have ever met. He knows everything, but he knows nothing. He's a living vat of information...but I don't think he understands any of it. He'll give an answer that's right...only he doesn't know why. So naturally he rather stinks when it comes when it comes to trying to teach us philosophy of education which we can use when we go out to teach the bright and eager shining youth of the country. I was sitting out on the knoll with Dick who has the same class too, waiting for the bell to ring announcing another hour of torture. Well, we got to talking and I heard the bell ring but thought...let it ring. It's nicer out here. Dick didn't hear it and I didn't let him know what time it was until about ten to four, when I was good and sure it was too late to go. He was kinda mad and didn't say much until we got to Dayton's tent and had ordered.

Sound: juke box in b.g. soft

Dick: What did you make me cut that class for anyhow...I didn't want to...we both had to go to it.

Betty: Why?

Dick: Why? Why? Because Stiggs says so. He doesn't want you to cut class. And now you made me cut another one. And on the day the term papers were due.

Betty: Hand it in late...he won't care as long as your paper agrees with his ideas.

Dick: Besides it's near the end of the quarter. He might have said something important.

Betty: He hasn't yet.

Dick: No, but he might.

Betty: What? O.K. you win. But you gotta go to class. And you gotta hand in your term paper and you've got to listen to his drivel whether you like it or not...because if you don't he won't pass you and if you don't pass...you don't graduate in a week. And when I stand on that rostrum and receive my diploma I can say thankfully to the world...I have managed to sit myself through Stiggs' class for two quarters and because of that I'm ready to take a place in society? Nuts!

Dick: You've had classes from good profs too...what about Reines?

Betty: Yeah, the greatest teacher in the world...and half his staff sneers at him.

Dick: Because he's so much above them they can't even see him.

Betty: That's right. He's one of the few profs I've met here who knew what the purpose of teaching was...and who sincerely tried to get it across.

Dick: And did he succeed?

Betty: With some people yes...with others no I suppose not. They're past all hope.

Dick: Too many Stiggses?

Betty: Yeah...and that's why they don't like him. He symbolizes to me everything that's wrong with the world...and I know too many people like him.

Dick: And that's how you're going to stop him...by cutting class?

Betty: No...but I can keep out of his way.

Dick: Just avoiding won't help to get rid of his kind...

Betty: Who wants to get rid of him...I'm no superman...but let him go his way, and I'll go mine.

Dick: Even if his way is wrong and is doing damage?

Betty: Well, what else can I do?

Dick: Fight him...fight everything that he stands for.

Betty: Oh don't be silly...how could I fight him...there are too many of him...and not enough of us...look at the world now...it's a mess.

Dick: Yeah. It's in a mess. And it's in a mess because too many people like us let the Stigges go to town while we sit and loaf.

Betty: But how do we know that we do the right thing? How do we know we're not just a different variety of Stiggs?

Dick: That's something you'll have to find out for yourself. I know it...but if you don't you'd better find out.

Betty: How can I be sure that I'm capable of fighting Stiggs? I can't be...and I probably am not. It might be better for everyone if I just ignored him.

Dick: That's not so, Betty.

Betty: I'm not so sure. I agree with you about Stiggs, Dick...but I have no real desire to fight him. I know he's wrong...but how do I know I'm right...and what difference does it make anyhow.

Dick: I can't tell you that.

Betty: And I can't either. But maybe Katherine can.

Dick: Katherine can't tell you and going into the swamp won't help.

Music: up and out

Sound: swamp noises

Betty: *(Off)* Katherine! Katherine! Where are you now...call out will you...you know that I can't see anything in here.

Adams: Very few can...there's not much worth seeing anyway.

Betty: (fade on) oh...hi Mr. Adams. You scared me. What's that you've got in your hand?

Adams: I scare everybody. Another rabbit.

Betty: Another rabbit...i thought you stopped killing rabbits.

Adams: I can't. They won't let me...they want to be killed. I don't even have to bait my snare...they'll run into them anyway.

Betty: My gosh...how awful. It must keep you busy.

Adams: Terribly. I get no rest at all...but I'm working on a snare now that I think will fix that...if this snare works it will kill all of 'em at once. Think of it...bing. All the rabbits dead. Utopia. I can loaf forever.

Betty: Have you seen my cousin Katherine, Mr. Adams.

Adams: Yeah. She's up in that big Norway fir in the center of the swamp. Last time I seen her she said she was headed for the top.

Sound effect: snap of snare

Adams: Oops...there's another rabbit...beats me how they keep asking for it. Well I'll see you, Betty.

Betty: So long Mr. Adams.

Sound: crashing of grass and sticks and woods, etc. Then splash of water

Hole: *(angrily)* oh for heaven's sake.

Betty: Hole? Hole. Is that you...I'm sorry I tripped over you again.

Hole: Look...I mean...I don't mind it in the spring now because I'm pretty full of water. But don't make a habit of it...last year you just about dried me out. Had the doctor awfully worried...he had to give me interswampage shots. So take it easy will you.

Betty: I'm sorry but I've got to go find my cousin.

Hole: She's up in a tree.

Betty: Thanks.

Sound: crash of underbrush

Betty: Katherine, Katherine.

Kath: *(theatrical and annoyed)* What do you want?

Betty: Well, really Katherine what are you doing up there.

Kath: *(delightedly)* Betty? Dahling, I'm so glad you came...just a moment I'll hop right down.

Sound effect: very heavy crash...Kath ad libs ouch

Kath: I'm sorry I was so rude but I just missed that silly porcupine again. He can't get used to the fact that this tree is my observation post.

Betty: Can you see anything up there?

Kath: See? I can see miles and miles from every side.

Betty: Well, what do you see?

Kath: Swamp. Nothing but swamp...but I'll keep trying...you never can tell.

Betty: Katherine...why don't you come out of the swamp. You've been here so long you must have forgotten what the rest of the world is like.

Kath: no, my chile, when I come out of the swamp it will be for good. I will not be like you are...undecided. Here one day and gone the next and back soon after.

Betty: But I can't stand it down here long and I can't stand it back there. What am I going to do?

Kath: Make up your mind, my dear. Make up your mind.

Betty: Are you happy down here, Katherine? I want to be happy.

Kath: I know a form of contentment, dear...

Betty: Don't you miss Ralph? I miss Dick all the time.

Kath: Ralph...he hasn't remarried has he?

Betty: No... but he misses you an awful lot...

Kath: *(fading off)* Good. When he stops missing me is the time to worry.

Betty: Wait, Katherine, don't go yet. I want you to cheer me up.

Kath: I can't cheer you up, my child. You have to do that yourself.

Betty: Oh you're just like Dick... 'I can't tell you that. You have to learn for yourself.'

Kath: He sounds like a nice young man.

Betty: How? How Katherine...how can I learn?

Kath: Find your way dear...find your way out of the swamp for good.

Betty: Riddles...riddles...I can't do that and you know it.

Kath: You can if you try dear. *(fade off more)* and that is why I must go back up in the tree.

Sound: zoom and off crashing of limbs. Kath ad libs off an ouch or two

Betty: *(petulantly)* I don't think you're ever going to find anything up in that tree.

Kath: (outraged) Betty...Betty how can you say such a thing? How can you?

Betty: Well I'm sorry, but that's the way I feel about it.

Kath: But don't you see dear. At least I'm trying...I'm looking...that's more than most of the people in the swamp are doing. More than you are yourself.

Betty: Yeah, you're looking all right...but you never find anything. Why don't you look down here?

Kath: There's nothing down here. Now go away will you, dahling. Take a short walk and stop bothering me. I'm really frightfully busy.

Betty: *(mad)* All right! Good bye. Oh, I hope she chokes...here I came all the way down here to get cheered up and what happens...she's up in a pine tree. I don't know why I ever came here at all...it's dark and dank and wet and nasty and I hate it.

Sound: slap

Besides, the mosquitos drive me nuts. But it's no good back home either. The people are mean and conniving and I hate them.

Sound: crashing of woods for ten seconds

Now what's that under that log...it looks like something I know...why Jim...Jim Gong what are you doing here.

Jim: Go away Betty...I don't want to be bothered now.

Betty: But what are you going to do down here in the swamp?

Jim: Swamp? Swamp? What are you talking about...don't bother me please. I have a final and I have done absolutely no studying for it.

Betty: What are you studying down here for then?

Jim: Down where? I'm studying my final where I always study...in the library. Go away now, Betty, and stop bothering me.

Betty: But you're not in the library...you're down in the swamp!

Jim: Go away...I don't know what you're talking about.

Bim: Betty! Betty. Have you seen Calvin?

Betty: Bim? You down here too? Why aren't you at the theater?

Bim: Where do you think I am? I live here. Come on now. We've got to get that set finished...it's almost time for the show to go on...have you seen Calvin?

Betty: But Bim...we're not at the theater...we're down in the swamp.

Bim: (*hurriedly*) Yes, yes. Come on now though. Come and help. We've got to get that set up.

Betty: How can you when you're in the swamp?

Bim: What swamp? What are you talking about.

Betty: You're in the swamp...can't you get that through your head...

Bim: Yes, yes Betty but I've got to get going (*fading off*) Calvin...

Betty: Wait Bim wait...answer me yes or no... are you in the swamp or aren't you?

Bim: (*humoring her*) We're all in the swamp (*fade off*) good bye.

Stiggs: (*fade on*) Miss Hanson...Miss Hanson...where were you in class this afternoon.

Betty: Mr. Stiggs...Mr. Stiggs...you here too?

Stiggs: Of course I'm here. No answer my question. Where were you in class this afternoon.

Betty: You mean you're in the swamp and know it?

Stiggs: What swamp?

Betty: Go away...go away. I came down here to get away from you and here you followed me. I don't understand.

Stiggs: Neither do I. I'm in the swamp. I know just where I'm going. And I know what will have to happen to you if you don't come to class more often and hand in your work. Now I realize that you're busy, and I've tried to be lenient...but after all, grades have to be in.

Betty: (*resigned*) I'll get them in sir...already handed in three. Can I hand in the term paper the day of the final?

Stiggs: (*kindly*) Yes. I suppose that will have to do. But get to class Thursday. You see I'm a new teacher here and it's not good for my reputation to have very many cuts against me. And if you see Dick you might tell him the same thing.

Betty: I don't see Dick down here Mr. Stiggs...he hates the swamp.

Stiggs: Swamp? Swamp? I told you before, Miss Hanson...I don't know what you're talking about (*fade off*) good bye.

Betty: They're all in the swamp...they're all in the swamp...and they don't even know it.

Church: (*fade in*) I beg your pardon...but could you tell me where the council of the foreign ministers is meeting. I seem to have lost them and I would like to see Mr. Byrnes after they finish.

Betty: (*amazed*) Mr. Churchill? You?

Church: Yes...is that so strange?

Betty: (*comprehendingly*) No... not very. I'm sorry...all I know is that it's some place in London...

Church: Oh never mind...there he is now...*(fading off)* oh Mr. Byrnes
Mr. Byrnes.

Byrnes: *(fade on)* and as I was saying the affairs of Europe must be
handled jointly...and not by one nation.

Russian: *(accent)* Fine, fine and what about the Pacific area. You think
that should be handled jointly too?

Byrnes: *(fading off)* Well really now, that's a different place entirely.

Betty: They're all down here and they don't even know it.

Kath: but at least you know it don't you dear.

Betty: Oh Katherine...when did you get here?

Kath: I came down from my tree for a minute...I got worried about
you. But at least you and I know we're in the swamp dear...and
we're trying to get out...there's no help for the others until they
realize that. Come now, you must be tired. Let's go find a camp
cot.

Betty: Yes let's...I'm tired, and I always sleep so well in the swamp.

Board fade

Kath: Here we are now...just pull that string...and a cot will come
down from the tree.

Betty: Yes, I know...I've slept here before.

Kath: I've got to go now...(fade) I thought I saw a new trail when I
was up in the tree...I've got to go back up and find out for sure.

Betty: Good bye. Now I'll just pull this string.

Sound: plunk of camp cot

Betty: Gee I'm tired...it will be nice to get a rest.

Cot: You have to be careful when you sleep on me...remember I'm
ripped on the side.

Betty: Yes, I know...but it's never bothered me before.

Cot: It only bothers a few...if you're ready you can climb in any time.

Betty: Thank you.

Sound: rip of canvas

Cot: Oh, there now...I told you to be careful. I bet you ripped me again.
Don't move. Now just lay where you are and everything will
probably be all right. If only I wasn't an inanimate object and
could feel...i could tell you for sure then.

Betty: But I'm not comfortable.

Cot: You're not...you always were before. Well I can't help that. I
have to remain useful. I can't have everyone ripping me.

Betty: Well I hope I can get to sleep.

Cot: Goodnight.

Music

Cot: Wake up wake up.

Betty: I'm awake...I haven't been able to sleep...I kept thinking about those people...and then I got a back ache.

Cot: Yes, that's customary when you sleep too long.

Kath: *(fade on)* I'm glad to see you up dahling.

Betty: I've got a back ache (comprehendingly) I've got a back ache from too much sleep in the swamp.

Kath: You'll be going then...good bye.

Betty: If you sleep too long here you get a back ache...yes, Katherine...I've got to go.

Kath: Yes, you too...you've found your trail...I hope I find mine soon...*(fading off)* I'd better get back to my tree and look again.

Betty: *(calling)* you won't find it up there Katherine...you won't find it up there.

Kath: *(calling off)* Yes, I will...yes, I will...say hello to Ralph for me will you?

Betty: Hello Dick...I'm glad you came to meet me.

Dick: I came to the outskirts, Betty...and that's the nearest to that swamp I'll come.

Betty: You don't have to come that near anymore...I'm out for good.

Dick: Are you sure?

Betty: Everyone's down in the swamp, Dick...Stiggs, Bim, Churchill. They're all down there and they don't even know it. They're all fighting for themselves and not for everyone...and because of that they've forgotten how to live and are down there. None of they really know where they're going or why...and that's why they're there. They're all out for themselves. And that's why I was down in the swamp...but I'm out now for good...because I learned something down there...I learned that too much sleep gives you a backache and that you can't ignore people and keep your ideals...one of them has to go. I made my choice.

Music up and out

A Summer of Fire

In the early 1930s there was a big drought in Minnesota. That was the time of the dust storms in Oklahoma and the whole country seemed dry.

At the lake it was heaven. The water was cool and the weather was nice. Davy and Eileen Hayes and their mom came up for a couple of weeks. Auntie Hazel and Lucy Hayes sat in the water and talked and the minnows came up and nibbled on their toes. They were lucky. There were no fires when they were up, it was just ideal weather.

There was a dark side to all of the sun and fair weather. No rain meant things got very dry and campers really had to put out their campfires thoroughly. And there were fires all over Northern Minnesota and Canada, which was just 25 miles from us as the crow flies. So we had smoky air all the time. Sometimes it was a dense as fog, and all the time it stunk.

Finally, we began having heat lightning when for two or three hours each night it would lightning, usually around midnight. Sometimes faint thunder, but no rain. And, what was worse, when it did rain, there was a bunch of thunder and lightning but just a short shower. What happened then was lightning strikes on the dry trees on the lake shore. One summer we had two small fires on Hinsdale Island (our island) on the other side about three or four miles away. One of the fires was a jump over from a big fire on a unoccupied island about 100 yards off Hinsdale. That one was serious enough to call the forest rangers who had a fire crew in various areas they would send out. The smaller fires were dealt with by people living nearby.

There were two fires on Hinsdale, a small fire on Seven Acres Island which had to be put out. Hazel and Edward and I piled pails into the boat and set out. All of our neighbors were there with their boats and pails. Some were old friends, some we barely knew, but we certainly got to know them. Seven Acres Island was owned by the Hoyts and they had five people up at the time of their fire, and we all got it under control rapidly and hurried by boat to the two on Hinsdale.

The Robinsons were the only people working the fire there and they were glad to see the group of about a dozen people. We carried water and used shovels and axes to prevent the fire from spreading. This was really difficult because of the wind. And the wind did take the fire across about a 20-yard channel to a very small island made up of nothing but spruces. We saved half the island, but that was all.

I remember using a gallon gas measure to dump water and sometimes a minnow bucket. I was pretty small at the time—around seven or eight I think. We would put out a fire one day and a day or two later there would be another one. We did this until the fires were out, and then returned home. Sometimes we kept at it for most of the day.

Hazel got very nervous and began packing bags. She finally threw all her clothes out and packed her suitcase with old photographs. She said that memories were worth more than clothes. She could buy new clothes. But we never had to evacuate. I never got scared, and neither did Edward. We all just worked away and the general feeling. was that the fires had to be put out and we were there to do it. If things got too bad the rangers were nearby fighting other fires and would help us. They did come and check each time we stopped a fire. They made sure it was really out. That made Edward and the Hoyt boys mad. The wind finally stopped and the rains came for almost a week. A very frightening time. The only good thing that happened was that we got to know our neighbors better.

Teaching

As a kid, I thought school was dumb. I could think of hundreds of other things I would rather be doing.

I went into teaching because Frank Whiting, head of the University of Minnesota theatre department, told me it was a good option. Breaking into the professional theatre was practically impossible unless "pull" was available and employment was erratic even then.

Professional theatre has a poor work system, except for stars. Each play is separate. Getting a job in a play means you have a job in that play, no matter what your job is—prompting, technical work, or acting—the job is for that play only. After it is over, you must reapply. This is true all over. The only exception is repertory theatre and

A fresh-faced young teacher

there were few rep theaters in the U.S. then,

Teaching had some advantages, especially if you were located in a big city like Minneapolis. They had teachers' unions with a staff that worked for the teachers. Cities had pay scales, with increments each year and more raises for taking in-service training or going to the U or any college for that matter. It also had a good retirement system and if you taught for 25 or more years you really got a good pension which increased each year by about one or two percent.

I was able to combine several of my speech and theatre courses and the few electives I had led into a radio speech major too. So I had a double major, and I almost chose radio as a profession. I was doing a great deal of class and practical work in radio. I worked several days at the University radio station, KUOM which ran from six a.m. to nightfall when the radio station at St. Olaf College took over for about six hours. I directed shows, wrote, used the sound board, looked up music cues for drama programs, organized current problems programs and children's programs. I did a lot. So much, in fact I realized that I did not think I really wanted to go into the field.

So I had two choices, three, if I counted radio which I didn't. My decision was somewhat like an Indian marriage. I grew to get used to it, and then to love it. I am glad I listened to Doc Whiting, he was right. So teaching was it. Things are easier in the speech field now. Communications has turned up and people have learned it is important to learn how to communicate, and quite hard actually. Now you have majors like business communication, basic communication, communication in medicine—you name it. And there are other jobs than teaching and better pay too. In today's climate though, they may or may not have pensions, and this is really important when you get old.

When I graduated, Doc Whiting made sure I got some offers to teach speech, and one was a dandy, but the town was near the Iowa border. I was seeing Paul constantly and we were planning on getting married, so that was out. I took a job in a town about 20 miles from Minneapolis teaching junior high English and physical education. Good Grief! After that year I got married and entered the U again to get my M.A.

There was a problem. Paul was at the U too as a graduate assistant in speech on the agricultural campus and earning a salary of about $1,900. Even in those days, that was a lousy salary. Of course, his tuition was paid, but he also worked. He had four classes and if anything pertaining to his job interfered with his course work, like if a staff meeting met the same time a seminar he needed met, tough luck. He also was a returning soldier— had a Purple Heart even—and he got the GI bill.

I still had some money left from Grandmother's $3,000, so I could handle a quarter of college on that. Then I had a great idea. Substitute teaching. I called the Minneapolis public schools, told them my problem and they were just great. They told me to try to get a couple of days free and they would be glad to place me on those days. They needed experienced teachers.

It worked out beautifully, except for two unfortunate experiences. One, I was asked to teach a class of 12 mentally retarded kids. First hour was carving linoleum blocks with very sharp knives. I passed out 12 knives and only 11 were returned.

I went down to the office and told the principal. He called in every kid in the class singly and got the knife after about half an hour. I was famous in the lunch room. Seemed every teacher in the school heard about it.

The other was a physics class. Oh yes, I taught everything This one was studying refraction of light. I knew a little bit about light, and that was it. I got the kids starting their lab and then went around the room looking for kids who seemed to know what they were doing. I found one. Put him in charge helping me. He was quite busy.

After I got the MA, my mother got funny. She didn't want me to work. Said I should stay home and keep house. The best way to treat my mother, I had found, was to be friendly, listen, and ignore. On this issue Auntie Hazel helped. I stopped to see her in her library one day on my way home from the U.

"Rosemary, why don't you take the certification test for social work. They need social workers in Minneapolis and you would qualify. It's not a hard test."

She found a book and told me what to study, so I did and took the test. And she was right! I passed it. I was offered a job with Aid to Dependent Children. Auntie Hazel was ecstatic! I had passed the test that graduates in social work had to pass —and she helped me win a battle with Mom.

In respect to work, Hazel was more into women's rights than my mother. My mother, of course, was forced to work and worked with many men, who always got favored. So maybe she was trying to shield me. Hazel worked alone except for her clerks and did not face the prejudice that my mother faced She may have been trying to shield me too. Who knows?

The day after I was offered the job as a social worker I got an offer to teach speech, English, and remedial reading at Robbinsdale, a city about 20 minutes from where we were living. I took it, and annoyed both my mother and aunt.

"Good work!" Paul said. Got them both mad, did you?"

Robbinsdale was a good school and it was a good job. There were even people teaching there I knew, so we were able to commute together. I enjoyed the speech classes; English and remedial reading were weird for different reasons. Robbinsdale as a suburb was growing rapidly and this was putting a strain on the school. A new school was in the works, but that did not help the present situation.

One of my speech classes and my English class was held in a science lab with aquariums and tables with stools and sinks. This was absolutely lousy for speech and just weird for English, but no real problem I thought.

Ha! Ha! Ha! Who would think salamanders would be a problem?

I was beginning to enjoy teaching. The people were fun to work with, although of course there are some exceptions. But I never found a man on the make. I found some pig-headed. idiots, but they were not gropers. They just wanted to be big shots and boss everybody. I was not interested, but I never saw any woman on the make either. The people working as teachers seemed genuinely interested in their job and in helping the kids learn and mature.

In every class there were some kids who did not seem to be able to learn. Some teachers worked hard to teach them. Others did not and in senior high we hit the teacher specialists who feel they are experts in their subjects and if the kids can't follow them, flunk them. And they do. But it is really not as cruel as that. Most teacher agonize over this. They do try to help the kids, but things operate against them. In high school adolescence, there are distractions besides their hormones such as jobs, family problems, love, other school activities, etc.

Every winter when I entered any senior high where I was teaching I smelled feet and I heard feet. Basketball players were practicing in the gym. They had been at it from 6 a.m. They also practiced after school until 6 p.m. Did this develop their character? I have no idea. It certainly tired them out.

I had two boys in one of my classes who were welterweight wrestlers. In season, they had to meet the weight. On the day they were weighed, they sure didn't do any English and if they had a speech in speech class we heard about their weight problem and the little they were allowed to eat. I certainly was glad I wasn't a wrestler.

How do you keep them interested.? What do you do with the kids who won't do the work, or can't do the work? How do you handle them? How do you teach the junkies, the ones on pot, whiskey, drugs? Parents? No parents? Poverty? Absences? Bullying? Principals, Poor teachers. One principal I heard about one allowed each teacher just one piece of chalk, to save money. (In my day teacher would have purchased chalk from a store then—teachers still use their own money for school supplies.)

After my first year of teaching junior high English in the town 25 miles south of Minneapolis I knew absolutely that I was eager to spend the rest of my life with Paul Hagen. So I quit teaching and entered graduate school. There in the education department I was told by a no-nonsense professor that I should take some work in reading.

"Sounds good." I said. "I love to read."

She looked blankly. at me for a minute and then started to laugh. I had never seen her laugh before. That should have said something to me. It didn't take me long to discover that the course of study involved teaching kids *how* to read. This was a complete surprise to me. I had no idea of the number of kids in school who were unable to read; those who were reading English as a second language, the mentally retarded, those who had been really sick and never learned, those who changed schools all the time, lengthy illnesses or accidents which kept them home for long periods of time, those who had poor hearing, eyesight, those who were taught poorly, or couldn't understand the system of teaching reading that was being used.

Many kids, many reasons. One reason that could have been ended was the business of reading systems. There are many systems. I don't know what happened in the elementary schools, I didn't teach elementary school. I know it was common for secondary school teachers and principals to blame the grade schools for every problem they faced.

Methods to conquer the problem of kids who could not do the work seldom involved teaching them differently or giving them other materials. What was generally done was to throw them out of class, to flunk them repeatedly, and urge them to quit school. Reading teachers were the answer to the problem of quitting school. If they taught them how to read, they might stay in school.

Anyway, from my reading classes in college I got interested in reading classes in high school and after I married Paul I got a job in a Robbinsdale teaching reading and speech, with only one English class at 7:15 a.m. I remember I had a girl who was in my first period English class and fourth period speech class and I didn't realize it for almost half the semester. She was so different at 7:15 from 11:00 a.m. I hardly recognized her.

She was one of the speech class leaders. She gave funny speeches and worked well in discussion groups helped organize activities for the monthly TV shows the local station was sponsoring for area speech classes. Her name was Becky something. I remember she was at the top of my class list in both classes, so her last name began with an A. Probably Anderson; we were in Minnesota, land of Scandinavians. Not only didn't she talk at 7:15, I didn't even see her. She was slumped down in her seat, book up on the desk as if she was perusing it, and when I checked her one morning after I realized I had her twice a day, she was sitting with her eyes closed napping. Not a morning person!

That English early morning class was held in a biology lab because the school had too many kids for the school. Students had to share strange rooms. The afternoon teacher was a bubbling, enthusiastic teacher from Hibbing who loved kids, birds, reptiles, animals and smiled and talked about them whenever I saw her. I got to know her because I had speech class in her room which I knew was a big mistake in scheduling. She had aquariums all around the room. Some were filled with water and had fish or other things that liked water. Some just had a few leaves and a couple of sticks, for snakes. Many were filled with salamanders, because she was giving extra credit to kids who brought in salamanders.

She laughed when she saw me as I was going home and she was coming in.

"I must have 25 salamanders ready to put in the aquarium," she confided. "The kids were busy over the weekend. That assignment really got them out of the house and into fresh air!"

The next morning was the morning I always told Becky later that was her awakening. We were studying *Moby Dick*. This is a really interesting book, and Ahab, one of the chief characters is fascinating. I was going around the sleepy room. Why was Ahab so determined to get the whale? They all looked at me as if I was from a different planet, the difference between us being that I was being paid to stay awake. Then, to my amazement, Becky raised her hand quite excitedly—waving it.

"Becky!" I beamed, "You have something to say about Captain Ahab?"

"Mrs. Hagen," she squeaked, looking at her foot which had something on it. "I think I have a baby alligator on my foot?"

And everyone looked at Becky's foot. Then another and another student spoke up. There were salamanders all over the room. Twenty-two to be exact. They had escaped from their aquarium. So the kids woke up that morning.

For 15 minutes we gathered salamanders. I couldn't find the aquarium they came from. Greg found it and reported that the side panel had fallen off. We found a carton and put the salamanders in it. It was 7:35 a.m. I thought of Mr. Wrucke, next door. I did not know him well. In fact, I did not know him at all. He had never spoken to me. He scowled dourly one morning when I said hello. But, I thought happily—all science teachers love salamanders.

I told Greg and Becky that I was going to go next door to Mr. Wrucke and give him the salamanders. They both looked distressed.

"The Wreck?" Greg even said.

I had no idea what he was talking about and took the box next door to Mr. Wrucke, who taught biology and who was teaching biology when I entered his room. He was in his customary gloom and glowered at me. He was giving a test, and his class was busily working away.

"All of these salamanders got loose in my English class and I don't know what to do with them."

He looked at me sourly.

I swallowed. "Do You?"

"I don't want them," he snorted. "Throw them out the window!"

This actually was the best advice I received, but I was too stupid to do it.

"I can't do that!" I gasped, astounded. "They are alive!"

"Who cares! A few dead ones won't hurt, there are plenty of salamanders in the world. "

I pursed my lips and went back to my class with the box of salamanders. I told the English class that Mr. Wrucke was giving a test. They nodded understandingly. A chemistry student spoke up.

"Mr. Hagemeister has a workroom with across the hall, maybe he could store them."

I went across the hall to Mr. H. He was a plump, friendly guy who was busy teaching.

"Sure," he said "put 'em in the back. I'll talk to the afternoon teacher this noon." As an afterthought he said, "Be sure to close the box so they won't get out here!"

I did as instructed and went back to the class. Everyone was awake by then and we really explored Ahab and got to see what made him tick. The following Monday, an irritated Mr. Hagemeister saw me as I was going into English class.

"Rosemary" he said. "What is the name of that girl who teaches in your room in the afternoon. I want to talk to her. I forgot about the salamanders and they all died. You know, you don't need 20 live salamanders to show a bunch of kids what a salamander looks like." He paused, working himself up. "You could even show them a picture of a salamander. My room stinks, It's gonna be hard to get rid of that smell. One girl with allergies had to go down to the nurse!"

I sympathized and got out of there. But I was back in the same room third hour and Hagemeister got me again.

"I want to talk to that girl. My God, she is a goddamn menace."

It was turning out to be a rotten day.

"If I see her, I'll tell her," I said.

"You damn well better see her," he growled.

It was speech class and we were giving demonstration speeches the purpose being to learn how to explain a process through demonstrating. Dennis, a tall boy—he must play basketball, I thought—was going to demonstrate how to swing a golf club. I really blame Dennis' accident on Mr. Hagemeister. If he hadn't obsessed so crossly to me about the salamanders I would have been paying more attention to Dennis and moved him farther away from the aquariums. As it was, his golf club smashed into the fish aquarium and sent pregnant guppies all over the floor in a puddle of water.

"Shit!" I muttered. Beverly, who was next to me, looked up.

"What did you say, Mrs. Hagen?"

I looked blankly at her and then spoke.

"Dennis, you can finish the speech some other day. Find a rag and let's get this mess mopped up."

"Do you think the guppies will live?" Beverly asked.

"Oh, shut up," Dennis said and became my friend for the rest of the semester.

We couldn't find a rag, because they were all in Mr. Hagemeister's workroom and I was damned if I would go over there. But Zeke Olson donated his T-shirt. He said his gym T was in his locker; his mother had just washed it. I told him to go get it.

"I need a pass to get by the hall guards" he said. "I'm half naked, they'll be sure to see me!"

I was on my hands and knees wiping up water and scowled at him

"If anyone bothers you, send them to me!" I barked. Five minutes later, the principal entered my room with Zeke in tow.

"Mrs. Hagen," he started. "What is this student—Oh, Great Scott, what happened?"

Later, I went to the principal and told him of my plight. He listened and shrugged his shoulders.

"The only other room available is the old lunch room anteroom in the basement and it has mice!"

I smiled. "Mice would be a real relief!"

So I was able to move the speech class. I asked the 7:15 class if they wanted to move. They voted no. They didn't like the lab, but they thought they would like the lunch anteroom even less.

A couple of years after I left they built a new school

My First Job Really Teaching Reading

I got on this kick, after I lost my first baby, a girl with blond hair lying there in my crotch in my hospital room, quite dead. I got on this kick that if I was going to teach, I was going to do more than just entertain kids, particularly kids who had a lot of talent anyway. I'm talking about the kids who sign up for speech.

I had four speech and one English class at Robbinsdale the first year. The second year I had no English, but two reading classes of about four kids each plus four speech classes. What Robbinsdale was really looking for in a reading teacher was a special education SLD (special learnings disability) teacher. I was not qualified for special ed nor was I interested in entering an entire new field. I wanted to teach reading to kids with normal or above normal ability who could not read.

I don't know if Robbinsdale was interested in that idea or not, because I didn't go back to Robbinsdale after I lost the baby. I wanted to start fresh. So I applied to the Minneapolis School System and got a job teaching remedial reading at Northeast Junior High. I had one English class. I had a tiny room overlooking the sidewalk and grass. I remember this place because of the third-floor geography teacher.

Although I guess she tried to teach, she didn't have much luck. That fall chairs came flying out of the window, along with notebooks, blackboard erasers, and a stray bench. They settled opposite the windows of my room. Gave my students a different view.

The problem was handled in a typical bureaucratic way. She was sent down to the board of education office where she became an assistant consultant in charge of geography. She was to help with materials. So she got out of teaching because she couldn't do it and got a nice cushy job. Figures.

My reading kids were a mixed bunch. I had a bully who had spent so much time bullying that he never learned to read. I had a hyperactive kid under the care of a psychiatrist. I had another boy who never remembered his pencil. I mentioned this to his mother at an early PTA parent's meeting

"That goddamn kid has at least 500 pencils at home. I'll kill him," the parent said.

I winced. I talked to her a little about the rest of her family. She had four kids, one six months. Chris, the pencil forgetter was her second. Her daughter was in tenth grade at Edison High. The mother worked part time as a school clerk. She applied, I found out later, to Northeast, but Liz, our counselor said she would quit if they hired her, she was so disorganized. So she went to a grade school three days a week.

Her husband worked in downtown General Hospital as a nurse's aide and had a rotating schedule so was home three days a week, when he took care of the baby. Her mother did it the rest of the week except Saturday and Sunday. The tenth grader filled in sometimes when the father got overtime and the mother was working, and Chris was chief substitute.

"Except that he hasn't had to do anything yet!" the mother laughed. She admitted that there was a lot of confusion in the home. Two kids were starting new schools and were nervous about it. The grandmother was sick with the flu right now so unable to help with the baby. The father has been able to trade times with another worker but will have to double up next week. The tenth grader will have to help with the baby, and Chris too, if he can be trusted, which she doubts.

I saw Chris a while later and told him I heard he sometimes took care of his little brother. He gave me a scared look and then laughed a short laugh.

"Yeah, but I don't know how to change diapers!"

"What's his name?" I asked. Chris looked at me blankly.

"I dunno." he said. I don't think they named him yet."

"You have another brother too?"

"Yeah he's in first grade."

"Can he help at all?"

Chris started to laugh and would not answer.

I had 10 poor readers. The best reader in the group test wise was Chris. He tested at fifth grade and was just entering seventh. By rights he shouldn't be in the class, but we conferred—his counsellor, his teacher and I—and decided he needed some special attention

Stephanie was a girl who loved to stare off into space and day dream. Her mother told me she liked to sew. I mentioned her to my good friend Maybelle Berg, the sewing teacher.

"Oh yeah!" she said. "Excellent student What's she doing in your class? She reads patterns beautifully. She's a leader in class!"

I was beginning to understand my students. There were reasons why they couldn't read. Immaturity was one; the pencil forgetter was young for his age. He'll do better when he learns how to follow a routine and keep at it. The bully needed to learn how to read. He was a strong athletic kid. He was poor in school and didn't like it. The hyperactive kid needed something to really interest him which also taught him to read. All six needed different materials and different approaches. The girl needed review on how to divide words of three or more syllables. She also needed to start reading for fun. In a reading test she checked out at third grade level although she was in seventh. Actually that was where most of them were except for Chris. He was the best reader. He checked in at the middle of fifth. His record in sixth grade was terrible. F in just about everything, but he passed.

Mr. Hyperactivity fell in love with the Sears Roebuck catalog. He got to read that when he finished his drills. I corrected his reading drill and went to talk to him about it. He was perusing woman's underwear in the Sears catalog. He shut it guiltily.

"Everything's there, Bruce," I told him quietly. "Nothing in there to be ashamed of."

His eyes got big. I found some U. S. Army basic readers for the bully. He enjoyed working on them and made good progress. He stayed with me for about six months and made it back to regular class. One nice spring day a kitten came by the window and Bully reached down and pulled it in through the window. He petted it, and it sat down on the front of his desk and it watched him read. When the bell rang, he put the cat out the window and left the room.

Stephanie the seamstress was not doing well. She was working terribly slowly. I asked her how she did in math. OK. I asked about problems. Yes she had trouble reading them. So she brought her math book and we read problems. Once she understood that she was not understanding the problems because she didn't know some of the words, she began to work on syllables. Her slow reading helped her in math, and she improved a little in general reading. I talked to Maybelle about her. She was amazed.

"I can help," she said. She put Stephanie in charge of clean up— each girl had to clean her dressing room after she had her dress fitted, and the room had to be really clean. Scissors had to be counted. And it had to be done fast. Stephanie learned to move.

Maybelle also had her make a poster listing things that had to be done to clean the room and to clean the dressing rooms. Her sewing vocabulary was growing beautifully. But so was her ability to work out all words. She finally started to improve. Out of the 10 kids I had, the Bully, Stephanie, and Bruce, the kid on hyper pills that calmed him, made solid improvement. Chris was still immature forgetful, easily distracted, unable to concentrate. No test improvement. But he did not go down. His final reading test score was about the same.

That was the story for the other kids too. They stayed the same. I wondered how they were able to handle their other classes. Stephanie, of course, had good grades in home economics and was passing math. Bruce got a C in math. In fact, many poor readers do all right in math.

The Bully, however had learned to read and was able to be sent back to regular classes. He had been so busy being a big shot he lost confidence in his ability to do school work. He began working in junior high and as the other kids grew in size he stopped much of his bullying. He became a good average student and after the half year with me, I never heard much mention of him at all. I would see him in the halls. now and then.

Sometimes the teachers were more of a problem that the kids. If they were lucky I took one or two of their kids each hour, for that is how I chose the kids I got. The kids got taken by testing—oral and written, references from grade school, talks with the counselors or complaints from the teachers.

Most of the kids I got were serious enough about school and wanted to do well. They simply could not understand the text books or the vocabulary the teacher was using. My students were unable to read much of the material given to them as assignments. Secondary school teachers really did not understand poor readers. They were trained in subject areas, not in basic skills, and knew nothing about teaching reading. They taught with one book and lectured often. It was a change from grade school, and many of the grade school kids had real difficulty in making the transition from elementary school to junior high, which is one of the reasons junior high got junked and middle school got started.

The problem did not go away, but the kids stayed in the same school and the new teachers had the former teachers to confer with, which did help quite a lot. It was easier on parents too. Basic problems I had with junior high teachers (for middle school did not come in my day) was that there were only a few poor readers in their classroom. I felt they could adjust their teaching by using books the poor readers could handle. This was easy for a number of subjects such as geography, science, math and some English novels the kids were assigned.

The teachers did not want to do this. They had 25 to 30 kids in a class and did not really have a great deal of time. Actually I believed that if they took the time to help the poor readers with assignments they could handle it would save them time. Some agreed; other said it was coddling the kids. Nor did they care to give special assignments where the student could read material at his reading level. This smacked of giving kids special favors. Teachers could wax forever on this subject, and democracy in the classroom. I never understood it. I would fight back and ask them to prove why giving a kid material to work on that he could handle was undemocratic. They finally laughed, because these people were my friends.

"Rosemary" they would say "forget them they are losers."

One or two of them got really excited about the poorer students and how to help. One teacher started to rewrite the geography text book, but she got pregnant and quit teaching. That was another thing I thought was crazy with Minneapolis. They loved to hire brand new teachers. Over fifty percent quit after the first year. And what kids did the brand new teachers teach? The poor students—certainly not the good ones, the parents would complain.

At a teacher's meeting I ran the meeting one time and handed out instructions in which the third word in every sentence was in Russian. Drove them crazy. They all started laughing and shouting and yelling.

"Hagen, what a joker!" The social worker said she loved it and went around collecting all the papers. Said she would use it at a workshop she was going to. Did it work? Who knows? I went home and cooked dinner for Paul and me.

Sometimes teaching reading got exciting. Once the man who was in charge of all of the announcements in the tiny room next door lost his temper at Bruce, who he found fooling around with his microphones before class. He grabbed him and put him on his knee and spanked him. Bruce started to cry and ran home to lunch five minutes early. I didn't report it to his mother, and she never said anything to me. I will say Bruce stayed away from the microphones after that, but the door to announcements got locked too.

Another time I got John, a handsome seventh grader who was going to break a lot of girl's hearts. He could not read at all. I never asked why, just got a beginning phonics book and worked with him orally in class. He had poor auditory discrimination. So we went over all the vowel sounds. He had a hard time getting the difference between the long A and the short. I would point to the word and say it for him.

"Cat," I would say.

"Cat," he would repeat.

"Cate, I would say, pointing to the word.

"Cat," he would reply.

"No. Cate," I would say. It got funny when we hit rap.

"Rap," I said.

"Rap," he said.

"Rape," I said.

"Rap," he replied.

"No, rape," I said.

"Rap," he said.

I spoke louder. "RAPE. Rap. Rape RAPE. RAPE!"

I looked up and there was Doug Harding, one of the counselors. I had made so much noise he came down to the room to see if I needed help. I glared at him.

"What do you want?" I growled and turned to John. "Mr Harding doesn't realize that we need the door open for air, the room is so small. RAPE."

John was looking at Doug.

"RAPE," he repeated.

"Good John…Say it again now."

"RAPE RAPE. RAPE."

Doug left.

"Well" we learned that word didn't we?" John grinned. Two years later as classes were passing a good-looking blond kid who was walking with a good-looking blond girl stopped and poked my arm. I turned and looked and it was John, all grown up and in ninth grade.

"John! How are you?"

The girl spoke up. "You didn't have her, did you—she just teaches the dummies."

I could have killed her. That was another thing my kids faced. Derision from their peers. Half the time I thought that was what ailed Chris. The kids thought he was dumb, so he became dumb. It was then I began to think that maybe the way we taught remedial reading in the secondary schools was not the best way and. began thinking of other ways these kids could be helped.

From Northeast I applied to a new school being started under a federal program at one of the junior highs in a poor section of Minneapolis. There we met and planned for half a year before we even started, and the object was to plan a curriculum that all of the kids could understand. We had a math and shop teacher, an English and remedial reading teacher, a counselor, a home ec teacher and a principal.

We worked out a curriculum that the kids could handle, but the building for the school was poor and noisy and there was no place for reading, so I raised hell and got myself transferred to another federal program as curriculum coordinator for Adult Basic Education, a program for adults from the complete illiterate to adults who could read, but we're unable to read well enough.

I loved that job, but it was part of the poverty program of Lyndon Johnson and it finally went broke and the Minneapolis Public School refused to continue it because of cost. Several years later it cropped up again with a national literacy program, but then I lost track of it completely. I went to Marshall University high school, the laboratory school for the University of Minnesota. There I taught remedial reading plus did the play and the speech team. I was there three or four years when Paul was eligible for a sabbatical, and I ran into Maybelle Berg from Northeast Junior High.

She and her husband had just come back from a sabbatical to Europe. I found out how to apply, wrote up a proposal and it was accepted. When I came back I continued at Marshall U high, but then transferred to Edison High. I had a system of teaching reading I wanted to try. Marshall U was into alternative schools and not interested in my alternative school. I got a math, social studies, English, special education, and reading teacher together. We taught the kids the subjects (but with materials they could handle) all morning. In the afternoon they could take their elective classes which they could handle and which they generally liked.

The school worked out well. Kids improved three grades in comprehension on a reading test and two in vocabulary. Most of them returned to class. The number of drop-outs went down and more kids graduated. We were so successful that we threatened Marshall-University High School and their alternative school program. We were accused of coddling the kids.

This was not a strange reaction at all. All reading teachers faced it. Parents of kids who are able to handle the work want them to be challenged so that they will succeed in the world. They saw remedial reading in the high school as an attempt to baby the kids. Principals saw it sometimes as an admission that there were students who weren't doing well in their school. Heaven forbid. We got some of that at Edison, but not much. They got a lot of it at Marshall U high because so many of the parents were U of M faculty.

Edison's parents were supportive and kept telling our administrators that they loved Edison's reading program. It started as a federal program. Money ran out, but the program was kept and the Minneapolis Public School paid for it. When I retired, it kept on, something which really pleased me. At Edison in the afternoon I was allowed to teach speech, and debate. I had state winners in speech every year I was there, and our debate team won several tournaments.

So I finished teaching doing what I wanted to do and doing it well enough to satisfy the school plus me. Plus me was important. The principal gave me a big hug when I left. I thought I deserved it.

The Good Book

One day Don Ryberg showed up at my reading lab. He was teaching Russian and history. He came by to talk to me about seeing his parents in Chaing Mai, Thailand on our sabbaticals and possibly looking up some friends of theirs in Nairobi, Kenya. I was disgusted with myself. I should have thought of Don right away.

"Don, you are working on your PhD in Russian, aren't you?" I said to him and showed him a book that had been palmed off on me during a trip to Russia.

He sighed. "Supposedly," he said "but two kids, a working wife and teaching full time puts a damper on it." He looked at the book, opened it and looked it over. it. "Looks interesting. I'll look. it over and show it to Emma. And by the way," he grinned maliciously: "Emma wants to see you."

I groaned. 'I have been notified about that by Al, (who was our school principal) yesterday," I said.

Emma was a professor of Russian at the University whose office was on the same floor as some of the classes of the Campus school, where I taught. My reading lab was on that floor and the kids I was handling were from grades seven through 12. I was working with an eighth-grade teacher and specific problems in her classroom. I was testing kids who she suspected might be reading cases. One of the boys she gave me was having trouble adjusting in her classroom, and she assigned him to me for a couple of days of testing and observation. His name was John.

John did not adjust well in my classroom either. He got in trouble by hitting the boy sitting next to him who socked him back. I had to break up a fight, which I did by taking John out into the school hallway and talking to him quietly. After about five minutes John settled down, but still insisted the other boy started it. I pointed to the floor and told him to sit there.

"You are going to have to stay out here until you cool off and can be a good citizen in my classroom," I growled.

He stared back at me stonily. We stared for a few moments and he finally sat on the floor and I went back into the room. I planned to go get him in about 10 minutes but got involved working with another kid. That was a mistake. In 10 minutes later Emma was in my room and had John by the nap of the neck. He had worked his way up the door of the Faculty Ladies lounge and was observing Emma washing her hands. It could have been much worse, of course. Emma was livid. She had already called Betty Jo, the junior high principal, who called Al, the high school principal and her immediate supervisor, who called John's counselor, who called John's mother. They were now getting to me again.

I had already been to a conference about this and more were on the docket. It was far from over and John was still suspended from school. Now Emma wanted to see me again. Don grinned sympathetically and gave the book back to me.

"Give it to Emma." he laughed. "It'll get her mind off John."

"That'll be the day!" I replied. On the way to see Emma I stopped to see Betty Jo, who had wanted to see me too.

"Sigrid Peterson will take John back in to her class," she told me. "John's mother said he reads all the time and doesn't know how he ever got into a reading class. He specializes in science fiction."

I grinned at her. "How does he do at home when it comes to courtesy and socking people?" I asked and gave her a last suggestion: "Maybe we should give him gym and he can climb the wall they have there."

She laughed and then looked serious.

"Bring it up at the next conference." she replied. I saw Emma and reported on John's progress. The good news was that he would be shunted downstairs and would not be near the faculty ladies' room. She grunted and then raved for a while about John.

I told her John would get counseling help and we would have a conference with all of his teachers to see that we all understand his strengths and weaknesses. She opened her mouth and then shut it. At that moment I handed he the Russian book which got her attention. She loved it. John was forgotten; this was the first book out by this author in years, and she was extremely lucky to get a copy of it. We became good friends because of that book. She read it and said it was a brilliant book!

Beni and Wally Cox, Beni's mom, Paul and me on a cruise.

Coon Rapids Book Club

I do not remember a single book that we members of the Coon River Book Club ever read. *Small is Beautiful* is one we touched on, but we got off on an argument about something else pretty fast.

I remember one meeting where Marian got up on Tom and Phyllis' coffee table to make her point. That was about the only way she could be heard. Everyone was yelling. It was always a stimulating get together. Much shouting, much yelling, much kidding and teasing. Much cursing about the people who didn't agree with us. It was a fairly large group. And we stayed together until members died.

I am the only member left. Lee Swisher died last year. She wrote a book about the Coon Rapids Book Club when she was 92. We had the following members. Let me start with the ones who didn't live on Mississippi Blvd. in Coon Rapids.

Connie and Dale Burchettt. This couple lived in a different part of Coon Rapids. Dale was the executive secretary of Operating Engineers Number 49. Connie ran for the State House of Representatives and won. Phyllis was her campaign chair and Paul and I and the Hilborns and Seversons helped. It was because of Connie that I got appointed to the Governor's Commission on the Status of Women. Dale died and Connie finally lost an election and moved to California to be with her daughter. She died in Ventura, California—I think.

Milt and Rosalie Goldstein. Milton sold men's clothes throughout Minnesota and was on the road a good part of the year. They originally moved to Coon Rapids, but to their amazement, for they had never encountered prejudice before, the people of Coon Rapids (Thompson Park development) were very nasty to them, particularly their next-door neighbors. They did not like Jews. Phyllis and Marian met Rosalie in League and invited them both to join the Book Club. They were good members. Here are the other members:

Ollie and Inez Severson. Ollie was a counselor at Marshall-University High School in Minneapolis. He was elected to the Coon Rapids School Board and eventually became chairman. There was a terrible argument one year because a new school got named after a former school superintendent. This annoyed half of Coon Rapids and the decision was made to have the school board name the new schools. Ollie decided they should be named after the presidents. The first one he named was Washington. He also got higher pay for the teachers and built a number of new elementary schools.

He quit teaching and he and Inez left for the Philippine Islands where he was a counselor in an American school stationed on a U. S. Army Base near Manila. That way he picked up retirement income from another source. They came back to the Twin Cities and got an apartment in the same independent living arrangement we were in for a year before we came to Englewood, Florida in 1982. Inez died first at 84. Ollie died at 100.

John and Jean Hilborn. John was a counselor in a suburb of Minneapolis. He left that and became dean of students at a new junior college in Bloomington, Minnesota. John was one of the Book Club's early deaths. He had diabetes. Jean died about 10 years later. She had a difficult death. The doctor allowed her to live much longer than necessary and she suffered too much.

Eleanor (Lee) and Jim Swisher. Jim sold insurance, was a ham radio operator, and also a substitute minister in the Methodist church. Lee was an Anoka County social worker. She worked with Paul and me on the Anoka County Mental Health Committee and was invaluable because of her contacts with Anoka County Welfare. We had a lot of competition from them.

Tom and Phyllis Forsberg. Tom was a lawyer who got appointed to the Minnesota Appellate Court. Phyllis was a Spanish teacher in a western suburb of Minneapolis. Phyllis died first of a series of strokes, Tom a few years later of heart failure. They lived across the street from us with their four kids, who in the summer came over daily to swim.

The Book Club discussed current events and yelled a lot. We didn't like prejudice, we didn't like poverty, we didn't like child abuse, we didn't like many of the politicians. We were a bunch of liberals who put their money where their mouth was. By then Paul was a professor of communications at the University of Minnesota, while I taught remedial reading and English in the Minneapolis public school system. Other members included:

Wally and Benester Cox. Wally was assistant dean of students at Kennedy Junior College in Bloomington. When the school started, Wally. was just leaving his job as a counselor at the Anoka State Hospital for mental health. The program was ending, and the mental health program was to go to the communities. Lee, Paul, Beni Cox, and I worked on the committees responsible for this.

Beni, Wally's wife worked in the Anoka Fire Department. Wally and Beni were black. Tom's law partner at the time sold them his lot, which was three or four doors from Tom's house, and found them a contractor. Two or three years later Wally's father and mother moved up from Dallas to a house right next to them. They lived across the street from Paul and me. Beni died before Wally; his parents died before any of us. Wally was seriously ill for some time and then refused to eat and he starved to death.

Marian and Bill Fletcher. Bill was a speech professor at the U of M. His field was technical, mostly devoted to the makeup of the larynx, esophagus etc. He met Marian when he was doing his Ph.D. thesis. He was photographing larnyxes and Marian had the perfect larynx. So naturally they married. He was killed in an automobile accident by a teenager charging out of a mobile home development. Their second child, Bill, was born two days later. Marian finally moved to Bow, Washington where she had a house on Puget Sound. We all visited her.

Paul became head of the Anoka County Mental Health Association. I was on the board as was Lee Swisher and Beni Cox. Paul also became chair of the Coon Rapids Democratic Club. Everyone in the Book Club was a member except the Swishers. They were not Democrats. They seemed to be Independent but would not say. The love Hubert Humphrey though.

Bill Fletcher ran for the school board and lost. Marian became chair of the Coon Rapids League of Women Voters. Ollie Severson ran for school board and got elected. He was on the board until he and Inez left for the Philippines. Dale worked and Connie got laws passed in the legislature. She was especially helpful with union legislation and work with the mentally retarded. She also got a law passed which stopped the practice of making woman pay five cents to go in a public bathroom.

John ran for county commissioner and lost, for school board and lost. When they moved to Bloomington he ran for school board again and won.

Jim Swisher became a Methodist minister and did a few services now and then for the local Methodist churches. He died way before Lee. Lee died last year. After Jim died she stayed in their house for a few years and then her kids arbitrarily moved her into assisted living. She was furious and called me, asking me to come and live with her in Coon Rapids. I didn't want to do that.

The kids maintained that Lee kept phoning them day after day several times and that she seemed uncertain. Laurel Severson (Ollie and Inez's daughter) checked that out for me and worked with Lee and the kids. Lee was mad, but not mad enough to do anything but tell her kids she was mad.

While Lee was at Walker Home she wrote two books and also was bean bag champ of her floor. She then had a stroke and was moved to the hospital where she stayed for several years. John, her son, called me last year to tell me she had died. I gave him the phone number of the Fletcher kids in Washington.

I suppose of all of those women I was closest to was Lee. At least she lived the longest. We played golf together and we talked on the phone. When Bill Fletcher was killed Marian called me to come over to be with her and I called Lee to come with me. She was a person who let me know her and who I trusted and could relax when with her. She didn't get excited easily, was not in politics, education, nor did she have many of my interests other than golf.

When we came back from Florida to visit, I always went to see Lee and Jim. Lee's mother who was staying with them, was a painter, and Jim had bought her some paper and crayons and colored pencils. She was drawing ducks, mostly, and laughing about her efforts. She had ducks all over the walls of her room. She gave me two.

We saw the Forsbergs at our UU church in Fridley along with our church friends. Generally, a party was held every summer and we tried to make it. I would then write Marian and tell her all about it. One year we went on a cruise with the Cox's, Beni's mother and some of their friends. Beni's mother won all kinds of money on the slots. I was amazed. As usual, I didn't win a thing.

All of these people are gone now. Just their kids are left. I see the Forsberg kids. Bill has a condo on Siesta Key which he uses in the off season and rents otherwise. He and his wife and son, Tom, have stopped by and we go out to eat occasionally. They adopted four kids from the Philippines, three girls and Tommy. Fred, the oldest son, came by last year. He and his wife were using Bill's condo. Fred called me one time last year in the middle of a hacking fright and told me what to do on my computer. He is a sweet man. His wife is a deeply religious woman, but managed to handle me, an atheist, quite well. We proved people of different political views can talk together.

I also keep in touch with Laurel, Ollie and Inez's daughter. She drove me all around Minneapolis the last time I was in Minnesota besides taking me to visit Lee.

I think of Coon Rapids often. Here were our neighbors, wild and funny and opinionated. I know no one now who will jump on a coffee table to make her point, and although I have many black friends I have yet to have one tell me, "Next time make that cake chocolate!" after a party.

If I were asked what part of my life I would like to relive I would say Coon Rapids time. The crazy Book Club, the cat Ho Ho, the river right outside our door the vegetable garden full of Anoka Roses…another term for sand burrs, the politics…mental health issues… snow up to our knees and once up to our waist from the boulevard to the house. Once Ollie came with a big home-made plow on his old truck and cleared the way for us.

Paul and I left Coon Rapids mainly because of my job. I had taken a job with Lyndon Johnson's poverty program which was attached to the Minneapolis Public Schools, so I didn't lose any tenure. I was curriculum coordinator for Adult Basic Education. I hired teachers, prepared the course of study, got them the materials, and visited the classes. The classes met at night. Coon Rapids was at least 30 minutes away from Minneapolis and sometimes an hour away in the winter and the classes I visited were practically in St. Paul. It was too much driving on the snow and ice and I hated it but liked the job. That was why we finally moved from Coon Rapids.

Of course, the program ended and I went back to teaching school, so we could have stuck it out in Coon Rapids. At the time we had an offer from old friends to take an upper modern duplex in Prospect Park which was a couple of miles from the University. It seemed like a great opportunity. Like most great opportunities it had its darker side and we left Prospect Park after a few years and went to Roseville where we remained for 26 years, living quietly on a pond with little excitement…except for the Coon Rapids Book Club which we still attended.

Bella Abzug campaigning in Minnesota for the ERA with Gov. Wendell Anderson

Status of Women

I was appointed to the Governor's Commission on the Status of Women by Governor Karl F. Rolvaag of Minnesota. I was put on the Employment Committee and was elected Vice Chair. This was in 1965.

Nationally the Status of Women was Eleanor Roosevelt's idea. John F, Kennedy called for it and Lyndon Johnson actually got it going. I got this appointment because of the political work I did for Connie Burchett of Rapids Book Club, who respected my ability to get things done. Also, I asked for the appointment. Things come if you ask!

Connie was a state representative from my district, my friend, and a member of the Coon Rapids Book Club. In an effort to convince the governor that I should not be appointed, the county chairwoman asked Paul to accept an appointment by the governor on a commission dealing with old age. He refused, clearing the way for my appointment.

Paul and I did not discuss this, he just told Kay, the chair, that he was not interested in that committee. So I never knew if he rejected it because he knew I wanted the Status of Woman Commission appointment or for the reason he gave Kay. I assumed he was telling the truth when he told Kay.

In politics someone could be personal friends with another but not on their side in some issues. It meant for strained relationships sometimes. We were friends with Kay, and her husband Bill, but in the year that Connie got reelected we ended up against them on almost every issue. The final straw was my appointment. I was removed from the Status of Women when Connie ran for state senate and lost. Kay got the post, and I gave her a hug.

The Status of Women came out with a report the first year. We pointed out the discrepancy in opportunities for women's training for jobs, job opportunities. For working women there were few opportunities for advancement on the job, lower salaries, even when doing the same job. (The employment committee made a big issue over not getting equal salaries for equal work. We still don't.)

The custom of keeping salaries secret from everyone was another thing we attacked. I was working on salaries in education, and I stressed the necessity of unions, collective bargaining, and rules which both the School Boards and teachers should observe. I stressed the necessity of salary schedules and standards which made it clear to all workers how they could get better pay.

I also got a change in a custom that had been going on for years. Extracurricular sports for boys paid much more than extracurricular sports for girls or non-sport extracurricular activities which took as much time, (and in some cases much more time), as sports.

Football and basketball coaches get large salaries and I did not contest this, because they also take in a huge amount of money which helps all programs. The other male coaches in sports such as track, tennis hockey, wrestling, or long-distance running were getting much higher salaries than any of the women coaches, who were spending as much time on their sports as men.

In addition, activities such as school newspaper, school annual, speech and debate teams, student council, National Honor Society paid peanuts compared to sports. A tennis coach in most schools got $1,500 to $2,500 for coaching tennis, which occupied his/her time during March, April, May and part of June. A speech coach got $375 and was busy with tournaments twice a month from November to June. A person doing the school annual started in October with the completed book coming out the week before graduation in June, got $375.

Because of my efforts the commission recommended that schools address this problem and stop the salary discrimination. This was one issue which resonated among school boards and was universally changed by the boards and also during union negotiations on salary. I also sent out a form to the Department of Education asking for sex of principals from elementary schools through high school in all of the schools in Minnesota. I sent a separate form to the Minnesota Department of Education asking how many school districts had women superintendents.

The figures I received were interesting.

None of the superintendents were women. More than half of the elementary schools had women principals. Eighty percent of the high schools had male principals. The argument for male principals in high schools was that women wouldn't be able to handle trouble with problems that come up in high schools such as obstreperous boys, gangs, or bullying. Of course, Catholic schools all had women principals for their girl's schools.

The assumption that women are only good with young kids comes from the myth that they belong in the home taking care of the kids. Men can't do that, they say. Men don't want to do that! I do believe that the Status of Women Commission was helpful in getting more men as teachers from kindergarten up to ninth grade. There are both male and female students in all grades and the opportunity to be taught by both male and female teachers is important.

The form asking for the gender of each school's teachers showed a preponderance of female teachers in elementary K-8 and over 80 percent male in high school except for the Catholic girl's schools. The Commission called attention to one fact: there are almost as many girls as boys in any grade. Certainly young boys need a male figure other than the principal; and girls do too. Principals are in charge of curriculum.

Perhaps one of the reasons there were no girls to speak of in science and math courses was that male principals saw them as mothers and homemakers. However, women themselves and the behavioral habits they have formed while growing up have cause a lot of their problems. Women don't like to ask. They feel if they do a good job, they will be promoted. Not necessarily true. They also don't like arguments and will not speak up. This is still a major problem with women. Attend any group having a discussion. The men do most of the talking. They have louder voices, an advantage, but they also are more aggressive. Women seldom contradict anyone in public. Manners! Some improvement since my time; not much!

I got a fairer standard for pregnancy leave. Many schools asked a pregnant teacher to take a leave of absence at seven months. For most school systems that meant the teacher lost the entire year on her record, for she did not finish the year. This interfered with tenure and getting tenure. In addition, another problem with pregnancy cropped up. I knew about it intimately: premature births. I lost five babies between six and seven months. I had two years of tenure. After each birth I lost a year of tenure because I did not finish the year.

This eventually began to anger me, because tenured teachers had many more rights and higher salaries too. I complained to the Minneapolis Teachers' Union and Selma Larson was put on my case. We discussed the problem, she reported back in two months. The problem was solved, and I had been given tenure. This is a good illustration of what a union can do for you. Yet at that time we had women teachers who would not join the union because many of the men were so "rude," "loud," and disagreeable. Women can have prejudice too!

Until the pregnancy rules were overhauled, some women could never get tenure. I don't know if they ever complained, or just left to stay home with the babies after they had two or three. It meant in some cases a person due to get a raise as soon as tenure came in lost her chance of tenure because of pregnancy. The schools really saved money because they loved to hire newly graduated women who often quit because of marriage or got pregnant and quit. The Status of Women also tackled this problem and recommended some state-wide standards regarding pregnant teachers.

The Status of Woman was trying to get all employers in Minnesota to treat their workers equally as far as gender was concerned. Much progress has been made; much is still needed. Governors in all the states eventually started similar commissions. They did well in areas other than women's salaries. Men generally made 20 percent more than women. This is still true, with maybe a one or two percent difference from 1965.

We emphasized the importance of pensions, and schools either strengthened or started pension. Unions helped, of course, and we had representatives from the AFL and the CIO on the Commission. I believe we also strengthened the unions. Not for long, though, for throughout the United States there are fewer and fewer unions.

And the Equal Rights Amendment needs just five more states and it will pass. Florida is one of the states which has not passed the ERA. For years the state Senate has passed it, but the speaker of the house refuses to bring it up before the House to a vote. He has the power to do this. A vote from the house could dispense with this power, but such a vote has never happened. Basically, ERA is dead in Florida because women are still unable to organize well enough to get something that controversial passed. It would insist on equal pay and equal rights. Business, especially small businesses do not want equal pay because their representatives say businesses cannot afford it.

We got agreement from the state and the employers in many areas. They responded positively to my report on extracurricular activities in schools,

Still fighting for our rights as women

and to other committees pointing out the need for more careful counseling of girls. Often girls were shunted into courses which guaranteed them lower pay. Counselors respond to parent's interests, and their preconceived opinions as to what the students want. Many times aspirations are not high, so it is up to the teachers to make all students, not just white boys, realize their full potentials.

Minorities historically did not get a fair break from teachers, counselors, administrators or employers. Things are better now, but not much. If minorities were getting the same salaries as white men, we wouldn't call them minorities, would we?

Visitors

About 7 a.m. on a summer Sunday the doorbell rang. I poked Paul. He did not respond. It rang again.

"Paul," I said, "the doorbell is ringing!"

He did not respond. I got out of bed looking for a bathrobe.

"Turn the coffee on as you go by it, will you?" Paul muttered, so I detoured to the kitchen to turn on the coffee. It turned out I had made the right move. It was the back doorbell ringing, not the front. And now there was banging on it.

I frowned. Who could it be at 6 a.m. on a Sunday morning? I saw no face through the door's window. The doorbell rang again. I opened the door and there stood two kids, maybe four or five years old.

"Well!" I said. "Good morning! And who might you be?" I had never seen them before in my natural-born life.

"I'm John, and this is Ellie," the boy replied.

"Hello!" I said and then called plaintively, "Paul, we have visitors!"

Ellie spied the toaster. "Do you have any toast?"

I blinked and looked around for the bread.

"You're hungry?"

"Sure," said John. "We haven't eaten for hours."

Paul appeared. He beamed at the two kids. Paul loved kids.

"What did you have for supper?" he asked.

"What's supper?" Ellie asked.

Oh those poor kids, I thought. They must be lost. I stuck some bread in the toaster. John looked at me.

"We like peanut butter and jam on our toast."

Paul looked for the peanut butter and got the jam out of the refrigerator. He put both of them on the counter and found a knife. John grabbed the knife and began smearing peanut butter on his toast, then jam. He started to eat and then gave the knife to Ellie.

"Who are these kids?" Paul muttered to me. "Where did they come from? Have you seen them around?"

I stuck some bread for us into the toaster.

"Why don't you ask them?" I muttered back.

He looked at the two kids eating toast and peanut butter. He gave them both a napkin.

"Where do you guys live?" he asked. They looked at him, chewing steadily.

"I live at 8700 Laurel St. Dallas, Texas," Ellie answered.

"Not lately" Paul said, giving her a look.

"We've moved," John spoke up.

"When did you last eat?" Paul asked.

"We had dinner last night," John answered.

"We had slices of pizza," Ellie said.

Well at least they have eaten I thought. They apparently don't know what supper means. I took the toast out and started to put some jam on it. John looked at me.

"Is that for me?"

"No. It's for me," I said. "We're hungry too. We haven't eaten for hours."

They looked at me impassively.

"Where is your TV? Ellie inquired.

"It's in the other room." John said running over to it and turning it on. "Look" he hollered to Ellie "it's Mr. Rogers."

They both sat down in front of the TV. Paul and I ate our toast and coffee. He tried a little peanut butter on his toast and liked it.

"Those kids have got good taste," he said.

"Right." I replied. "Who in hell are they? Are where do they live?"

Paul went outside and came back after about 10 minutes. I went out to the road, I looked all around. No one was up. I didn't see a soul.

"Has anyone moved in recently?" Paul asked.

"What about across the street and behind Coxes?" I said. "There are some new houses there"

"They were new last year, Rosie," Paul said. "No one new has moved in."

The kids sat happily watching TV. I went and turned it down a little.

"You don't need it so loud," I said. "You'll wake the cat."

They giggled at me.

"You think they are Johnson's grandchildren?" Paul looked over toward out neighbor on the left.

"Their grandchildren are adults, and their kids are teenagers, don't you remember them?" I asked. "They're the ones who came over to look at our boat."

"I don't know why you would think I'd remember that" Paul laughed. "Everybody asks when we are going to put it in the river."

The kids got up from the TV.

"We got to go home now." John said. And they headed toward the door.

"Back to Dallas?" I asked.

"Don't be silly, we live here now," Ellie replied and shut the door.

Paul and I looked at one another.

"Where?" he asked and followed them out. He came back in a few minutes. "The Christiansons must have sold their house."

They were our neighbors to our right. They had been away to Colorado, we found out later, and had decided to stay there for a year with their kids. So they had rented their home, which was next door to ours, for a year.

"So that's where the kids live." I said.

"And they came from Dallas," Paul concluded. And sure enough, in a few days we met our next-door neighbors. They asked us over for coffee and were surprised that John and Ellie knew us. Marie put her hand to her mouth to stifle a laugh.

"That's where they were Sunday, then," she said. "We wondered but were so tired we couldn't wake up. We were just getting up to go look for them when they appeared. Hungry as usual. Don fixed some toast and peanut butter for them."

The neighborhood kids having a great time

Living on the River

We bought the house because it was on the Mississippi River. It was located in Coon Rapids, a suburb thirty miles from Minneapolis. The house wasn't much— painted stucco and two bedrooms. We later added a big room overlooking the river. Coon Rapids wasn't much either when we moved in. When we left it had grown by about 30,000 people.

We liked water. I liked it especially, and I was very excited about being on the river. We put in a dock each spring and took it out in October or November. If we didn't do this, winter ice took it down river, and we would need an entirely new dock.

We brought the boat from Vermilion down to Coon Rapids and towed it up there again in June for the summer. We used it on the river in May, September and October and, if we were lucky, even into November, although we could have snow the first of November in Minnesota and sometimes did.

When it got too cold to use the river, Paul would get John Hilborn to help him and they would drive the boat down to the Anoka landing, pull it up on the trailer and bring it back to our front yard, where we stored it carefully covered by canvas until the next spring.

Paul and John worked together on boats. John had a big pontoon boat which needed storing and he had to have help with it. The Book Club members living on the river all had boats (except the Fletchers) and we helped each other when we were needed. The Swishers had a pontoon boat that Jim and John took care of and the Seversons, who were furthest down the river, had a boat Ollie and his son Paul handled.

At Vermilion we usually stored it at Arrowhead Point. My family had done business with Bill Gruben of Arrowhead Point. Bill and my mother had been good friends. Sometimes we used Dick Levine's marina, which was only a couple of miles to our cabin, and it was sheltered waters too, but a longer drive ending in 27 miles of gravel road, usually very rocky with slippery gravel that flew up and hit the car. But it was far more convenient to have the car at Oak Narrows Landing where Dick's marina was located. It was also easier to get to Cook and the range towns of Virginia and Hibbing.

However, we did not like to store our boat at Dick's because we did not like him. Dick was a pal of Eddie Woolverton and he did not especially like Paul. Dick also was a teacher and he liked the fact that on the Iron Range, where Lake Vermilion was located, men got higher salaries than women.

"Women have no families to support," he cracked. This burned me up. I mentioned the single women who supported kids or aged parents and his response was a laugh.

He had three kids, two girls and a boy. The youngest one, a girl, gave him a hard time and Evie, his wife, said to me once that the girl's marriage was not working out, that the husband was a bum with no money. The girl was coming back to live with them, bringing two kids. She had a job, but it didn't pay well, Evie said, and crabbed that men doing the same work made more money.

"Some people say women have no responsibilities and should not have equal pay," I said. Dick was there at the time so it gave me great pleasure to say that. Evie laughed.

"I know who you're talking about, too," she said. Dick's face got red, and the next time he saw Paul he said he would have to raise the docking and storage rates on all boats.

We liked having the boat in Coon Rapids, and it saved us a bunch in storage at Lake Vermilion whether at Arrowhead Point or Dick's Marina. We were on a stretch of the Mississippi which was really like a lake for a couple of miles, down to the Coon Rapids Dam. We went swimming in the Mississippi all the time and played there with a rope John and Paul tied to a tree limb sticking out into the river. We also swam a lot usually with the people on the other side of the road from us who were not on the river.

Bill and Mollie Tousignant and Phyllis and Tom Forsberg came over occasionally and when their kids found out they were over all the time. They loved the rope swing. They would stand on the river bank, kick off hanging on to the rope, swing out over the river and drop into the water. We adults did it too, but got tired of doing it. The kids never tired.

The Forsberg kids, Mark Tousignant, and his sister, Kathy came most often. They were over so much that one day Bill Tousignant came over with tools and started measuring for steps; we were ruining the bank getting down to the dock. He built us nice wide pine steps which made it much easier. Bill was a good carpenter. He used our cabin a couple of times and built us a good outhouse with the lumber we brought over for it, but never used.

Billy and Freddy and Mark used the rope the most, along with the adults. The girls, Nancy and Susie Forsberg, liked to swim, sit on the dock and use the rope when the boys were through. Phyllis and Tom came over occasionally to check on their brood and swim, but things were going OK. At times we had seven or eight kids there.

Wally and Beni would not let Anthony swim in the river. They did not think the Mississippi water was safe enough to swim in, although it had been cleared by the State Health Department as satisfactory for boating and swimming, but not for drinking. We never argued with Wally. Many people felt as he did and did not trust the water. We did, though, and had no health problems from it.

Paul and I got to know the other kids in the neighborhood because of the river, but not Anthony so much. Too bad, he was a great kid. He studied music and became a really great bass player, traveling all around the world with various groups.

We'd often have relatives up. My brother and his kids—Nancy and Di and Fred—came up and used the river with us. Of course they were up at Vermilion most of the summer and we saw them there too. Paul's relatives came up and I remember Al and Maxine vividly. Al was a big man, about six-three. He must have weighed over 200 pounds. He had never water skied. Paul and I told him how and he hardly listened. He just smiled and as the motor started he staggered a little and almost fell into the water. With a shrug he righted himself and with his strength pulled himself up and got the skis straight. No problem at all with that body.

Friends came up to ski and people from school came with their kids. I asked Maybelle and Bob Berg who taught home ec and physical education at Northeast and then Edison up to water ski. She was wearing a suit that was a little tight and as she was climbing into the boat after skiing I noticed Paul goggling at her. One of her breasts had come out of the suit and was bouncing around. Bob called her attention to it by sayin "Maabe."

She looked down and with no embarrassment at all said, "Oh!" and grabbed it and shoved it back into the suit. Bob was a gymnast and was a really good water skier, but Maybelle did OK too. Sometimes the Tousignants would bring their boat down the river to our dock and we would ski with a more powerful motor. We got to know Ed and Charlotte Fitzpatrick because of the river.

Tom Benson and his wife from the University came with his five kids a few times. Fun to watch the Benson kids. They had adopted a boy from the Philippines and he was much better on the swing and in the water. Tom laughed and commented that anyone could see he wasn't a real Benson.

Ed and his four boys loved the water and came every spring and fall. They were up at their own lake place during the summer. Because of the river, we came to know the Fitzpatricks. Ed was on the Mental Health Board with us and was a big help. I taught with him at Northeast for four years and at Edison for about twelve or fifteen. At Edison our rooms were next to each other and we would discuss Coon Rapids and State politics, for we were both active.

Paul was very active in the community when we lived in Coon Rapids. He helped get the Community Health Clinics started. He was chairman of the Coon Rapids Democratic Party and president of the Anoka County Mental Health Board. Marian Fletcher got that job for him. He never asked for it. Marian knew the head doctor of Anoka State Hospital. He said most of the people incarcerated as mentally ill could function in society if they had a clinic they could go to weekly or monthly or whenever they needed help, and he wanted the state hospital system junked. He was all for community clinics. Marian told the doctor that Paul Hagen would be a live wire for them and could get a group going that could do the job.

Paul took the job, put me on the board, got me to ask Ed Fitzpatrick and Lee Swisher. He tried to get Marian on the board and she refused. She was pregnant at the time and said she would be too busy. He asked Wally Cox, but Wally couldn't be on the board because he worked for the state hospital as a counselor. So he told his wife to be on our committee and Beni joined.

We then put out a call in the Anoka paper for people who would be interested in serving on the Mental Health Board and picked up three good members from the city of Anoka. We were in business, with a board that geographically represented the different areas of Anoka County. Ed was especially valuable because he lived on the border of Fridley and Columbia Heights, in southern Anoka County.

It took us five years to get a community mental health clinic in Anoka County, and a lot of work. We were the first county to start a clinic. Other counties wondered how we could do it so fast. We didn't think we were very fast. We got a lot of trouble from the county social work agency. They had many clients with mental health problems and the head of the agency really thought his organization should have been put in charge.

Lee used to work for the county social work agency as a social worker. She had many friends still working there; that was a big help. She got hold of rumors before they even got started, and we knew almost all the time what was going to happen. We worked with the group, we submitted a plan that was approved by the state, and our problems were over.

Paul and Ed and I used to sit on the dock while his kids used the swing and discuss the problems of the Mental Health Board and the Coon Rapids Democratic Party. Ed was active in Fridley politics and was a strong backer of Connie Burchett, who represented the Coon Rapids area in the state legislature.

Time passed, and the kids grew older and the rope wasn't used that much anymore. I still liked to take a ride in the boat after coming back from school. Down river about one hundred yards was a grove of spruce and balsam pines which gave the most wonderful smell when I drove the boat to them. The scent seemed to envelop me. It lasted all the way to the Dam and back when I went by them again and docked the boat. Just like that, all of the problems of school left me.

When I left Adult Basic Education and went to Edison High, I was given the debate and speech teams along with the rest of my job. In debate, I had this kid Tom Lynch, who was winning debates and in speech he was really good at extemporaneous speaking and took most of the prizes.

One of his opponents was a Rick Fitzpatrick; I never got to judge Rick so really hardly noticed the name. Later on, when Ed and I were together at Edison, he mentioned Rick and Tom.

"That kid, Tom Lynch, he's good," he said. "Rick cannot beat him, no matter how hard he tries." And it occurred to me then that Rick Fitzpatrick was one of the kids I used to swim with in the river. Now he was an opponent in speech.

Char and Ed had the four boys close together in age which presented a problem when they were sending them to college. Rickie was the third boy—Char put an "ie" on the end of three of the boys names, hence Jamie,

Chuckie, Rickie and Jon. Jon was never Jonnie. I never asked why. He was the one Ed said who always got it right. He got a job as a junior in high school at one of the leading grocery chains and worked his way up to a good job in produce. He worked in that job through college and helped pay his way.

Rick, on the other hand did an interesting thing with his college education. He went to Canada and enrolled at McGill College in Montreal. Ed said the tuition there was much cheaper and Rick's education was cheaper than any of the others. He never even thought of doing what some of the Edison speech and debating students did: go to West Point.

Tom Lynch went to West Point, as did another one of my speech kids, Larry Kinde. Ed laughed at the cheap tuition at Rick's Canadian college because McGill is ranked as one of the best universities in North America.

Tom and Phyllis Forsberg sent all of their kids to the University of Minnesota, and Phyllis went too, majoring in Spanish. She got her degree a year earlier than any of the kids and began teaching in Osseo, a Western suburb of Minneapolis about twenty miles from Coon Rapids. Fred, the oldest, went to the Minnesota campus at Morris, Minnesota. The others stuck to the main campus. All of them had jobs. All of them went on to advanced degrees, too.

Bill and Susie became lawyers, Fred went into social work and Nancy business. Tom Forsberg, their father, got appointed to the Appellate Court and worked there for the rest of his life.

We kept up with the river kids. Mark Tousignant went into the trades and was one of the first to marry. Jamie Fitzpatrick used to ride his bike down from his house to visit us in Prospect Park when we moved to Minneapolis The ride got to be too much for me when I transferred into Adult Basic Education for four years and worked nights for part of the week.

Last year Fred and his wife stopped in to see me here in Florida. I got some help from them on the computer and we talked about their kids, whom I haven't seen since they were little. One is a computer expert, the other was a Peace Corps worker in Namibia. We had a great talk about Africa, for they had gone there to visit her.

Bill and Jenny Forsberg have a condo on Siesta Key in Sarasota about an hour away from me. They rent it out during the season but come down often the rest of the time. I see them and their son Tom frequently.

Tom and Phyllis have died, as have Ed and Char. Their kids live on, reminding me of my earlier days fifty years ago. Rick Fitzpatrick is a broker, Chuck works at a tool and die place. Jamie has a job with the state of Minnesota and Jon works as a legal aide for a group of lawyers in Plymouth. He and I were in touch a year or so ago about our lake island, which we sold to Ann and Patty Nevin, Eileen Hayes' kids.

Eileen lived across the street from me. Eileen has died, and so has her brother Dave, who I played with during most of my childhood. The next brother in line, John, lived in Mom's duplex in the back yard of her house. He and his family were a big help to her when we moved and she was retired and pretty much alone in the house. It got tough when she got older, and we finally had to hire a lady to come in and live with Mom.

Paul and I came home from New York to live in Minnesota. He took a job at the University of Minnesota in General College. Paul died in 2001. I miss him and am occasionally angry he is not around. He was far more popular with the kids than I was. He would kid with them.

I remember one time in Coon Rapids, Phyllis sent the four kids walking the half mile up to the fruit stand on Highway 10. She was so pleased that she found something for them to do so she could take a nap. Paul saw them walking when he was in the car and gave them a ride. They were back in ten minutes with the stuff they were supposed to buy. Phyllis laughed about that for days.

"That Paul!" she said. On bad days I really miss him.

"Where are you when I need you!" I yelled the other day when Edward's girls were trying to regulate me. A rough period which I hope is over with them. Most of my memories are happy memories, particularly of Coon Rapids and the Mississippi River, the boat, the tree and the swinging. Lee was a big help on the Mental Health Committee that Paul chaired. We were the first county to get rid of the Mental Health Campus where people were kept if they had mental health problems.

Lee was a good watch dog for us. She knew the people in the community and let us know when opposition was developing. When the teenager drove his car into Bill Fletcher's and killed him, the police came to tell Marian, and they insisted that she give them the name of a friend for them to call immediately. She told the police to call me. Before I went, I called Lee and we both went over to help. Marian had Billy three days later. It was a very difficult time. Tom and Phyllis went with her to the hospital.

Tom couldn't get it into his head that she didn't know exactly when she should go, she would have to wait for contractions. Phyllis went at a fixed time because she had Cesareans.

When Bill was about eight or nine Marian moved to Washington and got a house at Bow, Washington on Puget Sound. She had relatives there. Paul and I visited her there several times and I think most of the Book Club did too at one time or another. Billy and Marna, her and Bill's two kids, are doing well. Billy has married, has two girls, and has a job demanding some time in Alaska. Marna married a psychiatrist who practices near Bow and they live in Marian's house. She died about four or five years ago.

I remember the friends I had in Coon Rapids. Lee Swisher, the last member of the Coon Rapids Book Club other than myself, died last year. She and I did many things together when I lived in Coon Rapids. We golfed together. She had this theory that you should be able to use only one club golfing, plus the putter. She was always trying that. I did too sometimes. We had fun. We were not very good golfers and it really made little difference how many or how few clubs we used. The result was the same. We were terrible. "But healthy" Lee would say laughing.

She called me about four years ago and asked me to come up to Minnesota to live with her. Her kids wanted her to go into Walker Home, an assisted living home. She didn't want to leave her home on the river. She had happy memories of it with Jim, and later on her mother moved in to the guest room. I remember the walls were full of her crayon drawings of ducks. Lee's mother would look out the window at the ducks and draw them.

I would visit her when we still lived in Coon Rapids, and later when I was in Minneapolis and got out to that area. She always told me to choose a duck drawing. One time I chose two and she got a kick out of that. I told Lee I couldn't give up my house in Florida to come to Minnesota to live with her, and I thought it was terrible what her kids were doing. But they did it. Her kids put her into Walker Home against her wishes.

Laurel Severson, the daughter of Ollie and Inez called me and I talked to her about Lee. She told me Lee called her and that she was talking to the Swisher kids. They explained their reasons to her and she said we could talk about it when she saw me that summer.

I went up to Minnesota after a long time to see Connie Metcalf and Marti and Sig Reckdahl. I stayed with them both for a few days, and during that time Laurel picked me up and we talked about Lee and why the kids thought she should be at Walker. Then we went up to see Lee at Walker Home in Anoka. Lee was delighted, and we ate lunch in Walker's dining room.

"It's nice enough," Lee said. The kids told Laurel that Lee was calling them three or four times a day and this worried them. Walker had a sudden opening and they decided to take it and did not prepare Lee well for the change; they really did not have time. This did not make it easier for Lee.

She decided to adjust to Walker, and the first thing she did was write a book about the Coon Rapids Book Club. She called me when it was finished, and I notified all of the kids of the members of the club. She then wrote a book about her mother. Her son John did most of the typing and she certainly kept him busy. She wrote to entertain herself. She said there wasn't much of that going on at Walker.

We went up after lunch to her room and talked about her books. She was delighted that I had notified all of the Book Club kids. Many had written her or called her and bought her book. Then there was a knock on the door and a good-looking young man entered. It was the recreation director. He wanted Lee for the bean ball game. She was Floor 4 bean ball champ and it was playoff time. He looked at me and Laurel and acknowledged that she had company.

"We can do a make-up game with you and Floor three tomorrow" he said. I looked at him as he left. Bean bags! For her recreation. And she has just written two books. Laurel shook her head and turned to Lee.

"Are you going to write another book, Lee? Or are you going to visit some relatives or friends?" She refused to mention the bean bag championship. Lee paused, and grinned at both of us.

"I'm starting a book about my father," she said. "That will be my third book. I will have written more than Jim, and the second book sold more copies than Jim's sold"

Laurel and I laughed. That really tickled her, that her book had sold more books than her husband's. Now Lee and Jim are gone but their books remain and I have memories of both of them, all good—some sad, others happy enough to make me accept life in spite of problems and corruption of the world.

I think of the river, still flowing. I am 94. The house is still there, though we are long gone from it. The oak tree still stands, a new rope is tied around the big limb, and some kid soars over the Mississippi, and lets himself fall knowing he will hit the cool, deep water. Life goes on. You live and die. I am ready to die, and my relatives are prepared for my death. Do not worry. It is bound to come.

Sauna at Mike's

Mike was the former caretaker for a dentist and his family named Barlow. They owned a huge section of land on Smart's and Dismal Bay. When Dr. Barlow died, that was the end of Mike's job. The first person who bought Barlow's place was a taxidermist named Bartnik and his wife. They lived there all year round and became good friends of Mike's. He worked as a handyman for them, but they were no source of much income. In fact, they needed money most of the time, and after about three years they left.

I was sorry to see them go, because at 13, I was interested in science and taxidermy and animals. I had already skinned a rabbit the cat had killed and even tried a porcupine but quit because it was too full of swollen wood ticks and I couldn't handle the tail. But I loved going to visit the taxidermists. I went over there in the outboard two or three times a week and helped. They were a lovely, friendly couple who were preparing dead cats for college labs. The cats were sent up to them from Chicago. I learned how to be objective, do the job, and not feel sorry for the cats. After all, they were long dead and were going to be of use to college students.

After they left, Mike became something of a hermit, and I lost touch with him completely. He lived about three or four miles down the lake in a deserted section of Dismal Bay just before a bog. You had to walk up a rocky path about a quarter of a mile to his house, which was completely hidden from the water. Once you got there, you were in for a treat. It was a beautiful well-built building. He built it himself, with a sauna in the back yard.

The siding was rough pine which had been done by a sawmill. They had brought the wood in by trucks over the ice in the winter. It looked like the lake homes 1 saw in Finland when I traveled there about fifty years later. He also made his chairs and tables from the birch trees in his yard. He was a great craftsman and our neighbors, the Franklins, had some of his chairs. They were really neat.

Anyway, the big thing with Mike was that he was lonesome, Chris Peterson reported. Chris was from Chicago and owned a small garbage hauling business. He strained his back and came up to Vermilion to rest. He liked it so well he bought the Hoyt's old place on Seven Acres, and he got Mike to help him refurbish the place.

One day, Chris invited us to Mike's Sauna. He said that Mike was having it the next Friday. He said that Flo, his wife, was going, and asked if we'd join them.

I was married by then, so Paul, my husband and I went. Ivy Budd was there too. She lived down the island from us and had been my mother's nurse when she was in the hospital, so we were old friends. She knew Mrs. Peterson. I had never met her.

Mike sent the ladies in first. So I followed them into a sparkling clean dressing room, made out of smooth pine boards next to the steam room. In the steam room there were boards to sit on from the ground half way to the ceiling. A depression in the front of the seats was full of hot rocks which were heated by a wood fire. There were some logs nearby to keep the fire right. The rocks were almost red hot and so was the whole room.

The Finnish way was to get naked and really wash. I was a little surprised, but I stripped naked as Ivy and Flo were doing. When we were about to enter the steam room Ivy apologized and introduced us. I told Flo I felt like an old friend by then, and she laughed.

When we entered into the steam room, Ivy took a bucket of water and poured it on the rocks. More steam rose and settled through the whole room. We stood there with perspiration running down us, even through our toes. Ivy then gave us each another pail and told it to pour it over us, which we both did. Then we soaped down and got shiny and very hot and red.

There were a bunch of birch branches in a corner. Ivy handed us both wands about three feet long full of leaves. I turned to ask Flo what the branch was for and she whacked me with the bough.

"This gets your circulation going!" she chortled and whacked me again. She was a fat lady who turned out to hate the lake She had a big red scar

126

down her belly that was hard not to look at. She told me immediately that it was from a recent operation in Chicago and dammit, she missed that town.

Ivy poured some more water on the rocks. Steam shot up all over again, and Flo hit me again with the birch bough. She laughed again.

"My bridge club should see me!" she giggled.

So Ivy and I and Flo whacked each other's dripping bodies until we tired of it and then climbed up on the boards to sit and steam and rest.

Up on the boards, we removed the leaves sticking to our breasts and heads and feet and then Flo talked about how she loved Chicago and missed it and saw no sense to the lake. Couldn't understand how anyone could stand a place which was nothing but sky and water and woods. Not a darn thing to do. No movies for miles.

"Have you ever gone to a movie in the town of Cook?" she asked me.

"No" I said, "do they have good ones?"

She grunted. "The only one we saw was a terrible movie I had seen before. We had to leave at six p.m., drive the three miles down the lake to the road, and take the car 30 miles into town. Then at 11 we had to go back, and ride on this dam lake in the dark and Chris couldn't find the channel to our dock between the two rocks, so we had to row in. And the wind kept taking the boat. We had a hard time rowing in. What kind of a life is that? You gotta learn to row a boat in order to live."

I laughed and tried to sympathize.

"It's a job to get to Cook during the day. We only go there to get groceries. Of course, we like the desolation of the lake. We like to fish and walk and swim."

"You got that right," Flo said. "There's practically nothing to do here except look at the sky and fish. I've eaten so much fish I feel like a walleye."

"Well, you're looking good, Flo, "Ivy said. "The woods will put you in shape!"

We sat there for a while, thinking our thoughts, wiping the water out of our eyes. Then we went down and whacked each other a couple of more times soaped ourselves down and poured hot water all over us again. Then each of us poured a pail of cold water on us. We shuddered and jumped and squealed and ran into the dressing room and grabbed our towels.

"We should be running down to the lake" Ivy remarked., "but it's too far. That's what I did as a kid,"

"You're Finnish?" I asked.

"Right," Ivy said

"This is the craziest place I've been in yet," Flo said. 'but it beats fishing!"

I remember walking over to Mike's house without feeling the ground. I was that relaxed. I have never felt that way again in my life. The men went in for their sauna and when they returned we all had coffee and goat cheese and muffins that Mike baked.

It was a great party. From then on, whenever Paul and I were down that way we stopped in to see Mike. He stayed around for a few years, but then we went there one day, and his house was deserted, the furniture gone.

We asked around, but no one seemed to know where Mike was. Dick Lavine said he must have left in late fall. He either went back to one of the iron range towns about 50 miles away or died. Or maybe he had Finnish relatives and went to live closer to them. Northern Minnesota is full of Finnish people. He could have done that. The Petersons went back to Chicago and Ivy sold her cabin to a guy who thought the lake was wonderful and stayed up all year long.

He cut down all her beautiful Norway pines because he was scared of tornadoes, and her front yard was a wreck. We sold our cabin for $800 to a man from Iceland and bought a two-acre undeveloped island for $600 in Frazier Bay from Eddie, the old boyfriend my mother was hoping I would marry because he was good at fixing things.

The island, after a dock and a house got put on it, was very nice. And it is the reason we are in Florida. It paid our way.

Paul digging us out

Save The Scouts

I had joined the Roseville Bird Club after a bird walk I took with its president. Her enthusiasm for birds stimulated me to join the club. At about the same time I had signed up for a garden plot in Roseville, It was near where Margaret, the president of the club, came to watch birds.

After I finished weeding and watering my crops I would join her and watch birds too. I learned a lot. We lived on a pond in Roseville and it had many different water birds. I invited Margaret over a few times to sit on our balcony and look at the ducks, geese, and other water birds. Sometimes we would walk along the pond to the martin castle. She loved watching the martins with their babies and enjoyed seeing them grow up.

"I just love the Martins." she would say. And she would talk about how the scouts would come first in the spring to check if the weather conditions were satisfactory, and then they would start a few nests. The reason I am going into this before I tell the story is so that you will understand the routine of the martins, and the fact that to Margaret, who was the president of the Roseville Bird Club, they were very important.

Paul and I usually came back to Minnesota from Florida sometime in April. The exact date depended on us. We had to agree. We usually had quite a discussion about it because often one of us would want to stay longer, and this time it was me. Besides that—I knew I was right. Any fool would. Getting home too early in April was asking for snow. It always snowed sometime in April during the first two weeks. That is a given. Paul disagreed and said that he wanted to get home. There will be no snow, he assured me.

"That is your imagination," he said. Looking around him he'd say, "The weather is wonderful."

Off-handedly I mentioned that Florida was not Minnesota, but he wasn't listening. So I agreed. The disagreement wasn't worth our marriage. Off we went to the land of 10,000 lakes —all frozen I was sure. We got there, and I hate to admit it, but Paul was right The weather was wonderful The sun was out, the temperature was in the 80s—unbelievable for Minnesota in April.

During the night, though, the weather went through a change. It got cold suddenly. Very cold—from 80 down to 25 during the night. And all night long and through most of the day it snowed. And snowed And snowed When it finished we had 12 inches. Now a foot of snow may not sound like much, but it is. It piled up so high in our patio it was almost impossible to open the door for there was snow packed up against it. I managed to get the door open by pushing the snow that was there back down the steps. Some snow still got into the house, but I mopped it up. Paul shuffled to the garage and got the snow shovel and dug a path from the garage door to the front door. The dog then had a place to relieve herself.

We heard the snow plows coming. Although that was a good sign, it was also a bad sign. We needed the streets cleared, but the snow from the plow was going to block our garage and our patio door. There would be about four feet of snow to clear away with our shovels. And this would be hard packed snow. We dug in, I worked until I ran out of steam and went in the house to dry out and warm up. About an hour later Paul came in, exhausted but triumphant. The snow had been conquered and we could get the car out and open the patio door.

"In fact, it was very invigorating." he said as he went upstairs to change into some dry clothes.

I again made some coffee and brought him up a cup. While we were drinking it the phone rang. Paul handed me the phone.

"Your bird lady wants you," he chuckled. I took the phone.

"Hi Margaret. What's up? I asked. She was worried about the scouts.

"They have been back about a week. They will be frozen in their nests in the castle and will be unable to get out. We must free them! The Scouts need us! I'm coming over!" she said and hung up.

"She's coming over," I told Paul. "The scouts need us."

He looked at me. He looked out the window. All you could see was snow. He shook his head.

"I won't ask," he said. I finished my coffee and went down stairs. The doorbell rang and it was Margaret. She had a package with her.

"Rosemary" she said, pushing Chou-chou away from her, "we have to have a ladder. The martins will be high up in the castle."

We went down to the basement to get a ladder. But the. sliding glass doors to exit the basement were stuck badly because of the snow." We have to get out," Margaret said. "We will just have to push harder." And we did and the doors opened and snow packed against the doors fell into the basement.

"Get a shovel." Margaret said. "And a broom for the floor. We will dig ourselves out."

Paul appeared. He went out to the garage to get a shovel and came back down to us. He shoveled and got the snow out of the house and a short path outside. Margaret was ecstatic.

"You've done it! You've done it! You have saved the scouts!" she exclaimed. "All we have to do now is get the ladder down to them."

Paul looked at us and grinned.

"Have a good time, ladies." he said and walked away.

"Aren't you coming too?" Margert asked. "You're missing the best part!"

But he was gone I grabbed one end of the ladder and Margaret grabbed the other, and we stepped out into the snow. It was somewhat like stepping into the surf. After about three steps the snow was up lo our knees. It was soft snow and not particularly hard to walk through. We did have a distance to walk.

"Did you bring a screw driver?" Margaret asked.

"Brought a screwdriver, "I told her.

"You will need one to crack the ice off the nests," she said. We continued plodding through the snow dragging the ladder. We finally arrived at the martin castle. We fiddled with the ladder to make sure it was solid on the ground (wherever that was) and against the side of the castle's pole. I checked the hand crank. It was frozen with ice and impossible to move.

"I bought a pound of hamburger to feed the Martins," Margaret said. "I don't know that they eat hamburger, but they eat bugs and bugs are meat, aren't they?"

I tried to get the hand crank down again, for that would certainly simplify things, but I could not budge it. I swore at it, which did not help. Margaret grabbed the ladder again, and we fiddled with it to make sure it was steady and solidly on the ground which we found this time in the snow. I. threw caution to the winds and climbed up the ladder. I got to the first rows of nests and Margaret was right.

"Was I right?" Margaret shouted up to me.

"You were right," I shouted back. "The nests are all covered with ice and it is thick." I hacked at it with my screwdriver.

"Hack on it with your screwdriver!" she called.

"I am" I replied.

"What?" she asked and WHAM! the ice cracked and a scout darted out like a bullet, straight at my forehead. I ducked, and a chunk of hamburger came flying by my nose.

"Oh, the dear little thing!" Margaret cried and hurled another chunk, which hit the castle and stuck there. Another piece hit my collar. I hacked another nest and more hamburger flew.

"Take it easy on the hamburger, Margaret!"! yelled. "You are hitting me, not the castle."

"Are they eating it?"

I continued cracking ice off the openings of the nests. There were seven of them. All of the martins came out like bullets, the way the first one did, but I was prepared and leaned to the side after I opened the nest. Margaret kept at it. The meat flew by. The scouts ignored the hamburger.

"I was right." she said as I climbed down. "They don't eat hamburger, but there is plenty stuck there on the castle as a last resort. It was just an experiment. The poor little things were frozen in their nests and couldn't get out. You saved them, Rosemary! But how are they going to find bugs in this weather?"

"That's their problem, Margaret," I said. "We have done all we can do for the scouts."

"Oh, I hope they will be all right," she said.

So we plowed our way home. I made some coffee—tea for Margaret—and called up to Paul that we had some hot coffee or tea. He wouldn't come down. Margaret left after a while and at the next Roseville Bird Club meeting she reported on our adventure.

"Now we know the martins don't eat hamburger," Margaret announced.

That summer I was walking around the pond with my good friend Rosalie Goldstein and we came upon the martin castle. I told her about saving the trapped scouts and hacking away the ice. She looked at the castle for some time, quite impressed.

Then she asked: "What are all those little, splotches of stuff stuck all over the sides?"

I didn't answer for a minute or two.

"Oh" I said. "You're talking about the hamburger. It was an unusual experiment. The Roseville Bird Club has the whole thing written up."

Rosalie looked at me curiously.

"You'll have to tell me all about it later." she said.

But I never did.

Xmas letter, 2018

This has been a busy year. My grandnephew, Aaron, and his wife, Kristabelle, along with the new baby, Zachary, moved down to Florida but then moved back to the Midwest. I miss them and wish them well.

In January after a play at the Venice Theater, I tripped in the dark on a bad stretch of sidewalk, knocked myself out and was in Venice Hospital for two nights. At the end of September, I was in Englewood Hospital's emergency room for an irregular heartbeat. The day before Thanksgiving I reacted to the drug Cipro (for a bladder infection). It elevated my blood pressure and sent me to the Englewood ER again for the night.

On the fun side, I went to Cuba in February for two weeks. Cuba is poor. If the embargo were lifted, it would help. Cuba buys their food from China. How much easier it would be for them to buy from us. They have no homeless; their 1940 constitution, the one Batista junked, forbids it. Everyone has a roof over their head. Some of the roofs are pretty bedraggled shacks but are better than Sarasota park benches or Englewood beach.

According to WHO Cuba has one of the best medical systems in the world, and their education system is among the top ten. Blacks do as well on tests and in the classroom as whites. In a math test given to fourth graders in Caribbean and Central and South American countries, the lower 50 percent of Cuban kids did better than the top 50 percent of the others. Castro is dead now. It will be interesting to watch Cuba.

Here in Florida my friend Gloria and I attend amateur theatre. The recent Venice play *Billy Elliot* was as good as any Broadway production. Another good thing too; across the street was a brand new 100-yard sidewalk put in because of my January fall.

I work in the garden, walk the woods trail, or swim. I wrote and gave four speeches to four different organizations. I still am a Humanist celebrant and performed a memorial service for my good friend Linda LaSalle. Her husband, Bob, will do the same for me.

I was a precinct assistant in the election. It was interesting hard work, but the number of people who crab about the government yet refuse to do any political work really burn me up. It is almost becoming un-American to be active in politics.

On that happy note—enjoy your holiday-whether it be pagan, religious or have a nice break. Remember to be a good citizen. The world could use some. Remember the door is always open here

Xmas letter, 2013

This letter may be late. I have just returned from Colonial Williamsburg where I met my old friend Joyce Ostergren for five days of exploring. Joyce and met in 1942 at the University of Minnesota. We have been through a lot since then.

This June I went to San Diego to the American Humanist convention with Connie Metcalf from Minnesota. We have known each other since 1960.

When I got back to Englewood I had to enter Venice Hospital for four days. I had a reaction to the blood thinner I was on and needed some transfusions. Earlier, in May I had an operation on a melanoma cancer on my face; actually, it was five operations. The scars have healed, and the face is almost normal.

In February I went to Tanzania. I had planned to go with Charlotte Ackerman, another old friend whom I have known since she was born. However, her husband ended up in the University of Michigan Hospital, so it was impossible for her to go. I went alone and joined a group of eleven people and saw lions, giraffes, elephants, leopards, zebras, and wildebeests. Tanzania is where to go to see the most animals.

In September, Paul Spyropoulos and I had an art exhibit at the Unitarian Universalist Fellowship. He showed his acrylic paintings, and I showed African photographs and a few pastels and oils. In June, 2014, I'll be doing an exhibit on animals in the member's gallery at the Ringling Art Center's Englewood branch.

After ten years I finally resigned as president of the Gulf Coast Humanists and I am thoroughly enjoying going to meetings just as a member. I also helped start another Humanist group in Port Charlotte, which I visit as often as I can.

Paul's Death

Paul died in November of 2001. He was 81 and died of heart failure. His Alzheimer's was bad the last year, but even then he was coherent some of the time. It certainly was a contributing cause, as was his stenosis of the back which hurt him badly until Hospice came permanently.

He was aware most of the time of what was happening. He got help from Hospice once or twice a week. When they first came in Hospice wanted a hospital bed. I had to go through his primary care doctor for this and it was given readily.

Hospice changed his sheets, cleaned him, shaved him, and made him as comfortable as they could. He was incontinent, on diapers, which sometimes made him very angry and he fought them before Hospice took over. He no longer washed himself, nor did he know how. He refused to wash. I tried to wash him and he fought me.

He needed drops for his eyes. He did not believe me and refused his drops. It developed into a power struggle and continued with the nurse who was coming twice a week from the psychiatrist. Our primary care doctor had referred him to the psychiatrist because of the meds Paul was taking. The psychiatrist also put him on additional drugs which seemed to me to have no effect at all, but he sent a nurse to Paul twice a week, who sat with him and was able to get him to help wash himself and allowed her to diaper him.

After a few weeks she began urging me to put him in a nursing home. I refused. Paul did not want this. She then worked on him. He refused, and the whole issue turned into big argument. One of the main problems was that there was no available home for Alzheimer's patients that we were comfortable with.

We both had examined one close to us. It was a square of double rooms with two chairs outside each door. The square was completely enclosed except for an entrance, which also appeared to be its exit. The entire area was about the size of a third of a block and there was a sidewalk around the entire set-up, which patients could use for exercise.

The rooms had two beds and two dressers and a couple of chairs. They were not very large. They did have a TV, which Paul refused to listen to at home. It looked like the entertainment was TV and the other person in the room. The whole experience depressed us both.

A friend from the Port Charlotte UU, Mitt Austin, told me that veterans had special rights and that there were facilities available for veterans. Paul had served three years in the army, had a Purple Heart and some other medals. She made a lunch appointment for me and the wife of a veteran she knew. This meeting was very helpful. I learned about the vet's ombudsman help and made an appointment to see him in Port Charlotte. I met with the ombudsman and he talked about a new veteran's hospital at Land o' Lakes, Florida which had facilities for Alzheimer's patients. It sounded very interesting, and good but it was 60 miles away. No way was I going lo be separated from Paul.

The ombudsman said he understood my feelings, but Land o' Lakes was it. He also said a veteran's hospital was necessary in Port Charlotte. Our congressman was aware of the need. It was a matter of time, he said. This talk took place in 2000, before the Douglas T. Jacobson veterans' home was built there. All this was interesting, but of little help.

I decided that the best place for Paul would be his home, where things were familiar, where I and his dog, Blair, were full time. And the house itself was there where he could roam with his walker. He agreed and we decided he would stay at home. This did not sit well with the psychiatrist's nurse who intensified her arguing with me and Paul.

He could live forever, she kept insisting, and asked again and again "What will that do to you?" She got nowhere with either of us, and went on a two-week vacation. Then Paul stopped eating and refused his medications. He did not want to live any more. We talked to Hospice and they began to give him more frequent care and worked with the Hospice doctor about pain medication for his back, for it was bothering him constantly. They listened to him and helped him ease the pain in his back. He wanted no tubes in him, and the nurses agreed.

I don't remember the protocol. All I remember is that the helpless feeling I had went away. Paul had been in great pain and was being dealt with as an item. Hospice was a breath of fresh air. He finally was getting some effective medication for his back pain. Hospice was a godsend. Suddenly he was no longer in pain, he was no longer moaning and crying. Hospice had come. I remember Paul's cousin Mary Jo calling me from Arizona. She was a great, a wonderful source of reassurance.

"You will like Hospice, Rosie" she said. "They will really help." She was right, and little did either of us realize that Mary Jo would be under the care of Hospice in another few years. Paul's relatives kept me going. Paul's cousin Lee, in Germany, kept in touch. She and her husband Heinz had visited us when Paul had Alzheimer's but was still fun to be around.

He lived about three weeks under Hospice. They came in twice a week, bathed him, shaved him. I was with him at night.

Jim Seaman, the husband of Paul's dead cousin Judy. Phoned. He and his two kids, Judy and David, came down for a week right after Paul died. The psychiatrist's nurse came back from her vacation and the Hospice nurse told her she was no longer needed. Experienced nurses now worked with Paul and gave him pain medication. They sent male nurses in to wash him change him and clean the sheets when needed. They even got along with Blair, who tried to protect Paul by tripping anyone who came near him.

About three weeks later he just gave up. He refused to eat and would spit his meds out. He wanted no tubes in him, we had gone over that before. Because he was home, his wishes could be followed. The night he died he gave me a really big hug and kiss. We hadn't kissed for some time. That was a difference in our routine.

I went to the guest room where I was sleeping. I dozed off for an hour and then woke up and decided I should check him again. I went into his room. He seemed to be sleeping peacefully. I went over and sat by him. After a minute or two I realized he was no longer breathing and had gone. It was about 1 a.m. I didn't want to call Hospice and bother them, so I went into the living room and sat. I really don't know what I thought about. What needed to be done immediately, who to call, I suppose. It wasn't until later that I would reflect on our lives together.

Blair, the Bichon, finally left Paul and came in to me. I looked at her and smiled. She had always been Paul's dog.

"You'll have to learn to live with me now, whether you like it or not." I said. She looked at me morosely, and lay down by my feet, and later got up and went back to be with Paul. I sat in the living room until around 5 a. m.

At one time I remembered my friend, Marian Fletcher, and her actions the night she found out that Bill had been killed in an auto wreck. Paul and I were staying with her. She was due to deliver a baby at any time. She asked us specifically to leave her alone that night, that she needed time to think She was right.

The time was helpful. Around five I phoned the Hospice nurse on call and she chewed me out for waiting so long. I told her I didn't want to bother her so late at night. She said she was working all night and it would be no bother. She called the mortuary and they came and took the body away. The men were concerned about the dog.

"Will someone please hold the dog?" one asked. "We've been bitten several times by dogs."

Blair was in the way—she was down by their legs. I picked her up and held her, and we watched as they put Paul's body on the stretcher, covered him and wheeled his body out of the house.

Around eight I called Margaret and she came over and called Herb Adams, our UU minister, who drove down immediately from Port Charlotte. He called my niece, Nancy, who she said she would notify the rest of my family. Then he called Paul's cousin Jim and told him and that took care of Paul's side. The nurse left, Herb went, and Margaret and I were left. We went to the funeral parlor to make arrangements for Paul's cremation. She drove me home. We had a little breakfast and then she left. I started to go to bed and remembered I'd better take the dog out. So we went for a walk around the yard and came back in and I went to bed.

The Unitarian Universalist Service Committee in WW II
2012 Speech, UU Fellowship of Charlotte County

UUSC advances human rights and social justice for everyone everywhere in a world where all can realize their full human rights. We work with grassroots organizations on economic rights, environmental justice, civil liberties and rights of people in times of humanitarian crisis.

I have been a member of UUSC ever since my husband, Paul, and I joined the Michael Servetus Unitarian Society in 1965. In this congregation we had a man who worked as a team leader at Honeywell. His name was Peter Meyerhof. He and another friend taught me how to play tennis, and Pete was co-chair with Paul and me for our annual auction one year. That was the year someone donated his time share in Hawaii and we made all kinds of money.

Peter explained one day to my seventh-grade class why he had a number tattooed on his arm. This was 1958 and the kids were saying there was no such thing as the Holocaust. When I questioned why they believed this, a boy who was a poor student but a leader spoke up.

"There's no proof," he said. "Have you ever seen anybody who has been in a concentration camp?"

So the next week they met Peter and learned about Dachau, Germany. Peter and his wife, Rose, were allowed to come to the U.S. because he had an uncle here. His uncle's family in America were the only relatives Peter had. Rose had lost everyone. They all died in Dachau concentration camp. Peter was very aware of what the UUSC had done for refugees in World War II and he got me interested in UUSC history. Let me tell you a little about it.

Our story begins with two people in Wellesley Hills, Massachusetts, Martha and Waitstill Sharp. Waitstill was the minister of the local Unitarian church. He and Martha had contacts in Czechoslovakia and Germany and spoke fluent Czech and German. British Prime Minister Chamberlain and other leaders met with the Germans and agreed Czechoslovakia's Sudetenland could go to the Germans. He gave us peace in our time except that it wasn't. The Sharps were asked by the UUA to go to Czechoslovakia to help frantic people wanting to get out of the country.

They had two small children, three and eight. They left the kids under the care of friends in the church and went. They gave up their jobs – he as minister of the church, she as a social worker.

On the way to Czechoslovakia they stopped to see friends and officials in various places and began to set up a network which helped them later register the refugees, get attention from other embassies, promises of jobs. When they got to Prague. They set up shop and proceeded to even get people out of prison and arrange travel to safer places.

At about this time Robert Dexter, head of the UUA's department of social relations, came over with his wife, Elisabeth to look at conditions. They decided that the Unitarians should establish a relief office in Lisbon, Portugal, one of the few neutral nations during the war and virtually the only safe port in Europe at that time. The Rev. Charles Joy, an administrator in the Unitarian church, would run it. The Dexters and the Sharps would be field agents. Waitstill's job would be to establish routes of safety from France, Germany, and eastern Europe through Spain to Lisbon. The group decided to work mostly with the east German and east European area.

At the same time, in Holland another relief organization run by the Universalists was working closely with the churches doing virtually the same thing that the UUSC was doing. So both branches of our church worked hard for human rights during World War II. I only know about the Unitarians and that is because the Sharps' grandson, Artemis, did research on them which won an award for the Sharps from Israel called the Righteous Among Nations. The Sharps were the second and third persons awarded this honor.

Let me give you an example of how the Sharps worked. A name was sent to them from Lisbon. Martha took it, got a taxi to an apartment in Prague. As she got out of the cab, she saw a Gestapo patrolman coming. She flattened herself out against the door of the apartment and waited for him to pass, then dashed up five flights of stairs. The woman who answered her knock insisted she did not even know a Mr. X, the person Martha wanted. Martha argued and flashed her passport which the woman grabbed and slammed the door in her face.

Martha stood there for five minutes wondering if she would ever get her passport back. The door opened and a man stood there who told her he could take a message to Mr. X. Martha said there was no time for messages, that Mr. X had to come immediately. He slammed the door in her face, but a moment later he opened it and appeared, dressed for winter.

"I am Mr. X," he said, and gave her back her passport.

They walked through the snow to the British embassy passing two German guards to whom Martha waved her passport and said, "Americans, Americans." At the British embassy, they met a Gestapo officer who made them stop and state their business. Martha began to complain loudly about the lack of taxis, the weather and their wet feet. She then asked the Gestapo officer if he would run into the embassy and tell the people that they were late to the meeting on the second floor, but that the Sharps were coming. He snorted and waved them on to the embassy. After she had taken care of Mr. X, Martha returned to her apartment and met Waitstill coming in. He had been on a similar mission.

She was responsible for rounding up 29 children ages eight to thirteen, getting IDs, statements from parents, the guarantee of homes in the United States, and transportation to Lisbon. She bought 20 tan berets and put them on each head and took public trains to Lisbon. She got 35 adults and two kids, whose parents had committed suicide, to Lisbon. When the U.S. didn't want to take Jews—a wartime poll determined that 48 percent of the American people were prejudiced against the Jews—she sent them to other countries, to Ecuador, Sweden, to whomever would take them.

And so the Sharps stayed in Europe and helped rescue 3,000 people. That was their choice, and their two kids got raised by several different families in the Unitarian church of Wellesley Hills.

The chalice symbol UUs honor has a cloak and dagger beginning also. It became an icon during the war and was used repeatedly by the Sharps and other agents. One of the pictures I saw on the Internet showed Martha at a milk station with about two dozen kids and adults. She was standing by a sign that said milk depot with the flaming chalice next to it. The chalice offered hope and safety to people wherever they saw it.

Rev. Joy decided after repeated failures with people having little or no identification papers that our allies needed a logo or symbol which people could trust. Those were suspicious times. For all they knew the a refugee could in reality be a spy or a criminal, yet they were expected to care for them, send them on to other people on the escape route. Joy raised the issue. A German, Hans Deutsch, had been on the run from Paris and finally reached Lisbon. He was an artist and his caricatures of Hitler got him in trouble in both Germany and France. He drew the chalice. Joy liked it and kept it. The work of the UUSC so fascinated Deutsch that he joined to help it. And his words to Joy at that time have been kept. Here they are:

I admire your utter self denial and readiness to serve, to sacrifice all, your time, your health, your wellbeing, to help, help, help. I am not what you may actually call a believer, but if your kind of life is the profession of your faith, as it is, I feel sure...then religion ceases to be magic and mysticism, and becomes confession to practical philosophy, and what is more to active really useful social work. And this religion, even a godless fellow like myself can say wholeheartedly – yes!

And what about the Sharps after the war? Their kids didn't recognize then nor did they accept them as their parents. The Sharps' relationship with one another was badly damaged because of the stress connected with being hunted and hunting. Shortly after they returned, they divorced. Their daughter, Mary, 16, said when the judge asked her which parent she wished to live with, said "neither."

It was not until Mary was married and in her 30s that she really realized just what her parents had done. Her son, Artemis, who began sifting through thousands of documents across Europe and the United States, found refugees that his grandparents had rescued. Artemis said:

I want to inspire a new generation of people to do this kind of work. I'm interested in what we are going to do to stop the world from allowing a genocide like this from every happening again.

And it was his work which gave the Sharps the Israeli award...Most Righteous Among Nations.

In 1960 my husband, Paul and I were in Europe and we went to Germany and visited Dachau. It is a few miles outside Munich. It was not hard to find Dachau village. But we had to ask several people before we could find the concentration camp which was open to the public. We saw the towers, the gun ranges. More people were killed with guns than poisoned by ovens in Dachau, but we saw the ovens too, and the railroad tracks with some of the box cars which brought the people to the camp. We saw about 16 barracks labeled *jude, komunist, katolic*. And I discovered that many Catholic priests had died fighting the Nazis.

And why were people in the concentration camps? Again and again I have asked myself that question. It made no sense then and it makes no sense now. Look at Darfur. The UUSC is there, people like the Sharps, the Dexter's and Joys trying to help. Recently, a speaker discussed Darfur at our Sunday morning forum at the UU Congregation of Venice. He was grim.

"There is a famine in Darfur, and the people in power want the good land, so they kill to get it," he said. "But the willingness to kill, to maim, to rape, stems from rivalries between tribes. People from other tribes are the enemy. They are not human and deserve to die. "

We sigh at this and think it terrible. But it has been going on for ages in both the civilized and tribal countries. Look at Rwanda. Look at the Holocaust. Look at us in Abu Ghraib, the jail in Iraq. Look at the history of the United States. Since the Civil War blacks have had to struggle more than whites to get decent jobs, decent homes, decent educations. And what about our wall in Arizona to stop people from coming in. Some say illegals should be given no schooling, no health care. Yet in the next breath we hire them, paying them less than the minimum wage, rationalizing that they don't need as much money because they are used to being poor and are basically different from us.

Robert Burns, the great Scottish poet spoke to this in the 18th century when he wrote:

Then let us pray that come it may
(as come it will for a'that)
That sense and worth o'er a' the earth
Shall bear the gree, and a' that
For a' that, and a' that
That man to man the world o'er
Shall brothers be for a' that.

So let's talk about what the UUSC is doing in Darfur. Genocide has killed 400,000 people and displaced 2.5 million. I wrote to the Rev. Bob Keim who is the southwest Florida district representative of the UUSC, about Darfur.

"I cannot think of any subject which distresses me more than Darfur," I wrote. "Nothing except rape, killing, beatings, starvation, robbery and lies have succeeded in Darfur. Is there any way we can get some refugees out of the horror and into the USA? Could we sponsor some of the people? Could the UUSC and Muslims and the Jews get together and work on getting one or two families here? We have a working relationship with the Islamic community in Charlotte County. We just finished a dialogue with the Jewish rabbi and the Muslim imam. Our minister, Pam Allen-Thompson, facilitated it. Minnesota, my original home, is full of Hmong and Somalis who drive most of the taxis and usually are able to find their way. We ought to be able to get a few Sudanese in Florida. But not to pick tomatoes. "

Bob answered:

"Since you asked and since this seems to be a politically unsolvable problem, there are currently 'refugee emigration' efforts going on. I'd love to explain the process to you, but because those involved want to protect the identities and whereabouts of both the refugees and the operatives carrying out this work, we've been instructed to keep a very low profile. Let's just say that UUSC is one link in a greater chain. To date, just in our version of this operation, more than 350 refugees have been relocated to safe havens in Europe and this country, and more are being spirited out as I write this. And given that other religious and human rights organizations are carrying out similar work—many using the model we established—the number of relocated people is actually probably a good bit higher."

P.S. in my conversation with the operative, there was one moment of laughter and glee you might enjoy. Seems a Somali border guard was getting too close to what was going on, when one of the camels coughed up on him, shall we say, quite a hairball. As the other two guards burst out laughing he waved the operatives on in a cloud of expletives about camels in general. That hairball helped four parentless children get out. They now have homes and welcoming, loving families. So at least the camels are on our side.

It's a pleasure to share with you some points of success in the 10 camps where UUSC is working since we began our program just over two years ago. The program has trained the UN security police to implement a new effective model of firewood patrols. Women are now willing to participate and those who do can safely collect firewood. Now 50 to 60 percent of the community police in the camps are women. Before there were none, and as a result, there is a much higher incidence of women reporting to the community police.

Camp leaders have appointed gender committees in eight camps to deal with women and security issues. Over 400 women can now earn income within the camps. Over 2,000 women are attending the women's centers courses and trainings and as a result have access to mutual support, common discussion of their problems and skills training and income opportunities. This has enabled them to raise their issues with the camp authorities to improve their security. The UN forces recognize that the gender-sensitive protection training has been effective in improving civilian protection and increasing trust. One way we can make a difference is through support for work like the work that UUSC is doing.

So we know what the UUSC is doing in Darfur. Some of it is similar to what it did in World War II. The UUSC also helps and has done work in the union of Myanmar (Burma), Afghanistan, Kenya, Mexico, Guatemala and other countries. Here in the USA it is still working on the Gulf Coast helping victims of Katrina get their lives straightened out. In California it has been working with people to develop viable water systems, and Gov. Schwarzenegger has just signed four water bills which will improve everyone's access to potable water. This water package is the most comprehensive since 1960.

So here you have the story of the Unitarian Universalist Service Committee. It started on the eve of World War II and is still functioning in the refugee camps of Darfur. For eight decades it has been trying always to help people who have been treated inhumanely by other people, asking little, except that they be allowed to do their work.

Global Warming
2007 Speech, UU Congregation of Venice Forum

What kind of changes are taking place in the Arctic now? Average temperatures in the Arctic region are rising twice as fast as they are elsewhere in the world. Arctic ice is getting thinner, melting and rupturing. For example, the largest single block of ice in the Arctic, the Ward Hunt Ice Shelf had been around for 3,000 years before it started cracking in 2000. Within two years it had split all the way through and is now breaking into pieces.

The polar ice cap is shrinking. Images from NASA satellites show that the area of permanent ice cover is contracting at a rate of nine percent each decade. If this trend continues, summers in the Arctic could become ice-free by the end of the century.

The melting of once permanent ice is already affecting native people, wildlife and plants in the Arctic. When the Ward Hunt Ice Shelf splintered, the rare freshwater lake it enclosed along with its unique ecosystem drained into the ocean. Polar bears, whales. walrus and seals are changing their feeding and migration patterns, making it harder for natives to hunt them. And along Arctic coastlines, entire villages will be uprooted because they're in danger of being swamped.

The contraction of the Arctic ice cap is accelerating global warming. Snow and ice usually form a protective, cooling layer over the Arctic. When that covering melts, the earth absorbs more sunlight and gets hotter, And the latest scientific data confirm the far-reaching effects of climbing global temperatures.

Rising temperatures are spreading. In Alaska, the spruce bark beetle is breeding faster in the warmer weather. These pests now sneak in an extra generation each year. From 1993 to 2003, they chewed up 3.4 million acres of Alaskan forest.

Melting glaciers and land-based ice sheets also contribute to rising sea levels. threatening low lying areas around the globe with beach erosion, coastal flooding and contamination of freshwater supplies. (Sea level is not affected when flooding sea melts). At particular risk are island nations like the Maldives. Over half of that nation's populated islands lie less than six feet above sea level. Even major cities like Shanghai and Lagos would face similar problems as they also are just six feet above present water levels.

Rising seas would severely impact the United States as well. Scientists predict as much as a three-foot sea level rise by 2100. According to a 2001

Environmental Protection Agency studies the increases would inundate some 22,400 square miles of land along the Atlantic and Gulf coasts of the United States primarily in Louisiana, Texas, Florida, and North Carolina.

A warmer Arctic will soon affect weather patterns and thus food production around the world. Wheat farming in Kansas, for example, would be profoundly affected by the loss of ice cover in the Arctic. According to a NASA Goddard Institute of Space Studies computer model, Kansas would be four degrees warmer in the winter without Arctic ice, which normally creates cold air masses that frequently slide southward into the United States. Warmer winters are bad news for wheat farmers wo need freezing temperatures to grow winter wheat. And in summer, warmer days would rob Kansas of 10 percent of its moisture, drying out valuable cropland.

When we burn fossil fuels, oil, coal and gas cogenerate electricity and power our vehicles we produce heat-trapping gases that cause global warming. The more we burn the faster churns the engine of global climate change. Thus the most important thing we can do is save energy. And we can do it. Technologies exist today to make cars that run cleaner and burn less gas. We can generate electricity from wind and sun, modernize power plants and build refrigerators, air conditioners and whole buildings that use less power.

As individuals, each of us can take steps every day to fight global warming.

Incarceration In America
2016 Humanists Speech

After decades, people across the United States are realizing a simple fact: Too many people in the United States are behind bars. This incarceration crisis is having a terrible impact on our country with the human and economic costs rising daily. Our penal system is adding to our nation's serious economic and racial disparity.

The United States has the highest incarceration rate in the world. As of 2009, the rate was 743 people in jail for every 100,000 people in the United States In comparison, Rwanda had the second highest at 595 per 100,000, Canada was 123rd in the world at 117 per 100,000, and China had 122 per 100,000. The United States has less than five percent of the world's population and 24 percent of the world's prison population.

One out of every 32 persons are held by the justice system in the United States. Many people in our jails should not have been put there. In the 25 years since the passage of the Anti-Drug Abuse Act the United States penal population rose from 300,000 to more than 2 million.

The United States has a higher percent of imprisoned minorities than any other country in the world. It is at record highs in local, state and national jails. U.S. Attorney General Eric Holder states: "Incarceration has a role to play in our justice system, but wide-spread incarceration at the federal, state and local level is both ineffective and unsustainable."

For forty years our correctional system has had the mantra that handing down extreme sentences and criminalizing activities like drug use deter criminal behavior and keep us safer. Instead, prisons have become jammed, and one in four Americans are saddled with criminal convictions. Too many of these convictions are for minor crimes such as being the middle man in a $10 sale of pot.

The American Civil Liberties Union states public and political support for these policies is waning, evidenced by resounding public support for taxing and regulating marijuana in Colorado and Washington and strong poll numbers in states around the country in support of criminal justice reform.

When looking at specific populations within the criminal justice system, in 1997 there were just slightly more than 11,000 incarcerated females. By 2004, the number of women in state or federal prisons had increased by 757 percent to more than 111,000; the percentage of women in prison has increased every year at roughly double the rate of men, since 2000. The rate of incarcerated females has expanded at about 4.6% annually between 1985 and 2005 with women now accounting for seven percent of the population in state and federal prisons.

The American Civil Liberties Union is pressing for reform, including eliminating mandatory minimum sentences which the judges say tie their hands; increasing eligibility for release; reducing low-level felonies to misdemeanors; eliminating the incentives that lead to overly aggressive and racially biased policing tactics; and recalibrating drug policies, starting with decriminalization of marijuana possession, and instead investing in substance abuse prevention and treatment.

In states like Louisiana, which has the highest incarceration rate in the world, Oklahoma, Maryland, Mississippi, and Idaho activists are working for changes such as marijuana reform legislation and law reform that would eliminate nonviolent offenses as triggers for extreme sentencing. Throughout our nation thousands of people are serving life sentences without possibility of parole for nonviolent crimes as petty as siphoning gasoline from an 18-wheeler, shoplifting three belts or stealing a women's bagged lunch.

Also, solitary confinement is being used too frequently on nonviolent prisoners. It is especially damaging to young prisoners. Reforms here are very necessary. Many of the people imprisoned are mentally ill. They have been jailed and imprisoned for vagrancy, homelessness (some cities ignore the homeless—jail is the answer) for bi-polar disorders and more serious mental illnesses. An estimated 65 percent of people currently sentenced to life without parole are African American. Mentally ill minorities are arrested more than white mentally ill. It is a vicious circle. Treatment is needed for these people Otherwise they land in jail.

These sentences are cruel and disproportionate to the conduct they seek to punish. They do not make sense. And they cost the American taxpayer $1.7 million dollars a year! The American justice system can and must do better.

A Reading Program in India

Paul and I had been married for 15 years when we went on our sabbatical. We had to be in Washington D.C. and Cecelia Johnson, our old friend I met through Auntie Hazel at the lake, was working there in the State Department library. She put us up in her apartment opposite Watergate.

It was because of us that Cecelia joined the Foreign Service. Interviews for the State Department overseas employment were being held in Minneapolis. Paul and I and his friend John Bystrom and some other people we knew all went down to be interviewed. They wanted people who spoke a foreign language really well and that wasn't us. But they also wanted librarians, and we thought of Cecelia. Not only was she a librarian, but she spoke fluent Swedish.

She went down to be interviewed and they accepted her. She got sent to the Philippines for five years. So much for the Swedish. She then went to Malaysia and ended up in India until she was called back to Washington D.C. to finish up her contract. She never used her Swedish. She said it was probably because she could stand the heat and humidity of Southeastern Asia.

Cecelia was a big help on our sabbatical. She found reference material on various countries for both of us and also uncovered an India program in Lucknow dealing with teaching literacy to a huge number of people. We were able to make arrangements to visit it, and for the first time I found a good working program sponsored by the UN and a private foundation.

We were invited by them to stay overnight, but our contacts in the Department of State in Calcutta had made reservations for us on the late plane to Delhi where we were headed. So we arrived in Delhi at three a.m. and were met by a U. S. Marine who took us to our hotel. That was the result of writing to our congressman Don Fraser for help on contacting people knowledgeable in other countries about our sabbatical subjects.

The next day we were awakened by a phone call. It was a representative from the reading program we had just visited. One of the sponsors lived in Delhi and wanted to meet us. She was in her 90s and very proud of the program. She also lived in Connecticut very near Paul's mother and dad, so we visited her in Connecticut too.

She talked about problems financing the program, and also the trouble they had getting Indians to use the program. The most popular and successful thing they tried was an anti-smoking school held at night with movies in color discussing the evils of tobacco. It went over big, and because it was so popular they put out pamphlets in 20 different dialects and proceeded to teach those people who couldn't read them how to read. They did this with pamphlets on farming methods, health, instructions on how to repair water pumps.

This was the big divide in teaching reading I ran into around the world. Teaching skills related to specific jobs or industries through teaching them the skills vocabulary and helping them with pamphlets on the subjects versus the method used by the Swedes in Kenya and by adult education in the U. S.—graded readers with a controlled vocabulary and teachers able to help the students. There was no research which indicated if one method was superior to the other.

This approach worked for India and certainly is more meaningful and immediately useful. Obviously it does not create general literacy.

Russia and Copenhagen

In 1968, the year before we took our sabbaticals, we had a chance to visit Eastern Europe and the USSR ending up Copenhagen. The Reading Association was offering a tour which would explore Problems in Teaching Reading in Czechoslovakia, Hungary, Romania and the Soviet Union ending in Denmark for a brief two-day vacation.

Prior to our visit, it was hard to visit USSR. Nikita Khrushchev was in power, however, and he wanted tours which would explain the Soviet Union to its visitors. I thought that learning about problems the Russians had with their poor readers (along with the other nations) would be valuable to me as a remedial reading teacher and would give us a chance to see these countries too. Indeed it did.

We visited Prague for two nights and went out into the countryside to a neurological clinic which dealt with severe learning cases, to Hungary where we got lectures on the Hungarian educational system and the difficulty of the Hungarian language and how it developed. We were in Romania for only a day and a half. In Romania there was concern about their language, Romansch, which was different from all of the other countries around them. This made communication with them difficult. They had problem readers but were far more interested in their international communication reading problems. Otherwise we toured Romania and what I saw of it was very interesting.

I was sick when we got there and worse when I left. My stomach was mildly upset from a night of partying in Hungary. The Romanian bus driver recommended in his broken English some seltzer water he was drinking as being helpful for what ailed me. He was taking it and it was a real tonic. As I usually do, I trusted his diagnosis and drank the water. A few hours later I was really sick. I had bad cramps and diarrhea. So I saw very little in Romania except bathrooms and the back of the bus where I was assigned during our Carpathian Mountain tour. I was too sick to take notes and that is about all I remember except. some excerpts from the tour guides talk.

Romania has oil. I didn't realize that. It has beautiful mountains. The bus driver cared for me for as he and I stayed in the bus touring the walking portion of the tour. He brought me some of his cold water, which I appreciated. I missed some good trips, Paul reported, including one to one of the original Unitarian Churches. I would have liked to have seen that. They also heard. a lot of lore about Dracula, and visited some Dracula sites.

In late afternoon we were taken to the airport and put on a plane to Moscow. In the middle of the flight, I realized that I was feeling better, had no more stomach cramps. Paul came up with the answer, and I think he was right. It was the seltzer water. I was taking a drink to cure constipation. What was helping the driver was giving me diarrhea!

In Moscow we stayed in their newest hotel, a very modern one, practically next to Lenin's tomb which we could see if we wanted to stand in line for two hours. One or two of the group did. We were all given a nice tour of the city and then met with a reading official. This lady was in charge of what we would call curriculum. She spoke on language problems in the USSR. What she said was unexpected.

First of all she went into a thorough discussion of the English language. It is the hardest to learn of all languages because it has so many exceptions e.g. words such as thought, through, though. No rules at all for words like that and there are many. Russian, on the other hand, is completely phonetic and easy to learn. The Soviet Union has very few people who cannot learn Russian—except for the brain-damaged.

She then went into the rest of her talk, and discussed what in the USA were called "culturally deprived," a polite term for delinquents and problem kids. She said they had kids in the USSR who did not succeed in school because they were in gangs, were bullies. petty thieves, teen age criminals. She regretted to say teen age gangs are very common in the Soviet Union especially in the large towns.

This problem, which exists all over the world, is caused by poverty, joblessness, and poor nurturing by parents she said. She remarked that though students like these were poor students, reading difficulty wasn't the problem. She stopped, opened up a box and remarked that she had some books on language recently published in the USSR, and handed eight or 10 books, some quite thick, to our tour leader, an Arizona professor whose name I cannot recall, but whose first name was Anita.

I remember the books well enough, because when we left the Soviet Union to fly to Denmark, Anita found that she didn't have room for all of the books in her luggage so handed most to whomever was near her. I got a skinny, 175-page book on the Russian language. In Denmark, I tried to give the book back to Anita.

"It's yours," she said, "give it to someone at the University of Minnesota who is interested in Russian."

I figured I was lucky, I got a good book! Little did I know how handy that good book would be.

In St. Petersburg we had two adventures one in St. Petersburg and the other in Moscow. St. Pete scared Paul and in Moscow I wondered if Paul was going to jail.

In St. Petersburg it was the bathroom problem again. Three of us women had to go. As we were walking through the summer palace grounds I saw the ladies room symbol, poked the two and we veered off without telling anyone, sure we could catch up with the group. There was a line; It took longer than we expected. When we came out our tour was gone. It was near noon. We knew they were planning on eating because we had all heard the Russian guide talking to Anita.

There were four restaurants. Which one was our group going to eat at? None, it turned out. We struggled through the crowds to each restaurant, got in arguments with the waiters, but insisted on looking for our tour anyway to no avail. What to do? A large, blonde emotional lady was with us. She began to cry. We had ruined her research on Russia. All she had done was explore stupid restaurants and now we were lost and she would learn nothing. Her complaining upset the other teacher who suddenly became aggressive and started shouting at the big one.

"Forget. your research! It's a dumb idea anyway. We are lost in a place with millions of people and don't know what to do!" They glared at each other. I thought they were going to come to blows.

"Let's go to where the buses are," I said. "They would never leave without us."

"Wouldn't they?" the blonde cried. Whining, she came along with us, and after about 20 minutes of pushing and being pushed—it was very crowded in the summer palace gardens—I saw a sign in several languages including English saying, "Tourist buses." We were found. Shortly after we discovered our group which was waiting angrily.

Paul was glad to see us; Anita and the Russian guide were furious. We would be unable to eat. The blonde lady started to howl. (This quieted us all quickly). She gave her talk about her research and the Russian interrupted her and said we were taking too much time and most of our tour was lost. The others were mad because we did not have time to eat.

I told them that we had gone to the restaurants and it turned out that our group was going to eat at a cheaper restaurant on the road. Anita said to me stiffly that she had appointed Paul to wait and take us back to Moscow by train if we didn't show up, but at the last moment we had. The three of us were sullen.

Blondie settled down, but did not speak to me for the rest for the rest of the tour. I did not care. A salesman who came along with his wife, a reading teacher from California, sympathized with me. He was the only one besides Paul. But we all got over it when we learned that we were having a farewell dinner in Moscow that night, which is why we weren't having a big lunch. And on the bus ride home from St. Pete, we stopped for coffee and little cakes, so the group forgave us and we became the same rollicking crowd of old.

Paul began joking with people and we had settled into a convivial group by the time we hit Moscow. An hour later we met in the banquet room for our final dinner. It was huge. We could not find our table. There must have been over 50 tables. We finally found ours, carefully labeled "USA Reading." It was next to the Mexican table.

While we were all sitting down, Paul was looking at the Mexican table with another lady whose name was Lillian. Mexico was loaded with sweets, compared to us. Lillian wondered why. Then she pointed to a platter.

"Look Paul it's those marvelous cupcakes we had on the way back. Why do the Mexicans get them and we don't? I would just love some more of those cupcakes." So Paul reached over and took one and gave it to her. Lillian was thrilled. She opened up her purse and slipped it in after first wrapping it in a paper napkin. We then waited patiently as usual, for the waiters to appear.

Finally three waiters showed up with another man who was dressed as a chef, hat included. They looked upset. They wanted the head of the tour. Anita raised her hand.

"Someone from this table has stolen food from Russia!" one waiter intoned in English. We all were shocked. Who would do that? I wondered if it was a huge amount of food, and what kind.

The waiter pointed to the chef. "Our cook has counted the cupcakes at the Mexico table and one is gone!" he declaimed and pointed to one of the waiters: "And we saw someone but we do not know who the person was who took the cupcake from the table."

Anita was brick red and very angry.

"I don't believe this!" she said. "No one in our group would steal a cupcake!" She looked fiercely at each one of us.

The other waiter said, "This is a crime against the state, and someone must pay for it."

Paul looked up. "I took the cupcake." he said. The waiter snapped to attention and came over to Paul.

"You will come with me."

Paul got up. "Where are you taking me?" he asked.

The waiter gestured at him to follow them and they moved off. There was deep silence from the group after Paul left. Anita finally spoke. She drew herself up and said to the entire group:

"Your husband has brought shame to the group. What will they think of reading teachers. I looked at her and she made me mad.

"Oh shut up! I said irritably. "It's bad enough without you ranting and raving."

"That's right!" Lillian chimed in. "Think of what is happening to Paul and what we can do to help him."

The salesman's wife spoke up and said: "Someone should have gone with him!" The salesman started to stand up.

"I can go," he offered.

Anita looked confused. The blonde lady spoke up.

"Nobody does anything for anybody around here" and sniffed. Lillian was whimpering. Anita straightened up and glared at me.

"Your husband has brought shame to our group! What will they think of American reading teachers?" I looked at her and got mad. Paul is in big trouble over a cupcake and she is worried about our honor.

"Settle down and shut up!" I snapped. We all sat quietly, some of us sipping water. I was frankly scared. Just then Paul returned, with a Russian policeman. My eyes bugged. A cop. My gosh, what are they going to do with him. The policeman took him to his seat, smiled, and left.

The group was beside itself and wanted Paul to explain what had happened. Paul was laughing. He said at first it was scary, but that the one waiter did speak some English. The chef was upset because of the cost of the cupcake and that now he would have to provide the Mexicans with another cupcake and that would cost some money. Paul mentioned that our group liked cupcakes too and had wondered why we didn't get any. He didn't think taking one was that important.

"No! No!" the waiter exclaimed. "The Mexicans were on an A+ tour." The reading tour from the USA was only on an A. This meant no cupcakes. They all stared at Paul. Paul offered to pay for the cupcake. The cook looked confused. He did not know how much a single cupcake cost. He would have to look it up. They finally found the price—about USA 25 cents.

Paul didn't have the change, so gave them a USA dollar. Lillian was contrite and kept apologizing to Paul.

"Thank goodness we left the next day" Paul said as he reminisced about it later. "she could have been apologizing for the tour."

One would think getting lost in St. Petersburg and arrested in Moscow would be enough excitement for us on this tour. But no. We had more excitement coming in Copenhagen. On the plane we ended up sitting by the California couple. The salesman and his reading supervisor wife. He was very sympathetic to Paul and took his Players Club card from California.

"They have a Player's Club in Copenhagen. We can all go there and have a good Danish dinner and something to drink besides shots of vodka,". he exclaimed. So later on that evening we got a cab to go to his club. The cabbie frowned at our destination. Our friend showed him his membership card. The cabbie bit his lip and gave us a small smile.

"This club is not the same in Copenhagen."

Our friend asked what he meant.

"It is different," he said.

"Do they serve food?" our friend asked.

"Yes," the cabbie said reluctantly.

"That's good enough for us! The food is good isn't it?"

"Of course, all Danish food is good!"

"Then take us there!"

The cabbie shook his head but did as he was told. We got to the club and it looked like an apartment building. We went inside to something which looked like a very small exclusive hotel. It had a dining room in the back, a table with easy chairs around it as you entered and a counter with a well-dressed lady behind it. The reading teacher and I sat down and started talking about Scandinavian food. A well-dressed fortyish man was at the counter, took a card and proceeded down the hall to a room which he entered. The lady behind the counter finally turned to our husbands.

"We would like a table for four," the salesman said. The lady behind the counter looked shocked. She spoke softly to the salesman. He looked shocked and said something to Paul, who also looked shocked. They came over to us.

The salesman said to his wife, "The Players Club in Copenhagen is a whore house." His wife looked at him and started to laugh and I did too. It struck the two of us as terribly funny. I then began looking the place over very carefully, for I had never been in a whore house.

It certainly looked impersonal, and discreet. No one was around. All business was apparently handled by the lady behind the counter, and buzzers to the various rooms. There appeared to be about a dozen down the hallway. All of this was legal in Denmark. The lady behind the desk had called a cab, which came right away, and we left. The new cabbie looked shocked when he saw two women exiting the whorehouse and the two of us got the giggles. Paul and her husband shoved us into the cab and we went someplace else to eat. I don't know who recommended it, but of course it was Copenhagen and any place in Copenhagen has good eating.

A Hospital in India

Our trip had hardly begun, and I didn't know any of the tour members. That was to change. By the next evening, I was famous. We were going into a hotel in Jaipur when I and another person noticed a movie theater next door. He saw me looking at it and poked me.

"How about seeing a, movie later?" he asked.

I nodded. "Let's do it!" I said.

The tour director heard us and said he would be glad to go with us, for it was a good movie and it was about Old Delhi which we had just seen. So after we had unpacked I told my old friend and roommate, Barb that I was going to a movie. I asked if she wanted to come along. She said she did not want to come along that she was tired and was going to read her tour book and go to bed.

So off we started. It was only a block way. As we turned in, I looked over at the busy street next to us full of cars. bikes, motor bikes and elephants and marveled...INDIA! And at that moment I bumped my hand against a cement barrier in front of the movie house. It hurt, but I ignored it, positive that the pain would vanish in a few moments, which it did.

But—as I searched in my purse for Indian money for the movie, I saw that I had blood all over my hand. I had done more than bump the hand, I had scraped the skin off and it was bleeding profusely. I put a piece of Kleenex on it and told the tour director. He was very methodical. First, he took my money to buy the ticket. Then he looked at the hand. Then he asked the ticket taker where the Red Cross station was. I was impressed. A Red Cross Station…well, they are certainly prepared compared to a movie house in the States.

There they just have some band-aids at the Candy Counter. The ticket taker smiled at my tour director and said we could try the Candy Counter that he was sure the man there had some band aids. So things in the two countries weren't so different after all. The man—I should say kid—was about 14 or 15 looked a little shocked when we asked for help with my wound which by that time was oozing happily a bright red all over my hand.

He looked among the candy bars and rooted around. And found a key. He opened a drawer under the counter…shoved around some caramels and came up with band aids. My wound was a scrape. The skin was off and it covered half my hand. They did not have a band aid big enough.

The boy looked upset and said several sentences I did not understand. He gave me his hanky which he pulled out of his back pocket. The tour director intervened. "I have a clean handkerchief," he said to me and pulled this lovely new carefully folded hanky out of his jacket breast pocket, wrapped it firmly around my hand and then led the way to our seats in the movie.

We enjoyed it a great deal. The photography was wonderful and Old Delhi was fascinating. The two main characters were so poor they had to sleep on top of some of the buildings in Old Delhi and make love there too. It was a very good movie, although it is true I don't remember much more about it than I have written.

After the movie we walked back to the hotel and nothing exciting happened to me this time…both my companions commented on this. I smiled my "good sport" smile and proceeded to my room. Barbara was asleep but woke up long enough to ask If I had liked the movie. I started to tell her about it, and she started to snore so I went to bed.

The next morning, the hand was still oozing blood when I got up, and when we returned from breakfast around nine. I unwrapped it and it looked bloody, splotchy and irritated. Barb and I discussed it. both of us agreeing that it looked bad, that if it was not infected it certainly could be unless it was dressed and bandaged.

Barb suggested I call the tour director and ask for the hotel doctor. I thought that was a good suggestion, so did so. The tour director said he would get back to me. And he did, in about an hour.

Scenes of India

"The doctor will see you at 5 p.m." he reported. "It is the only time she can see you."

So we proceeded with our activities in Jaipur for the rest of the day. At 4:30 I met the tour director and found the rest of the tour with him. They had all become curious about my wound. They wanted to know where I was going, if it was in the hotel or some other place. The director calmed us all. "We are going to Dr. Panniker's Hospital," he said." That's where she will examine Rosemary's hand. And only I will accompany her."

Barbara shrugged and stepped back with the rest of the group. We went in a Tuk-Tuk, a three-wheeled vehicle and the director paid for the ride. I was impressed. The Tuk-Tuk was different and quite noisy but comfortable. It was only a couple of blocks, we could have walked it easily, but with a sore hand you got a ride in a Tuk-Tuk.

The hospital was four townhouses connected together with a huge sign at the top that read, DR. PANNIKER'S HOSPITAL. We went in and were told to wait; the doctor had not arrived. We looked at the folder describing the hospital. It had six floors. The fourth floor took bed patients only. The hospital was used by a gynecologist, an orthopedist, an internist, a diabetes specialist, a gastro person, an ophthalmologist and a surgeon.

Dr. Panniker was the internist. She arrived in a few minutes. She was about five feet tall and should have weighed 25 pounds less. She wanted to know all about the injury, all about the medications I was taking, and all about my medical history. She listened to my heart. It was beating. A nurse appeared. The doctor gestured to me.

"We will go upstairs," she said. "There we will fix your hand. Come." And she left the room with the nurse. I followed her.

The tour director stayed—reading a magazine in one of the comfortable leather chairs. I followed. We came almost immediately to an elevator which in the USA would have been called antique. It was a bunch of iron bars with a bottom and a top. With an angry squeak it started up, slowly. It stopped at each floor, so we could have a look around. I was glad it did, for I was curious. There were offices on the second and third, but when we came to the fourth floor, food was being served and people were in rooms with beds.

There were nurses in uniforms around and trays. It looked cozy but hospital-like. When we got to the sixth, we all got out. Down the hall was a door, and it opened to the operating room and, I guess, a storage room. The right wall was piled high with tightly sealed cardboard boxes.

In the center of the large room was an operating table. I was told to climb on it and lay down. I protested mildly. After all it was just my hand. The little doctor glared at me so I did what she wanted. They pulled out a thing-a-ma jig for me to rest my arm and the nurse unwrapped the dirty hanky from my hand. She proceeded to wash it gently but thoroughly with soap and water. The doctor then came and sprayed it with something and scrubbed it. When she was sure it was clean, she sprayed it again and sprinkled some powder all over it, and in a couple of minutes it stopped oozing blood. She stood triumphantly away from me and the hand.

The nurse approached with a box of Johnson and Johnson Bandages. She began bandaging my hand. The doctor and I watched silently. When the box was half out of bandages and my hand was completely bandaged at least a half a dozen times, the nurse halted and gazed at the doctor.

"Use it all," The doctor said with a wave.

When she was done, the hand looked like a boxing glove. They both smiled and helped me very solicitously off the operating table. I tried to object. After all, it was just my hand.

"No, no," the nurse said, came charging up with a wheel chair. I was told to get in it. Then I did object, and with reason. I thought they were adding charges to a bill which I feared could be very high.

"My gosh," I thought "nurse, doctor, operating room, painkillers, disinfectant. Did she operate? Would you call squirting powder on a wound operating? On an operating table, of course. Good Lord! All I have for the whole trip in cash is $300. I hope she takes a credit card… or a check."

I began to really worry, chewing my lip. The elevator squeaked down to the lobby. They were still eating on Floor 4. The whole procedure hadn't taken very long, I noted. We got to the main floor and proceeded to her office. The nurse vanished. The tour director appeared. I assured him I was fine.

We went into the doctor's office and settled down in a couple of leather chairs. She rummaged around in her bottom drawer and pulled out a form. I swallowed and then asked, as she was itemizing away, how much it was going to cost. She looked up, smiled, and handed me the bill.

"Twenty dollars", she said. My eyes popped out… "Twenty dollars—" But that was all I was allowed to say.

"Twenty dollars!" my tour director shouted, jumping up and waving his arms madly. "Twenty dollars? That is too much! It is highway robbery! It should cost no more than four!"

I looked at him in surprise as I thought, Four dollars. Is he out of his mind?

Dr. Panniker smiled sweetly. "Oh, I think twenty dollars is a very fair price. I operated on Mrs. Hagen's hand, we cleaned it, treated it, and dressed it. In addition, I gave her some antibiotics with vitamins. On top of that I am sure Mrs. Hagen has. trip insurance which will cover this visit. You do have insurance, don't you Mrs. Hagen?"

I looked at her. She was right. The tour required each member to take out insurance. I had forgotten this in my panic. But insurance was no issue, I certainly could afford $20. I nodded at her dumbly.

"It is too much! It is too much!" The tour director continued.

"It's all right." I shook my head at him. "I will pay." And I did.

Dr. Panniker gave me a receipt and smiled.

Suddenly I thought of another question. Looking at my hand the boxing glove bandage, all wide and round, I asked "How do I keep it dry when I shower?"

The doctor rummaged in her drawers again, pulled out a plastic sack similar to those we get at our grocery stores. "Wrap this around it," she replied. "And leave the bandage on for a week."

We proceeded back to the hotel in another Tuk-Tuk. The tour director was silent. He shook his head a couple of times and looked out the window. I said nothing. I was relieved to have everything turn out so well

We pulled up to the hotel. The entire tour—all 12 members—was waiting. As I got out of the Tuk-Tuk they crowded around me. Our self-appointed leader, Janine, asked. "How much, Rosemary? How much did you have to pay?"

"Twenty dollars!" I answered.

"Twenty dollars?" they all echoed me in wonder, as if they were a chorus.

There was a stunned silence.

The tour director spoke up: "It is too much, I know."

The Americans started to laugh.

He continued: "I tried to get her down, but I couldn't."

And we laughed all the way into the dining room, where we had a nice Indian dinner.

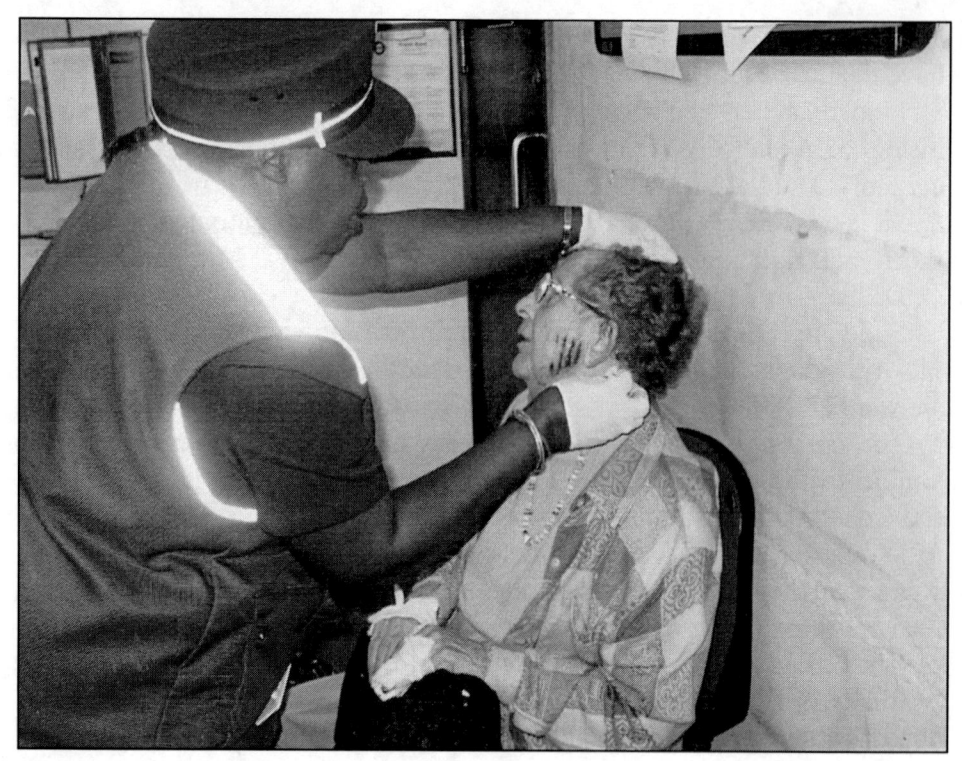

Merle Brunzell, my friend, after her accident in London as a station official attempts to stanch her bleeding.

Getting Sick or Injured in a Foreign Country

I have written about getting sick in India, how I depended upon the hotel doctor who turned out to own a hospital and was very efficient and inexpensive. The other thing I did not mention was that I had sickness insurance. It is required if you are with a tour, and easily available if you're traveling alone. I was so tickled at the cheap $20 total charge that I just kept the bill and paid the $20 myself, but I could have reported it and received payment.

We did have a single woman who became ill during the trip. She had insurance. She was seriously ill and slept on the bus and was in a wheelchair when we were walking. At the hotels, she was reported to the hotel doctor. We stopped on the bus twice, and one heart specialist recommended hospitalization, but she and the tour director did not want to do this. On the way back she was given a seat with an empty one next to her, that was all. In Miami, her daughter met her and she stayed in a Miami hospital for a week. I called her a couple of weeks after we were home and she said that the insurance covered everything.

I have two more examples illustrating sickness and procedures to follow in a foreign country. I got a urinary tract infection in the Canadian Arctic—in Iqaluit, the capital of Nunavut. I informed my tour guide that I had to see a doctor. It was night time—around 7 p.m. so he drove me to the Iqaluit hospital and left me in the waiting room with an Inuit mother and her sick baby.

A young woman doctor appeared almost immediately and after finding out why I was there referred me to the lab for a specimen, and took the sick baby and her mother into her examining room. It was a small hospital. The waiting room was probably 24 x 24 feet and the lab a bit smaller. There were rooms for patients, but I did not see them. The hospital was new—Iqaluit was new itself as was Nunavut, the newest province, so everything was in excellent condition.

Later, when we talked, the young doctor said that she had just graduated from medical school and that had signed a contract with the government of Canada to work for it after graduation, because Canada paid for her medical training. I believe her assignment was for two years, and she had some choices as to where she wanted to go.

She seemed happy enough in the Canadian Arctic. Canada took my insurance. She prescribed some pills for me and the pharmacists went into a huddle. They had no idea what to charge me and finally just made a guess, and my insurance accepted their bill.

For our sabbaticals, we took out term insurance for one year. We caught a couple of colds, and I had to get a gamma globulin shot because I had a conference with a lady who had active hepatitis. We were younger, healthier. So in 1969-70 our medical expenditures were limited to some Japanese cold pills and a preventive shot given me in Uganda.

In London, my roommate, Merle, a Minnesota friend, had a serious fall and broke her collar bone and a finger. and had a terrible gash on her face. We were on one of the subway escalators which go almost straight. up. She was adjusting her raincoat and the belt got caught in the escalator mechanism and tumbled her backward.

She screamed my name for help and I had no idea how to stop the damn machine, but another person did this promptly. We helped her up the steps and an ambulance was called. The station clerk proceeded to try to stop the bleeding face. An ambulance arrived in five minutes and so did a nurse on a bicycle fully equipped to deal with an accident victim.

Many times, the ambulance driver said the bicycle beats the ambulance because of traffic and has the equipment necessary to save lives. The ambulance driver was bragging about the time it took him to get to the subway—seven minutes—beat the bike by 30 seconds!

Merle was transferred to the nearest hospital and I went too. There she was in intensive care for nine hours with a doctor by her almost constantly watching, ordering x-rays and checking her responses hour by hour. They were worried about a concussion. I kept her company. They discovered her broken collar bone and finger, did not bandage them, nor did they give her any pain killers all because job fear of a concussion.

We finally went back to the hotel where she spent an incredibly painful night. She was allowed to take Tylenol only, and they refused to bandage her broken bones until the next day, just kept it in a loose sling. She stayed in the hospital then for an entire day. I stayed with her and gave up a tour of England with an English friend, Joan Baringer, from Englewood who was visiting her family.

She was an amazing patient, chirpy and upbeat no matter what. She got to talking to the cleaning lady and found out she was a Russian who got the job for six months so she could learn English. She urged us to try the sandwiches at a nearby department store, so I went down the street and bought some sandwiches. The next morning we took a cab to the hospital (the cabbie told us to sue London).

We were sent to a huge room where specialists sat in designated spaces. We were shown to the orthopedist, who greeting Merle cheerily, explained their fear of a concussion, looked at her x-rays , questioned her briefly, gave her a pain prescription and sent her to a Nurse specialist who bandaged her collar bone and finger. Merle asked the doctor how much this was going to cost. He laughed and replied he had absolutely no idea and had no way to figure it out. So she never got a bill.

Of course, she *did* have a serious accident on one of London's escalators. On the trip home, Delta refused to give her first class even though she had enough points for it but placed her in coach next to an empty seat.

All of these things happened in 2005. Things have probably changed. But the insurance you *must* buy for a tour will cover any sickness, and occasionally the country itself will pay. Do *not* expect Medicare to pay for any accident or sickness outside of the country. You will have to have separate insurance.

Iceland

I just returned Friday from a 10-person, 12-day Elderhostel tour of Iceland, which I thoroughly enjoyed. It was not so with my dog, Blair. She is so insecure after my absence that she follows me around incessantly, even into the shower. A cold, wet, nose in a shower is an unforgettable experience. It is not for the old. It probably is not for anyone.

Her behavior reminded me of a great passage by Halldor Laxness, the Icelandic author who won the Nobel literature prize in 1955. He describes the love of a dog in his truly wonderful epic novel, *Independent People*

Bjartur did not make the journey back to summerhouses til the following day. The dog padded along beside him in blissful anticipation. It is lovely to be going home and whenever she was a few yards ahead of her master, she would halt and look back at him with eyes full of an unwavering faith. Her reverence for her master was so great that she did not presume even to walk ahead of him. A dog finds in a man the things it looks for.

Iceland is on the Arctic circle, therefore we had 24 hours of daylight during our visit. But this also means that during the winter, Iceland is mostly dark. Icelandic poets like to write about the spring, when light again shares the night

This is an excerpt from a poem in an Icelandic book of nature poetry called *Cold Was That Beauty*.

Spring equinox, a wonder of the world. (that fast-sprouting tooth of time) I count the hours on my fingers to confirm it all adds up. Now it's as light as it is dark
O just allocation of light! I wake up for this.
For this!
And pronounce winter's short days deceased. In veneration.
I believe in the resurrection of the grasses
And the sprouts everlasting.

Iceland.is an old country. It started in 874 AD and has records proving it carefully preserved on sheepskin. Iceland never had kings. The reason people went to Iceland was because they hated kings. The cold, the volcanos, and the earthquakes were a fair exchange for no kings!

Iceland has come a long way since 1940, when the British invaded it. Later, the Americans came and built an airplane run way which is still being used.

Before the British or the Americans provided them with work and money and bought their meat and wool, Iceland lived in extreme poverty. We visited historical sod huts which were lived in during the 1920s and '30s

with the dirt floors, the open fire kitchens, the living rooms surrounded by beds, where sleeping, eating, spinning and preparing the wool was done.

In other parts of the huts the animals lived during the winter. The hut I took pictures of was the minister's hut, one of the finest at that time. Our guide remarked that a man in his 70s had come by a month ago who had been born in the house.

In Reykjavik, at the open-air museum, we saw more sophisticated versions of the same thing. The only difference was that their sod huts looked unused, and some of them had the sleeping-living room upstairs, which had to be climbed up to on a ladder. Beds were small, about five feet by three feet. Sometimes two or three people slept in the same bed. Laxness, in his book, describes the 13-year-old girl sleeping with her two teen-age twin brothers; she at the foot of the bed and they at the head.

World War II brought Iceland out of grinding poverty. Now they have one of the best school systems in the world, and the highest literacy rate in the world. Education is free until high school ends at 16. Then students go either to vocational schools or colleges for four more years. In 2009 they paid $300 per year to do this. After college, they may take advanced work at either of the two universities in Iceland, again for a nominal fee. Iceland believes in education. It has a thriving adult education system, and education begins at seven and goes on until the end of some people's lives.

Free medical care is available from birth to death also. Median income now in Iceland is a little less than $30,000 per capita.

Iceland is unhappy now with their prime minister, who likes to do things without consulting the Icelandic congress, the Althing. The Althing, created in 930 AD, is a parliament whose history is almost continuous to this day. It meets for two weeks out of the year and outside in a natural amphitheater which we visited.

Iceland became a member of the George Bush's United Nations coalition through the actions of its prime minister, David Oddsson. He did not send this request through parliament, but instead referred it to the foreign ministry committee where it easily passed. The first anyone heard of it, according to our Reykjavik guide Erikur Einnarsson, was after it happened. Iceland soldiers are responsible now for guarding the Kabul, Afghanistan airport.

Now David Oddsson is in a bitter battle with the President Olafer Ragnar Grimmsson, a person with virtually no power in an office created for a head of state, elected only to be a greeter; to publicize the country. He has one constitutional right, the right of veto. This he just used over the issue of media ownership, a bill which Oddsson pushed through parliament. He says the law is vital to defend democracy; his opponents say he is trying to silence his enemies. Because of the veto, which has never been done before by a president in Iceland's history, there will have to be a referendum. Polls say that the referendum will lose, mainly because Oddsson is so unpopular with the people

The USA is not popular in Iceland. My college friend, Barbara Whipple and I were told this many times. We agreed tht there were many things about the United States' current actions and activities we also do not like.

Though geographically as big as England, Iceland's population is only 290,000 people. Three out of five live in the area in and around Reykjavik, the capitol.

One thing which might influence immigration is Iceland's geology. Iceland sits atop the North Atlantic Ridge, the fault line where two of the earth's tectonic plates are slowly drifting apart. As a result, Iceland is getting wider at a rate of 1 cm. a year.

On either side of the ridge. which we saw clearly several times, earthquakes and volcanos are commonplace. Iceland's location gives it one of the most volcanically active landscapes on earth, peppered with everything from naturally occurring hot springs to a string of unpredictably violent volcanos, which have regularly devastated large parts of the country. Indeed, as we traveled we saw lava field after lava field. Sometimes the lava rock was old and covered with moss, those fields were from the middle ages. Others were new and craggy with huge lava boulders and rocks strewn around.

Earthquakes come and go, with few people hurt or impressed. Icelanders like to brag that in 1998 during a fairly major quake, the national opera performed right on through an earthquake without missing a beat.

And the Icelanders take advantage of the volcanos. They sink pipes down into the soil and mine the heat. All of Reykjavik and most of its surroundings is heated by geothermal heat. Up in Akureyri, geothermal doesn't work because the hot pools and hot spots jump around and last no longer than a year or two. Then new wells have to be drilled and the process is not cost-efficient compared to hydroelectricity.

Iceland has waterfalls major and minor, high and low and they get 80 percent of their electricity and heat from these waterfalls. It is so cheap that the power source is attracting industries from other countries. Aluminum is the newest Iceland industry. Bauxite is shipped in from Australia; electricity and heat is so inexpensive that is cost-efficient to manufacture aluminum in the country. They are even able to export energy and are working hard on this problem by laying pipes along the ocean floor.

When we arrived in Iceland, one of the first things we noticed was that there were few or no trees. The climate is harsh, and the growing season so short that it takes a tree 30 years to grow 20 to 30 feet. Birch (dwarf) and fir trees are the most common wood in Iceland. There are reforestation projects, and the farmers are urged to start windbreaks around their houses. It will take 30 to 40 years for the trees to grow, which is discouraging.

Women's rights in Iceland are there, but not entirely there. The history sounds good, and it is, but there are noticeable gaps. The country elected the first woman president Vigds Finnbogadottir, in 1980. But presidents are just for show and Finnbogadottir never used her veto.

Icelandic women were the first in the world to get the vote. But it turns out that only women who owned land were able to vote. There were very few of those. According to the women who spoke on modern Iceland, women are not getting equal pay for equal work. They make about seventy percent of a man's salary. And even though the salary scale seems to be equal, men are promoted faster and given bonuses on the side. They work hard. Our guide at the beginning, Sonja not only was a permanent guide, but also worked at the travel office often.

Even at night in Reykjavik, at the end of our trip we met Sonja again. She was filling in on another tour for a male guide who had been away from his family for 12 days and didn't want to work that night. It required an hour's drive both ways for Sonja. I suppose she got home around midnight.

Erikur Einarsson , our Reykjavik guide has only one job. He is a research librarian. He gets a six-week vacation and spends part of it every year guiding. Maria, our Akureryi guide, had three jobs including guiding.

For a 12-day stay in the beginning of summer, Iceland is idyllic. Everything was well organized on the trip; the lecturers were interesting, the saga stories fascinating the scenery breathtaking. The horses and sheep convivial and most people spoke English well. They were friendly, helpful. Everything was lovely, but because of the rate of exchange, quite costly. A beer or a glass of wine was almost $10. Postcards were almost a dollar each. It cost me $17 to get some pictures developed. (in the United States it would have cost $7.99).

We got thorough information about various industries. We learned how to commercially fish cod, halibut, herring, and three or four others I never heard of. We learned about the various netting systems. We went to a fish factory and saw the fish being packed on ice to go to Reykjavik immediately, or being frozen and packaged in fillet form. We met workers, saw some teen agers shoveling ice and packing fish. We saw a bunch of women working on freezing and packaging fish with a black woman supervising.

Then we were taken to a fish meal factory. Fish meal is used as a fertilizer and as a supplement to animal food. Not too much to the cows though, or the milk will taste fishy. To top it off our teacher took us home and his wife served us coffee with cookies and sweet rolls. He also recited Shakespeare to us.

The agriculture man told us how to raise chickens, hogs, sheep, cows, cattle and horses in Iceland. They are raising chickens and hogs like we do in the USA. I asked if they had trouble with manure from these huge buildings holding 500 to1,000 chickens or hogs. The manure is spread on the fields, he said. I inquired about fertilizer run off. It runs off into the ocean, he replied. So far it has not harmed Iceland.

Iceland has some agricultural problems. The soil is volcanic, poor, and sandy. They have only a few crops; the major one is hay. They also have some barley and cold weather vegetables. We dined on cabbage and potatoes daily, although sometimes mushrooms, turnips, and carrots were included.

Sheep are everywhere in the country side. Maria said there was too much lamb. Iceland cannot sell enough of it, and farmers are urged to stop raising sheep. Sheep, horses, and cattle are good for Iceland. They graze between the lava rocks and make use of the land. We ate a lot of lamb, and it was served much better than it is here. The slices were thick and we got five or six at a time. And it was rare or medium. Never well done. I loved it. We visited a thriving farm of about 1,000 sheep. In a barn a ewe gave birth in front of us, and the farmer reached over casually as he was talking, grabbed the legs of the lamb, and pulled her out for the ewe.

He also raised horses. Iceland raises many horses. The Icelandic horse sells well. It is a little larger than a pony and is the same horse that was there in the Middle Ages. No other horses have ever been allowed in Iceland, and no artificial insemination has been allowed between foreign horses and Icelandic horses.

Iceland eats horse meat. About fifteen percent of the meat sold is horse meat. But the main use for the horse is riding. They have riding clubs, with trail rides all over the island. The Iceland horse has five gaits instead of the usual four. The fifth is between a trot and a canter and makes for very easy riding. The horses are also very mellow and docile. They are easily trained and do well in horse shows. They are a popular export. But once a horse leaves Iceland, it can never return. The Icelanders are afraid of imported horses bringing disease.

Iceland has a thriving dairy industry and provides milk, cheese butter and other dairy products for the country and for export.

They have started using greenhouses to grow vegetables, and are successful with roses, and with tomatoes. But there aren't more than a dozen greenhouses. The Icelanders resent the expense of heating and lighting in the winter.

Poets and writers complain of the weather in Iceland, and certainly in winter it is dark and snow storms can be severe. But it is under the influence of the gulf stream. Summers and winters are mild compared to our Midwest. In winter, it rarely gets below 20 degrees Fahrenheit and in summer it stays between 40-60 most of the time. Nearer 40 when we were there.

Iceland has also discovered the tourism industry which now accounts for fifteen percent of its industry.

Icelanders say that their humor is an acquired taste. For instance, they love the story of an Iceland woman who married a Turk. When the marriage failed, a legal battle ensued for the children. The Turk won, and took the children off to Turkey. To get her revenge, the woman ate Turkey for Christmas!

A man was hauling in the line on a fishing boat when it pulled violently and a cord severed two of his fingers. Horrified, he ran to the bridge to show the captain. "Look," he said, holding up his hand to reveal the bleeding stumps. "I've lost two fingers."

The captain eyed him for a moment and then said, "Not in here."

Like I said, it's an acquired taste.

Iceland is into hydrogen. No, Iceland is not the only country that is into hydrogen. They do have a hydrogen bus, however. The hydrogen bus is part of a two-year experiment being done by the European Union in five major cities in Europe. There are ten hydrogen buses in Reykjavik. They are easy to see with their great "H" on them and steam pouring out of the exhaust, on the roof of the bus.

I was determined to ride one. So, my roommate, Barb, and Joyce, a lady from Cleveland traveling alone, went to try out the bus. It was just like any other bus. It stopped at the end of the line for fifteen minutes and the driver talked to us.

It was cheap; he didn't understand the process which split water into hydrogen, but said it was an inexpensive process, and running the bus didn't cost much. The bus itself ran well except on steep hills. More power is needed there. But the real problem was the cost of building the buses, about 9 to 10 times the cost of a regular bus. He said that hydrogen vehicles will come, but probably not for another ten years.

There is much more I could say about Iceland; I have not talked about the way they classify their names, I have not mentioned our two boat trips.

I have not even mentioned their greatest saga historian, Snorre Sturlason, who died in 1241. He also wrote the history of the Norse kings which was carefully kept on Icelandic sheepskin. A copy of part of this book was lent to me by Gloria Scoboria.

Closing words. Another poem from *Cold Was That Beauty*. By Jon Ur Vor

Armed peace
An old cannon
In a grass-covered fortress looks skywards
With its silent eye-
And a bird has made
Its first nest
And chosen a place for it in the wide barrel.

What Is A Narr?

It was June or July, 1970 at the end of our sabbatical year. We were in Berlin and were leaving. for Le Havre, France and our ship to New York the next day. Germany was still divided into East and West Germany; and Berlin was the perfect example. To get on the road to France we had to go through East Berlin. We had finished up our research and interviews with the sabbaticals. The only thing we were exploring in Berlin was fun.

There was a film festival going on— an American Film Festival showing old American movies in German close-captioned in English. For our last night in Berlin, we decided to see an old Fred Astaire and Ginger Rogers film. After the movie, I remarked that I had learned a new German word: *narr* which means idiot or fool. Paul didn't seem particularly impressed by my new word for my limited German so I let the subject drop.

Narr was to become more important to us than we could imagine. The next day we left early and at East German customs there was no line. We were lucky. Paul took both of our Passports and for some reason was gone a long time. He finally appeared, looking annoyed and worried.

"They won't give me your passport, and they refuse to tell me why." he said. I started a little, sat and thought about this and of course asked why. Paul didn't have time to answer, for suddenly a German soldier appeared at the door of the car. He smiled kindly at me, and I smiled nervously at him.

"Bitte, aufstehen" he said finishing the request by pointing up toward the sky. Now I spoke better German than Paul, who spoke none at all—he spoke pretty fair French if he was allowed to think—I was nervous and did not recognize the word aufstehen which is a common enough expression and means get up! My hearing is bad and I thought he said regen (which means rain) because he had pointed to the sky. Therefore, I answered in my poor German.

"Nein, night heute." (no not today). I could see immediately that this was the wrong answer. I bit my lip and looked at him in my most friendly fashion. Paul groaned quietly by my side. He could tell I had fouled up. The soldier looked sternly at me. He straightened up, snapped to attention and roared: Auf Stehen! It came to me suddenly what he wanted. He wanted me to get up and I got out of the car in a hurry. He glared at me.

"Kom mit mir!" (Come with me).

Paul got that and started to tell me what to do.

"He wants—"

"I know what he wants," I said and I followed him. When we got into the office, he showed me the form Paul had filled out. I read it hurriedly, saw nothing wrong. He shook his head at me and pointed to my passport information. I looked at the form again. I saw that Paul had put the wrong date down for my birthdate.

"That idiot!" I thought and narr came to me just like that. I smiled at the soldier reassuringly and said in my limited German which was coming to me:

Herr Hagen ist ein Narr! Mein Gerburtstag ist funfundzwanzig night sechs. (Mr. Hagen is an idiot. My birthday is the 25th, not the 26th).

The soldierwas so delighted with my answer he came around the counter and gave me a big hug! We parted good friends, laughing about the whole thing. When I got back to the car, I didn't say a thing. I decided I would kid Paul. He gave me a funny look but didn't say a word and started the car. We drove about half an hour toward France, and then he could no longer control himself.

"Why did that German soldier hug you?" he asked very casually.

I countered: "Why can't you remember my birthday?"

"Oh was that it," he laughed. "Didn't I put down the 26th?"

I started to laugh. "That was the problem. It's not the 26th!"

He was silent for a minute or two.

"Well, when is it!" he demanded.

I looked at him sweetly. "I'll never tell." I said.

And we left it like that for a mile or two. He thought about my answer and shot a question back at me:

"How do you expect me to remember your birthday when you celebrate it for a week?"

"I give up," I laughed. "It's the 25th!

Torture: 2006 Speech—UU Congregation of Venice

Torture has been with us throughout the ages. It is still going on in Latin America, specifically in Guatemala and Columbia. Countries deny torture. Then it is discovered and stopped for a while. At the ACLU convention I met a man who worked for an international group exploring Latin American torture. I asked if it was finally accepted as a fact in Latin America.

He laughed, said it was a fact. Also said the worst torture example his group had found was the elimination of an entire city by torture, approximately 200,000 people. I didn't go into this with him. In Minneapolis, my home town there is a center for victims of torture. So do not think that Britain and the United States' behavior in Iraq is unique to civilization. It is not; it is completely normal. What about Iraq? First, the U.S. denied the torture. Then a bill was passed stating that the field manuals of the various services must be followed and Geneva Conventions must be observed. Now we are told torture is eliminated.

The U.S. does not torture. Except on Oct. 12, 2006. A marine sergeant, 23-year-old Heather Cerveny confirmed that torture is going on in Guantanamo Bay. In an affidavit, she states she met several navy prison guards at a club on the base where they described, over drinks, harsh physical abuse.

One sailor said: "I took the detainee by the head and smashed his head into the cell door."

"Yeah this one, you know, really pissed me off," one of the guards told his buddy, "so I just punched him in the face."

"Everyone in the group laughed at their stories of beating detainees" Cerveny recalled. She said the guards also talked about taking away detainees' privileges "even when they're being good," and denying their requests for water. In her affidavit she states she was told "they do this to anger the detainees so they can punish them when they object or complain."

The investigation into these new allegations comes as the military and the White House insist any problems in the treatment of prisoners at Guantanamo have long been fixed.

In Iraq, the causes of torture were many. Troops were unprepared for the chaos after the easy victory and so were their leaders. After the official war ended, the guerrilla war began. In attempting to control this, sweeps were made and people were gathered like minnows in a net. One of the reasons so many prisoners were taken was because we did not have enough soldiers in Iraq.

A Department of Defense document about a prison in Tikrit notes that:
We observed a lack of standards for detaining and releasing persons. The

detention facilities throughout were overcrowded and there appeared to be no standard release criteria. It's like the roach motel, 'they can check in, but they cannot check out.'" The detention facility at Baghdad International Airport was growing at an alarming rate. Built to handle 300 persons, it is currently handling 800 persons. We asked numerous officers and NCOs who had the authority to release detainees after it was determined that they were not criminals or had no intelligence value. Every person had a different answer, most being—I don't know. Because of the sloppy way people were arrested, it was almost impossible to find the bad guys. Interrogators were urged to get more information. Finally it was made clear from as high as it could go that any method that worked with 'incorrigibles' and thought guilty was OK. Torture was used, then ordered to stop when Abu Ghraib was exposed. From this maltreatment, suits by the injured were filed. For example: Evidence of torture and claims against U.S. army. Below are three case studies, claims for compensation made by victims of American torture in Iraq taken directly from occupation records.

Claimant is a Canadian citizen born in Egypt seeking compensation for torture and other abuses inflicted on him when he was captured and held in Camp Bucca, Iraq in 2003. Claimant member of a peace organization called Rights And Freedom Int'l. He was in Iraq on a mission to convince the Iraqi leaders to step down in order to avoid a war. He was tortured for three weeks with beatings, withholding of medicines and medical treatment, putting the muzzle of a gun to his head, seeing other detainees being beaten, solitary confinement, being hogtied for hours, being kept under the hot sun, uncomfortable positions for extended periods, and threats he would be sent to Guantanamo if he complained about the beatings. The detainee went on a hunger strike, after which he was beaten by a female officer. He was then deported to Egypt.

Claimant is an Iraq of Swedish citizenship arrested in Baghdad in September 2003. Was imprisoned in El-najaf, then Dewaniya and then taken to Abu Ghraib. He was subjected to many hours of torture, beatings assaults and sexual humiliation, threats and "unspeakable and demoralizing acts." In one instance the claimant and 12 other naked prisoners were roped together by the genitals while a laughing guard pushed one of the detainees onto the ground, causing pain to others. He was shocked with an electric stick, kept awake with loud music, had a belt around his neck and was dragged about 70 feet. A dog was used to intimidate him. In another instance an American guard shot randomly into a crowd, killing five prisoners. A reply from the army claims service acknowledges receipt of the claim and asks for more information stating the military claims act requires that the alleged torturers be acting within the scope of their authority when they cause an injury to a claimant.

Claimant was a night patrol guard in the village of Annana. On July 18, 2003, U.S. marines attacked the village and claimant was shot six times. The village was off limits to American soldiers. He was taken to a hospital and later to Abu Ghraib. The combined joint task force offers the person who was shot $1,000 to settle, stating in a letter to his mother that it "appears U.S. forces were negligent in shooting your son. In addition, he should have been released from the hospital and instead was arrested and transported to Abu Ghraib prison. Payment was approved and made.

In debate in Congress, Sen. Patrick Leahy had this to say about torture.
"Passing laws that remove a few checks against mistreatment of prisoners will not help us with the battle for the hearts and minds of the generation of young people around the world being recruited by terrorists. Authorizing indefinite detention of anybody the government designates without any proceeding and without any recourse is what our worst critics claim the U.S. would do, not what American values, traditions and our role of law would have us do. One of the goals of the Iraq War was to give democracy to it. I leave you with the question: how well have we done that?"

Kenya Literacy Training: Part of My Final Report

I found no real evidence of reading teaching by UNESCO going on in Kenya. It is true we ran into a boy on the beach who had a phonics book. It is also true that I was not in the country long enough to see any class in reading. All I can do is go by the little I saw, and what they told me.

A Swede is in charge of UNESCO's literacy program. He is also getting money directly from Sweden which gives him some autonomy. He has found a printing company which will turn out primers in Kenya's various languages. Social workers in the larger towns are literacy chairmen and are responsible for obtaining students for literacy classes. Sweden is also able to pay the teachers about $100 per year, a good salary for a moonlighter, and classes are functioning. I have not witnessed the classes.

I asked him about integrating reading with agriculture and other industries and he replied that their basic texts did give some information, but that after Kenyans learned to read they were then fed into Kenya's adult education program. He also feared literacy money might vanish when combined with farm machinery and expensive trips from UNESCO by literacy and agricultural leaders. He agreed Literacy Village in India was doing a good job but reminded me that India and the United States give money to support it besides UNESCO.

All UNESCO seemed to be doing on its own in Kenya was giving work to its teachers, if the beach boy example was typical. He certainly could use the job, and a few words would be taught.

Kampala, Uganda. Dec 18-23: We met with Mr. John Assedri, Ministry of Community Development; Miss G. Pasano, a UNESCO worker in literacy; and Mr. John Tweedy, USIS Information officer We discussed Uganda's literacy movement with Assedri and Pasano. Miss Pasano had come from a sick bed and was bright yellow with jaundice. Later we were advised to get gamma globulin shots to guard against the infectious hepatitis.

Miss Pasano was dedicated to her work, which appeared to be a job with many problems and few solutions. Uganda can pay teachers very little and up to now the churches have done the teaching. Currently, the entire education problem has become a national project. The school dropout rate is very high between the ages of eight and 14. There is no publication center and it is almost impossible to get books for illiterates. The present political climate in Uganda does not appear to emphasize literacy.

Uganda And the Uprising

One of the things we learned after our trip to Uganda was that we should have learned more about the country before we got there. In fact, we should have done more homework on all of the African countries we were visiting. They all had problems, and all had become independent nations within the last few years. Some of the problems were political power struggles between those in power and those seeking power.

In Uganda's case it was a little different in December of 1969. The people in power, Milton Obote and Idi Amin, were corrupt terrorists and just getting started. The man who shot Obote by mistake was part of a movement against Obote and Amin but had failed because he shot the wrong man. Amin was not even in the country then. From what I read later, the Tanzanian soldiers anticipated the take-over and were prepared to provide martial law all over Uganda. Here is what happened in Uganda to Paul and me, according to my memory and our notes.

We knew nothing of Uganda's political or economic problems. All I wanted was to meet with my literacy specialist and both of us wanted to see the wild animals. Paul had no appointments in Uganda. Now, as I write about our adventure in Uganda, and read my notes, I am amazed that we behaved as we did. We forged blithely ahead doing exactly what we wanted to do. And we were lucky. We knew nothing, absolutely nothing about Uganda. We were worse off than the average tourist, who at least had his tourist agency looking after his life. We just assumed everything was safe. Upon reading Wikipedia, I found, more than 50 years later, that Uganda at that time was not safe and had not been safe for almost a year. Here is the story of our four days in Uganda.

When we got off the plane in Entebbe, a guard asked Paul about change he had left over from Kenya. Paul showed him his change and the guard took it!

We were taken to Kampala, where the American embassy was located, by the hotel van. The hotel was modern with full facilities. We asked for a room on the second floor because in Africa electricity often went out and it was wise to be close to the ground. We were out of luck; our room was on floor six. On the way up on the elevator, we found it crowded with people going up and the entire elevator emptied on the same floor. We worked our way through the crowd and found our room.

We had only four complete days in Uganda and I was the only one with appointments, so I immediately called the American embassy to contact my literary specialist. The operator advised me to come on over, that she couldn't reach the specialist, who was in the hospital with hepatitis, but that people were there who could help me. I talked to her office mate who said that she had not been feeling well for some time. I was horrified and suggested that he get to a doctor and perhaps get some sort of protection. He laughed and said it wasn't very infectious. Not inclined to shut up, I asked if that was why they called it infectious hepatitis?

Anyway, he knew nothing about what she was doing in literacy teaching, so my work in Uganda was over; I had no one else to see, and my whole idea of new ideas about how to teach illiterates from Kenya or Uganda seemed to be out the door. The Kenyan teacher had a phonics workbook. That was hardly unusual. So back to the hotel. We had a good dinner, wandered around the neighborhood for a while, then took the elevator up to our floor.

The next morning, Paul was still asleep, so I dressed and started down to breakfast without him. When I got out into the hall I stopped. All of the doors of the rooms were open. Absolutely no one was around. I walked down to the elevator and to the next hall, and finally all around the sixth floor. Empty. No one...doors all open. We were the only people on the 6th floor. I went back to our room, and Paul was dressing.

"There is no one on the 6th floor except us!" I said. He was still sleepy and out of it. I went to the window. On the ground were three soldiers with guns marching up and down. That news got him to the window. We hurried down to the lobby.

"There has been a coup," the first person we met said.

"No," the second said, "It was an attempted coup."

Tanzanian soldiers had been attending a meeting in Kampala. Immediately upon hearing about the assassination attempt, they took charge. I turned to Paul in frustration to ask if he had heard anything else. He was gone. Where had he gone? Obviously, to get his coffee.

I walked over to the breakfast room. He was sitting at a table reading the paper. He waved to me. I joined him, full of news. But he beat me to it.

"Well, the paper doesn't think it is a coup attempt or an assassination attempt." We sipped our coffee which did not taste like coffee.

Meanwhile, down the hallway people were flooding the ballroom. In a few minutes it was full, over 500 people. We asked the waiter what was up, and where were the people from.

"They are from all over Uganda," he said. "They are frightened."

"Frightened?" I asked.

"Of being killed," he replied and moved off. We sat in stunned silence.

"Well," Paul remarked finally. "In times of stress, you should eat." And he dug into his kipper and eggs. The waiter came with my order of oatmeal and said the soldiers were from Tanzania, "part of the military meeting being held here. We are very lucky. We are being protected by many soldiers from a friendly country. There should be no fighting. We are all safe."

We looked out of the spic-and-span breakfast room window to the soldiers leaning against their guns and chatting with one another.

"Can someone tell us what is going on? Who shot the vice president?" we asked.

"I do not know," the waiter said. And he collected our plates and went away.

We wandered into the ballroom. It was filled with people crowded together, talking. Kids were running around, babies were being bedded down. We began to get information from some men who were seated. The people were all English residents of Uganda. They came from all over the country. That was really all the information we could get. No one in the ballroom wanted to talk to us. The men said things were a little more hopeful. That was all they would say.

I asked them about literacy projects in their area and one of them replied that it was senseless to talk about that now. Of course, what was going on was that Uganda was led by corrupt dictators who did not mind bloodshed. The assassination failed. The English people faced the loss of their homes and probably would have to leave Uganda. Some might be killed. Some would continue with their jobs and be accepted by the Africans. Change was going on and we were in the middle of it.

Did we realize this then? I certainly didn't. If Paul did, he was quiet about it. Looking back, I can see why the hotel people were happy that Tanzanian soldiers were in Uganda at the time. The next day the Tanzanians were gone and the Uganda Army was in charge. What to do. We had two days left in Uganda. My solution was to call the American embassy and talk to our contact there. He was not in.

A Frenchman was going to tour Kampala by van with a driver.

"Why?" we asked him.

"To observe. To see what is going on," he replied. We decided to go with him. So off we went to explore Kampala. It was very quiet. The streets were completely deserted. This was in a city of over 250,000 people. There was not a person or a car in sight. We drove around downtown Kampala and to the outskirts of the city. We got out periodically to look around. At one time in a park around the business district there was a cloud of mosquitos so bad that when we walked through them we could hardly see, and I was sure we would get bitten and maybe get a disease. But they did not bite. They just swarmed.

The streets looked like a movie set ready to go, like someone would call "OK, action! Bring in the cars and the people." Our driver began acting like a guide.

"Let's go see the bitches," he said. "The one is a beautiful bitch. The biggest and best in East Africa."

The bitches, I thought. Maybe we are going to the horse barns. I turned to Paul. "I thought female horses were mares."

He blinked his eyes at me. Still thinking about the barns, I asked him, "What do they call a female cow?"

"All cows are female," he replied. I started to answer him but we approached Lake Victoria. The soldier stopped the van, and the three of us got out. He pointed proudly to Lake Victoria.

"This is Lake Victoria. It has the biggest bitch in Uganda."

It wasn't much of a tour. We walked around the beach a little. Kicked some sand and left for the hotel. Things were certainly NOT happening in Kampala. When we got back, the soldiers were gone and the ballroom was empty. It was as if nothing had happened.

We went up to our room. It was empty. All of our stuff was gone.

"Have we been robbed? Do you have the passports?" I asked.

"Yes," Paul said, "and I have all of our money." He got on the phone and hung up shortly. "They moved us. They thought we would be safer on the second floor."

"That's the one we wanted in the first place," I said. We headed down to room 212. Everything was in order. I looked around further. My nightgown was missing and so was my new Vanity Fair slip. I called housekeeping and reported this. We straightened out our luggage. Paul proceeded to write a letter. I waited for my nightgown and slip. They did not come. I called again after 45 minutes. That got some action. At the door a lady appeared with my nightgown.

"Where is my slip?" I asked. She smiled at me and waited. I repeated, "Where is my new Vanity Fair slip?" She waited.

"She wants a tip," Paul said. "Here." He gave me an American dollar. "She'll like our money."

I handed it to her. She smiled, kept her hand out.

"She wants more," I said.

"I just have a five!" he said. "Oh, what the hell…here," he said and gave her the five. She left happily.

"I got that nightgown on sale for $6," I said. "And now I had to pay another $6 to get it back? What will I have to pay for my slip?"

He was relaxing on the bed reading the American edition of the Kampala paper.

"Who says you are going to get it back?" he asked. "Why should I give her a tip for returning something of mine that she probably took?"

I grumbled. Paul laughed.

"At least you got it back!"

"That does it," I said. "Unless I get that slip back, I'm wearing jeans until I'm out of Africa."

Paul laughed harder. "Going against African custom, Rosie– you should be wearing a mumu all the time."

"Style!" I said.

"Custom!" he said, continuing to read the paper.

The next morning Uganda Army soldiers were out in front. We looked at them for a while, discussing what we were going to do that day. We wanted to go to the Nile River and see the hippos, but we didn't know how to get there. We could fly. Planes to the Nile were available at the airport. Paul pulled a face.

"Maybe not in times like this," he said. "And are the planes safe? And what is the cost? If we have to charter it alone, we probably can't afford it. It's better to rent a car—except I don't like to drive unfamiliar roads in an unfamiliar country."

Buses were not running. We went downstairs to talk to the people at the desk. It turned out buses were running but not to where the wild animals were. The best solution would be to hire a driver who would also take us to the area which surrounded the Nile where we could see some other animals too, like buffalo and giraffes.

"Is it safe?" I asked.

The African smiled at me. "The country is completely in the control of our army," he replied.

Paul looked at the ceiling and grinned. I caught it.

"Maybe I should call the guy at the Embassy again," I said. "He might know more about travel."

"Good idea," Paul said. I got hold of the man and had a very interesting conversation. He didn't know a thing, but like a good bureaucrat made it sound as if he was giving great information. No one had reported on the road conditions to the Nile. If we took that trip, it could be very helpful, for then the Embassy would know about the road.

"Know what?" I asked. There was a long pause.

"If it is usable," he finally replied. I didn't say anything and there was a long silence. Finally, he spoke again.

"If you decide to go, please report back to us the conditions."

"Of the road?" I asked.

"That too. There have been some storms."

I relayed this all to Paul. We talked it over. The embassy was not helpful. On the other hand, he did not tell us we should *not* go; the man was just noncommittal.

"We are their scouts," I said. Paul went downstairs to talk with the desk again. He came back.

"I think it's OK Rosie," he said. "President Amin is back, and things have quieted down. The Tanzanian soldiers are leaving. The Ugandan Army is in charge."

So, we decided to drive to the Nile River and see the animals. It was just about the only time we had in Africa to see animals. I called the Embassy and told my contact we were going. He replied again that things were quiet.

"Call us when you get back so we know how things are."

I began putting on my jeans and a long shirt and my boots.

"We both had better buy a good straw hat against the sun," I said.

"Saw them for sale at the gift shop," Paul answered. We grabbed a small knapsack and went downstairs to wait for our driver. It was about 11 a.m. We would be gone until around midnight. I went to the desk to tell them this. I also told them I hoped my nightgown would be safe, and that I had not received my Vanity Fair Slip yet.

He nodded. I looked at him. I had two responses. Smile or not smile. I was damned if I would smile. My underwear was missing! I needed the slip to wear with my very thin cotton dresses. I met Paul.

"I'm still mad about my slip. I don't think I'm going to get it back."

Paul laughed at me. "In times of real stress, deal with minutia," he said.

I glared at him and headed to the gift shop and purchased two straw hats for five dollars each. I rejoined Paul and gave him his hat.

"Here's some minutia for your head." And I plonked it on him. The driver then appeared and we started out to the Nile.

We drove through Kampala and there were cars in the streets now and business seemed to be starting. At the outskirts of the town, we ran into some soldiers on the side of the road. They had put up a sign saying STOP and our driver obeyed it, showed our credentials and one of the soldiers smiled and said, "Move on gentlemens!"

"Gentlemens!?" I asked and looked up. Paul grabbed me by the back of the neck and pushed my head down.

"Shhh," he said. The driver started up and off we went again.

The main highway from Kampala, the largest city in Uganda to the Nile River, was a two-lane dirt road. It was well designed, and had no loose gravel, and it was wide enough for traffic. What I am saying is that it was not as bad as the Tsavo Park road in Kenya where we met the elephants. It was far superior to that. But, it was nowhere near the quality of the highway we drove on to Tsavo Park from Nairobi.

We were driving on a well-packed gravel road. It was dusty and bumpy, particularly at 60 to 70 miles an hour. We hung on to our hats. Again, we realized that Africa was beautiful. The grasses were lush and long and blowing patterns—it was just lovely. There were occasional farms with crops well-tended and even some tractors. We rounded a curve. In the distance we could see a barricade and some soldiers around it. We stopped. A Uganda soldier approached staggering slightly, laughing and hiccupping.

"Greetings, gentlemen," he said, and came toward us.

"Gentlemen?" I said, and Paul grabbed my straw hat and pulled it down over my ears. "Shut. Up," he said and squeezed my shoulder. I shut up and listened. The soldier said something in dialect to the driver. The driver answered in English.

"These are my passengers. They are going to the Nile to see the animals. Here are their passports." Holding on to them, he showed them to the soldier.

The soldier ignored them and swept his arm toward us.

"Get out of the car gennelmens and disrobe," he said.

"Disrobe?" I squawked. Paul shoved me down beside him and shaded me from the soldier. The driver protested and began to speak very loudly, so that the other soldiers could hear.

"Their papers are in order. They are American tourists who wish to go to the Nile River. They do not need to get out of the car!"

Another soldier approached.

"Hey, hey," he said in a cajoling tone. "What is going on? We have Americans here? Why was I not told?" and he shoved the other soldier away.

"You go," he ordered. "I will take charge." The soldier shrugged and staggered off. The soldier looked in our window and spoke to Paul.

"I am the sergeant and am in charge here. I like Americans. I used to live in Los Angeles. Do you know Los Angeles?"

Paul shook hands with him. "Not well, but my aunt lives in Long Beach. Do you know Long Beach?"

"Do I know Long Beach? I sure do," the soldier replied and for five minutes he and Paul discussed LA and Long Beach. I sat and looked interested, straw hat practically down to my chin. And that was that.

The rest of the trip was uneventful and in about two hours we were at the Nile. We drove around the area and saw a huge buffalo. I got out of the car to take its picture. The driver was frightened and told me to hurry and finally

got out and escorted me back into the car. We went by some giraffes and I wanted to take their pictures. Our driver kept going. He wanted to connect with a tour boat on the Nile. We could see giraffes from the boat, he said. And he was right. We saw many giraffes on the shore from the boat.

He phoned a boat and then drove us to a landing and we waited only about five minutes and a covered tour boat holding about a dozen American tourists came up to the dock. We got on to see the hippos. Our driver would return in three hours. He would phone first. And off we went. On the River Nile. Wow! I was really thrilled.

The Americans had been in the area for a week and would be in it for almost another week when they would be driven to Entebbe Airport. They knew nothing about the assassination attempt and were not particularly interested. They were fascinated by the hippos and so were we. These animals are very large. I didn't realize how large. They are also fearless, at least the ones we were dealing with were. They also reminded me of the saying, "Like a bull in a China shop."

The mothers particularly kept crashing into the boat. When they did, it shuddered as if it were about to collapse. The first time this happened I grabbed Paul and yelled, "Hang on!" The others laughed hysterically.

"Not to worry. The boat is strong! Scary though, wasn't it?" one woman said. There must have been about twenty hippos in the area. About 14 adults and maybe five babies. The babies were the size of a milk cow. At least they looked that big. They all swam around the boat looking at us curiously. We traveled on the Nile River for about twenty miles, and we met and passed various pods, if that is what they call a hippopotamus group? The hippos pushed and shoved the boat and sent it rocking back and forth so that I had to hold on to the railings. Once they got under and lifted the boat out of the water. As I remember, we all thought it was wonderful, although I admit as I read this it doesn't sound very safe.

We had a nice buffet onboard ship with a choice of Coke, beer or wine to drink. It was a fun experience. Sure enough, after three hours the phone rang and our skipper pulled into a dock and away we went again by car to Kampala, this time at night.

The ride back was uneventful. We drove on at around fifty to sixty miles per hour and after about a couple of hours our driver stopped. He tooted his horn.

"What now?" I asked Paul. He looked worried, but shrugged. A young boy turned up at the driver's window. The driver turned to us.

"I hate to ask you," he said, "but my wife wants some bananas. The boy has no change, and we do not have room for a whole dollar's worth of bananas."

"Do you want change?" Paul laughed.

"As a matter of fact, I do," he said.

Paul held out his hand with change.

Our driver took 25 cents in Ugandan money and gave it to the boy. We waited, and suddenly three boys appeared with three wheelbarrows filled to the brim with bananas. The driver looked impressed. He turned to us to explain.

"They are for my wife. She likes bananas." They could not get them all into the trunk of the car, so we shared the back seat with about 200 bananas. They had spiders in them which I was afraid of. I reported this to the driver and asked him to stop so we could kill the spiders He refused and gave me a lecture about the lack of safety in Uganda and the danger of stopping.

"Except for bananas," I muttered.

Paul chortled.

We got back to the hotel late and staggered off to bed tired after a full, exciting day. The next day we were to leave. Paul went down to the desk to find out the airport van schedule. To the great regret of the hotel, the airport van was not running. It had no gas.

"How will we get to the airport?" Paul asked. The clerk at the desk looked at him sadly.

"I know not," he said. "I know nothing." And that was all he would say.

"Maybe that's all the English he knew," I suggested. "Perhaps if we go down again we would hit an English speaker."

"You try it," Paul said. "But give it a rest for a while. They may get some gas." Well, they didn't get any gas, and we got no response from them about the airport. Our plane was to leave at five p.m. We sat around the room. I phoned the Embassy and told our contact that the road was safe. He wanted to know about barricades and if the soldiers were Ugandans. We went to eat at noon. Asked at the desk, and the tourist desk. Asked many places – all over.

"No gas anywhere in Kampala," they said.

"Are we supposed to walk?" I asked.

Paul looked at me. "Did you ever get your Vanity Fair slip?" he asked.

Around 2:30 I looked out the window. There was an Ethiopian Airlines van. It had come to collect Mr. and Mrs. Hagen for their flight to Accra, Ghana.

The airport was a mad house. Long lines everywhere. We were put in the Ethiopian Airlines line to customs. After an hour we cleared customs and walked to the plane. We were both tired. I was unstrung and not sure we were at the right plane. Paul was wrestling with the carry-ons. A guard approached him.

"May I see any change you have from Uganda, sir?" he asked. "Oh sure," Paul said absently and handed the carry-ons to me.

"Here." He held out his hand full of change and then frowned and tried to put it back in his pocket. Too late. The guard took it and motioned us into the plane. I got to laughing and kept laughing until we took off for Ghana. Paul's last words in Uganda were, "Poor Scott. He's not going to get any Kenya or Uganda coins," but we got out of Uganda.

Africa with Paul, 1970

I went to Africa was with my husband Paul in 1970. We were on sabbaticals, he from the University of Minnesota and I from the Minneapolis public schools. I was studying illiteracy, for I was teaching remedial reading to high school students and for three years had overseen curriculum for adult basic education. I was excited about meeting literacy teachers in other countries and perhaps finding some different, perhaps even wonderful ways of teaching poorer students how to read.

Paul was dealing with curriculum in junior colleges. On the side, he was looking at foreign movies because he taught a class in film. And we got to see a number of interesting foreign films, and even met a Hong Kong star. We met her through my help—I inadvertently got into a scene being filmed so they had to do it over. The star had nothing to do while they were rearranging things, so she talked to Paul. She told him to go to Africa, he would love it!

From India we flew to Nairobi, Kenya arriving around Christmas time. We had decided to take time off for the holidays. First, we had some chores. I wanted to visit U.N. literacy classes, and the parents of a colleague wanted us to contact two Kenyan men about a living memorial for their son, As usual we checked in with the United States Embassy. We saw the Nairobi cultural attaché who clued us in on places and persons to see.

We had asked our congressman, Don Fraser to alert the attaché, and we had written so we were expected. The man we met I was from Minnetonka Mills, Minnesota and still owned a home there. He was a good-looking man who knew Walter Judd, the congressman Don had beaten. We avoided conversation about politics and got down to our specific problems.

Our Minnesotan attaché replied that the Swedes were working on literacy and referred me to the Swedish embassy, where I met with a tall, blonde, very serious man in charge of the Swedish literacy program in Kenya and who also taught classes. He would have nothing to do with the UN program. He maintained the UN teachers were inadequate and that the Swedes could do a far better job alone. I asked him to go into detail, and he replied that the UN teachers did not have skills or training, their program was poorly organized, their purpose did not always seem to be teaching literacy. Therefore, it could not be taught well.

At this time there were no classes in session and when they started again I would not be In Kenya. So that was that as far observing any Literacy classes from the UN or Sweden. I connected with Paul and we headed to the University of Nairobi to see the two men. Don Ryberg, a teacher I taught with at Marshall-University High School told us to look up his parents when

Mr. and Mrs. Ryberg and me in Thailand

we got to Chaing Mae, Thailand. They were teaching in a Presbyterian missionary school in Chaing Mai for a year. We prepared for the Rybergs by searching for something they could use in their teaching.

Ryberg taught eighth grade science. and in Hong Kong Paul found a beautiful set of real butterflies that had been captured, killed, pinned to velvet, and named. I put away my disgust at the killing of beautiful butterflies and agreed that a science class could get some use from them. We carried them carefully in a specially packed box from Hong Kong to Bangkok and finally Chaing Mai which was located in northern Thailand.

"Just what I wanted," Mr. Ryberg proclaimed. We arrived the day before Thanksgiving. The Rybergs invited us to Thanksgiving Dinner, said their church celebrated it. And the next day they brought us over to the Chaing Mai Presbyterian Church and with a bunch of Englishmen, Americans and Thais we celebrated an American Thanksgiving.

We had the works. Turkey, mashed potatoes, vegetables, cake. Delicious. The only thing the Thais could not manage was pumpkin pie. There were no pumpkins in Chaing Mai. The Presbyterians had also invited the United States Embassy attaché and his wife to Chaing Mai, and they in turn asked us to dinner the next night. There, we met some American field exchange students who told me about literacy teaching in Chaing Mai.

Paul with Frederick Kingu and Issac Onyinda

Paul met some college professors from St. Olaf College in Minnesota, which had a branch in Chaing Mai. They had much to tell him. So Chaing Mai was a wonderful stop.

The Rybergs explained their plan for a living memorial for their son, Charles, and why they wanted us to meet the two young Kenyans. Charles, an American infantryman, had been killed in Viet Nam. The Rybergs wanted to do something to remember him and decided on a living memorial in Charles' name. Helping the Kenyan students, whom he had met in an international relief workers' camp, in a significant way would be a suitable living memorial.

Paul contacted the two, and we met them at the University of Nairobi cafeteria, a large, mostly outdoor area with chairs and tables and a few shady spots one which we chose. The two had obviously prepared for their visit with us. They were both in their middle 20s and were nice-looking. Frederick Kingu, the shorter of the two wore carefully pressed slacks and a long-sleeved blue shirt with a blue tie. Issac Onyinda was taller, had a beard and was also wearing spic-and-span clothing carefully pressed. They both needed to put on a little weight, in my opinion.

Frederick presented us with a hand-beaded shoulder bag, which a Kikuyu women's group had made. Frederick was a Kikuyu, one of Kenya's over 20 tribes, and was proud of the bag. It was well done and had many colored beads. He wanted us to market it as we traveled. We had no time do that!

Paul, being a diplomat, admired the bag and after looking it over, responded that we would try to market it in Minneapolis, when we would have better use of our time. Then we discussed the Rybergs' offer with them. They were both amazed, and Frederick said that he didn't deserve such help. We assured him that this was what the Rybergs wanted, because of their friendship Charles. They believed that giving these two a better life economically would be a good living memorial for Charles.

Isaac, who was a refugee from the Sudan, caught on quicker than Frederick, who told me later that Charles had not been a special friend. Frederick was just as friendly with all of the people on the project, and he did not think he deserved anything special. Paul assured him that the Rybergs had thought this out carefully, and this was what they wanted to do.

When we asked them what the Rybergs could do to help them permanently in their lives, they did not answer immediately. Then Isaac kind of shrugged and said he would like to become an airplane pilot. They were needed badly in Africa for short hauls for Africans and tourists, and if he knew how to fly he would have a good income and be able to support his wife, Grace.

I looked at Isaac in amazement. Wow, I thought. He sure knows how to pick a good expensive vocation. No ordinary job. He sets his hopes high; he wanted to be an airplane pilot! How about an airplane too?

Frederick stared bug-eyed at Isaac, and then muttered to me that he would think about it and tell us when we were corresponding about the shoulder bags.

That was all we could get out of Frederick It was obvious that not only didn't he believe us he did not think he deserved such an honor. He sounded more worried about the shoulder bags. After all he was representing a group of his people and trying to get a product established in the USA. And he was sensing correctly that Paul and I were perplexed about how to market the bags not only as we traveled but in Minneapolis. We were teachers. What did we know about marketing anything? And could we find anyone to buy the bags?

As we left, I could hear Isaac scolding Frederick, "No! no! They mean it! They mean it! Anyway, give it a try!"

We had invited them both to visit us in Minneapolis. Although we did not realize it then, we were to see Isaac and a lady missionary from Chaing Ma in Minneapolis at our house for a few days. We would become much closer to these guys, and to my friend, Don's, parents too, for they meant what they said. They were lovely people, heartbroken about losing Charles and willing to spend a large sum of money for the two friends of Charles.

Without going into this story in great detail, for it all happened in the next few years, Isaac did get his flying lessons in an airport in Iowa. The Rybergs found a Presbyterian who was eager to help. He paid for Isaac's pilot training and certification for small planes and found a place for him to live.

Frederick was harder. In the first place, he did not feel he deserved any special treatment and really didn't want to impose on the Rybergs. What he did want was to get a lot of Kenyan shoulder bags to some store in Minneapolis. He wrote me a letter stating this, and asking for store addresses, which I promptly sent him. He then stated that if the Rybergs wanted to help him, he would like to become a salesman. We were leery of his choice. What kind of a salesman. Selling what? How? Where and when? He could not answer this in his letters, just insisted that being a salesman in Kenya was good job.

The Rybergs, back from Thailand, met with us, discussed Frederick and his plans, and Mrs. Ryberg took over. After extensive correspondence which lasted almost a year Frederick came to the United States and entered the College of the Ozarks on a scholarship.

I got to know Don Ryberg better when I got back to Minneapolis and school He was quiet about Charles but felt the Presbyterian Church would help. He said his mother was very persuasive and had a high position in the hierarchy of the church. There were wealthy people who wanted to help. The man who was paying for Isaac's training in Iowa owned a flying school in a small community airport and was excited to have a foreign student learning how to fly. And Frederick finally agreed to go to college. That was all Don said in respect to financing, and I think probably that the Rybergs financed the scholarship that Frederick won.

African Christmas

After we finished with the interview with the two Kenyans, we got ready for our African Christmas. We had planned to take some time off in Kenya to visit a game park and also to do some deep-sea fishing off the Indian Ocean coast. We were referred to Tsavo Park which was about 50 miles south of Nairobi, and probably the best game park in the area for elephants.

Our friendly cultural attaché said they were all over the place. We had to rent a car and wanted the cheapest rental possible. Paul, after much haggling, was able to get a Volkswagen. The renter objected to our choice and insisted a larger car would be more secure. Paul replied that he was a very safe driver. I nodded vigorously that we would be secure in a Volkswagen. The man shook his head mournfully.

"I suppose that is possible," he replied doubtfully. Both of us thought he was concerned about the cheaper cost, although we had some concern about the roads. I commented that Kenya's car rentals were just like the ones in Minnesota—out to make a profit by renting big cars to people with small incomes!

"But he didn't get away with it, did he?" I chortled.

The road to Tsavo was two-lane and black tar, a good sturdy road with little traffic, nothing to worry about. We reached the entrance to Tsavo Park at 2 p.m., which is what we wanted, for we were aiming for afternoon, so we wouldn't be charged a full day. We were on a strict budget and were trying to travel on $10 a day. In 1970 that was possible, if you were careful and avoided expensive game parks.

We drove under a sign announcing the park. Then we went over to a path where there was a map tacked to a palm tree. The lodge was about 15 miles away, and there were two roads we were going to have to follow. According to the map. I of course was navigator.

"OK, let's get started," I remarked cheerily. "Where is the road to the park lodge?"

Paul looked at me for a minute and shook his head

"We are on the road, Rosie."

"You mean this trail is a road?"

Paul laughed. "Yes indeedy, and you are my navigator!"

"Huh!" I said.

We bumped along and discovered that Kenya was beautiful. Part of what we drove through was jungle, filled with trees and bushes and grasses, so at least to us it looked as if no one could walk through it. Then we saw tall grasses in big fields swaying in the wind, making a circle in the fields as if a car was being driven through it. We were really enjoying this drive when we came up to a huge fork in the road. And standing on both sides of the fork was a small herd of huge elephants.

"Are they friendly?" I whispered to Paul.

"Do you want me to ask them?" Paul whispered back.

He then got serious. "I count seven elephants and two baby elephants. They are standing on both roads. It makes little difference which one goes to the park. How do we get them to go away?"

That was a really good question, because just at that minute, the whole group moved forward curiously toward the car. Soon they were a dozen feet from us.

"Maybe I should back up," Paul; said.

"No, don't do that. It might make them nervous. They are awfully BIG, aren't they? At least four times as big as the Volks—" I gulped. "Yeah, I

see what the rental car salesman meant about a bigger car being more secure."

We stared silently at them. They stared back.

"I'll try to circle around them," Paul said.

"You could try that..."

He did, and the elephants followed us around politely.

"Can we try driving toward them?" I suggested, getting tired of the whole dance.

"I don't think that's a good idea, Rosie. They could disable the car with a flick of their trunk."

I looked at the five elephants who seemed to have gotten a lot bigger.

"Oh, they wouldn't do that!" I gasped. "Would they?" We decided to wait. They would get tired and go home. I sighed in frustration. We sat and waited. I got restless. It seemed hours. I looked at my watch.

"How long have we been here? Give me back the map." I reached across the steering wheel to get it, and accidentally tooted the horn. The elephants tossed their trunks in the air, flared their ears and ran away, with the two babies chasing after them madly.

With the danger over, we proceeded on to the lodge and got there in good time. It was a deluxe lodge with big rooms and a lovely veranda overlooking a small lake where wild animals liked to feed and water. A buffet was served, and drinks were available. We were given a small house close to the lake and told that use of the lodge was included in the bill. We cleaned up and went to the lodge to eat.

As we sat out on the veranda several brilliant birds flew around, settled on the railings and begged food. One particularly caught my eye—a blue and red beauty. It was quite a thief too. We were sitting next to an Italian couple who turned out to be the owners of Harry's Bar in Venice. They came to Africa every year for their vacation. From Kenya, they were headed to Tanzania to see the wildebeest and zebras, We told them that we were headed to the Kenyan coast, to Mombasa to and then Malindi for four days, and hopefully some deep-sea fishing. Then through more Africa, finally ending Europe. They told us to be sure to visit Venice and see them when we were in Europe.

That morning at 3 a.m. we were awakened, handed a pot of coffee and asked to go to our bedroom window. There we saw the elephants using the lake. They were drinking water and squirting it on each other. The babies were rolling in the dirt, having a great time. I certainly could see why Tsavo was called the Elephant Park there were elephants all over the place!

We went up to the lodge a while later for breakfast and then left for Malindi where we were going to try deep-sea fishing. We had our eye on a motel which was advertised in a Pan American Airline guide book (they had them back then!). When we got there, we found there had been a change of owners. Instead of English owners, we now had German. Luckily, they spoke a little English, enough to handle finances, and people from two German tours were settled happily within. Our reservation was honored and we got our room.

Unfortunately, it rained that night and our roof leaked. We were moved to another room the next morning, but it did not have working air conditioning. We endured it. Actually, we stayed out of the room during the day. After eight it cooled off and we were able to sleep peacefully. We met several Germans who spoke English and who wanted to speak English, so I did not have to prove I spoke very poor German.

The motel had a big pool with many areas to sit, talk, read or play games. It was a clubby place, and no particular effort was made to make us buy

drinks and/or snacks. The second day we were awakened at 3:30 a.m. and driven two miles down the road to a huge boathouse and fishing boats. We were the only people fishing that day. It was a good day and promised to be bright and sunny with a light wind. Fishing had not been good lately, which is why there were a dearth of customers. Paul, who had been reluctant anyway, began to grumble.

"This is going to cost us a young fortune and we are not going to catch a thing," he said. "Just our luck. You and your big ideas.!" I walked away from him and enjoyed the sunrise.

We headed out in the boat, crashing gently over the surf and then picking up speed. We shortly got to the area our captain said was the right one and he lowered two spinning lures to attract the attention of the fish, and we put out our lines. He was alarmed that I was fishing because I was a woman and would not be able to reel in a big fish.

Paul started to laugh and got over his sulking about the cost. We began to admire the Indian Ocean and the variety of colors of the water when my pole went down suddenly.

"Fish, fish!" the captain hollered and I tried to reel in. The line went zipping out. The captain came and grabbed the pole, dug in his heels and pulled hard. That set the hook. He then turned to Paul with the fishing pole. I looked in amazement. But Paul did not fail me.

"It's her fish." he said. "Let her handle it." So I did. It turned out to be quite a job, for it weighed 62 pounds. I reeled and reeled, it pulled the line back and went with it wherever it wanted to go, jumping angrily several times. I got stuck in a corner and the captain and his assistant lifted me up. They carried me one on each hip around the boat several times and finally complained to Paul. If he did not want to take the line they would give up because they were getting tired.

Paul replied that I would kill him if he stepped in. And he was right! I finally got the fish up to the boat. They pulled it in and it began flopping all over. I jumped up on the gunwales and watched the man who was attacking the flopping fish. He put his legs between it and beat it to death with a sledge hammer. By that time Paul was up on the gunwales too, and the captain looked like he was thinking about it.

Once we were sure the huge fish was dead, we came down into the boat, and continued on with our fishing, avoiding the dead eight-foot sailfish in the bottom of it. The captain baited my hook again and threw out the line, but just at that moment Paul got a fish. It took him a while. His fish weighed 55 pounds, but he brought it in handily and started to grin. He grinned the rest of the trip. It was a good day.

Later, I caught another sailfish and again they carried me around the boat while I reeled. Paul then caught a mahi-mahi. It was late afternoon. We headed shore with four flags flying. There was a crowd at the dock waiting for us. They strung the fish up, weighed them, recorded everything on a big board and took our pictures with the captain. Then we were invited up to the owner's quarters where we were given two martinis. Mine gave me the most remarkable headache I have ever had in my life.

We were then told by the owner that we could not get a ride back to the motel for another hour. So we decided to walk back. It was only two miles. It was two miles of hell in the broiling African sun. And by the time we got there, we felt medium broiled. A shower felt good and so did the pool afterward.

The next day the word was out and we had become famous. Everyone decided they wanted to go fishing. The motel owners told us we should have insisted that some of the fish come back with us, after all we caught. The urged us to contact the boat owner and get some of our fish, and they would have a fish dinner for us. We had turned in the Volkswagen when we arrived in Malindi because we were flying from there to Uganda. So if we wanted to claim our fish, we would have to walk the two miles.

It was a cooler day and still morning so off we went. When we got there the owner laughed at us and said the fish had been sold the day before and that they had never been our fish! We had signed a statement to that effect which he happily showed us. He offered us another martini, which we both refused, and headed back to the motel, this time taking short cut by the beach he told us to take.

There, on the beach, wouldn't you know it, I found a Kenyan reading a book, so naturally we stopped. It was an English phonics book and he was a UN literacy trainer going over his material for his lesson he was going to have after Christmas. He was a young kid, maybe 18 or 19, wearing only ragged shorts. He worked as a fisherman's helper. He had learned some English from tourists on the boats.

He not only taught, but he found people who were illiterate. He said most of the village was illiterate. All he had to do was get them to come down to this part of the beach and he would teach them how to read English. I asked how many came; he said two or three, sometimes more.

I asked if there were other teachers too. In other towns, he said, or other places. It is not hard to become a teacher. I asked about pay. He smiled but would not answer. I thanked him for the information and we continued our walk back to the motel.

The Arctic: 2006 UU Congregation of Venice Forum Speech

Technically, the Arctic is the area between the Arctic Circle, an imaginary line that circles around the top of the globe, and the North Pole. The Arctic includes the Arctic Ocean, Greenland, Baffin Island and some parts of Alaska, Canada, Russia, Norway, Sweden, Finland and Iceland. I have been in the Canadian Arctic, Norwegian Arctic, Nunavut, and Greenland's Arctic.

Temperatures can get very low in winter. In Northern Greenland -70C has been recorded. About four million people live in the Arctic. The indigenous people of the Arctic are called the Inuits. It is also home to the polar bear, Arctic foxes, walruses, and seals. The narwhal is one species of the whale only found in the Arctic. Males have a straight tusk projecting from the front of their head that can grow over four feet long.

The ice of the Arctic contains around ten percent of the world's fresh water. The frozen ice sheet of the Arctic reflects sunlight, helping to keep the region cool. It also plays an important role in keeping our global climate stable. In 2005 when I was in the Northwest Territories the ice was just beginning to melt and the Inuits were worrying, although some saw it as something new and possibly good.

All of Iceland touches the Arctic Circle, and Iceland's glaciers are melting. This is helpful to Iceland, which is one of the few countries benefitting from global warming. Icelanders use the water melting from the glaciers to make hydroelectricity which heats and lights their country.

Later, when we visited Greenland, we saw another benefit of global warming. Greenland has planted potatoes and carrots; the first food crops the country has planted in 300 years. We were served carrots and potatoes every day for the entire time we stay at the Arctic motel and hotel. These two foods are so plentiful now that they are being sold in their grocery stores. This is important to the country because for years Greenland imported much of its food from Denmark and other countries.

Average temperatures in the Arctic were rising twice as fast as they were elsewhere in the world. Ice is getting thinner, melting and rupturing. The polar ice cap as a whole was shrinking. Hardly a day went by in 2003, when we were on Baffin Island, when the talk wasn't about the ice getting thinner and the freezing of Frobisher Bay starting later and later in the fall, because it was getting warmer. Polar bears had to wait for the ice to freeze which meant they went without meat for a month longer than usual.

Images from NASA satellites showed that the area of permanent ice cover was contracting at a rate of nine percent each decade. Since 1970 the Arctic sea ice has shrunk by more than 50 percent. This melting of once permanent ice affects Inuits, wildlife, and plants. Older ice usually doesn't melt and thereby keeps the Arctic cold. But now the older ice has given up and is melting.

Polar bears, whales, walrus, and seals are changing their feeding and migration patterns, making it harder for the Inuit to hunt them. And along Arctic coastlines, entire villages will be uprooted because of lack of food and the damage done by the ice melting. Melting glaciers and land-based ice sheets contribute to rising sea levels. This threatens low-lying areas around the globe with beach erosion, coastal flooding and contamination of freshwater supplies.

The United States is vulnerable in areas of dense population, along the Atlantic and Gulf coasts; primarily in Louisiana, Texas, Florida and North Carolina.

In 2003 Greenland also had a transportation problem caused by global warming. During the spring and fall the ice which used to be strong was now so weak that neither dog sled or snow mobile could be used, yet too dangerous for boats. For brief periods island people are marooned, and the only way to reach them was by helicopters.

Fifteen years ago I was in Iqaluit, the capitol of Nunavut, located on Baffin Island. We stayed in the dorm of Arctic College. Rooms at best could

be called basic. Arctic College teaches courses dealing with problems of the area. A law program, for instance insists on the graduates being able to read and speak the Inuit language, Inuktiitut, and that they understand the Nunavut Land Claims Agreement.

They have numerous certification degrees. Social work courses stress the area, insist on ability to know the language and to be able to translate the language. Courses are also offered in adult basic education which is paid for by grants from the Canadian government. There is a special diploma in environmental technology, and numerous opportunities in art, for this is a lucrative profession in the Arctic. Courses being stressed when I was in Iqaluit dealt with health and rescue.

Fishing is a profession in the area, and boat wrecks are common. One very interesting thing was the color of Arctic College, one big building painted bright pink. The choice was unusual but deliberate—the school wanted to attract attention. Arctic College used solar heating, which they said saved them 20 percent on their heating bill. What's amazing about their solar energy is that Iceland is completely dark for half the year.

One of the environmental problems of Iqaluit is man-made; garbage coming from the Gulf Stream from the United States. This garbage from the south was polluting the Arctic. And the people of Iqaluit had their own garbage problems. They did not want to pollute the Arctic Ocean, so they dealt with their garbage by burning it. The ground was mostly rock in the Iqaluit area, so it was impossible to bury the garbage, so instead of polluting

the ocean, they polluted the air. They avoided polluting Iqaluit with garbage air by burning the garbage in plants with extra tall chimneys which sent the smoke whirling away from them. This was being done in Greenland too, but in addition, they were using the heat from the burning of garbage to heat for the towns. In Greenland we saw open pipes up to two feet wide discharging into the Arctic. In Iceland they threw waste into the ocean.

In Iceland volcanoes pollute the air badly. Occurring about every three years, air from the volcanoes can hide the sky for weeks and travel huge distances polluting as it goes with the wind. In the Northwest Territories the Inuit are worried about the Canadian government wanting pipelines for oil which go through their land and possibly pollute their streams. They were forming committees and electing people to represent them and in the area we were in —Yellowknife they had elected women to lead. Yellowknife was a fascinating area.

On Big Slave Lake, the people living there described how they used the lake in the winter. A big highway went through it carrying supplies and produce to other cities on the lake. But in 2005 the temperature got warmer and for the first time the road was not open for heavy traffic, even in March. It runs sporadically now. The fear of the Yellowknife people is that global warming will affect the lake in the winter, and it looks as their fears were correct. In 2018 the people of Yellowknife were suffering from the melting of the permafrost which for years kept the ground solid under the houses where they lived. The permafrost is melting and houses are collapsing. Also, there are many more wild fires because of droughts.

As the climate changes some animals become extinct. Despite the furor about polar bears, they are in no danger of going extinct and are holding their own very nicely. Seals, when we were in Iqaluit—and Greenland particularly—were so plentiful that people were eating them, using their skins on the backs of chairs, encouraging hunting parties to kill and eat them, and pushing the exporting of seal meat, which reminded me a little of venison. It is tasty, but very rich. People had open season on seals in Greenland and Baffin Island and there was no limit on the number killed. It is not easy to kill a seal though. They live in the water and duck when they see you coming.

Polar bears get a lot of seals in the winter on the ice. The seals come up to their sea holes to breathe and the polar bears catch them then.

Where the land itself is changing, and the weather changes dramatically the people and animals living there suffer. Extreme weather goes with global warming. Drought, hurricanes, endless rains. People, plants and animals suffer from the unusual weather which has become usual. We have it here in the United States too. Perhaps the most important thing I discovered in respect to global warming issue was that it was all over the Arctic and its effects are being felt in all of the countries I visited.

Life on the Cold Edge

Yellowknife is located in Canada's Northwest Territories. Back in2004 we visited Tuktukaytuk, the last village before the Arctic Ocean. We had a complete tour of the town in two vans led by a Canadian woman who married an Inuit hunter and was starting her own tourist service. Her assistant was her daughter, who had just graduated from college with a degree in early childhood education and wanted to start a kindergarten.

The tour guide's husband, an Inuit hunter, had three snowmobiles, a dogs kept chained by the dog houses, a hunting cabin 10 miles from their home, and two boats—one for fishing and one for hunting whales. He got $30,000 from tourists for fourteen days of hunting if they got their polar bear. He was allowed a certain number of bear kills by the Canadian government. The couple had four children. All had graduated from high school and college. And all had captured and killed their whale, which appeared to be an Inuit requirement for adulthood.

The young daughter working with her mother talked about her kill. She didn't really think she should have been aided by her father. She said she had the whale and had gotten the harpoon into it, but she got tangled up bringing the whale in and it fought on and on. She said her father got upset because she was hurting the whale and not making a clean kill. He finally stepped in and finished the job. The mother spoke up then.

"And she got her whale!" she said. "All my kids got their whales"

The girl sighed.

"My brother will help me be better with a harpoon. I can't get what my dad wants and he gets disgusted. He thinks I cause the animals to suffer."

In that family the mother set high goals for her kids in a harsh environment. In Iqaluit, the freshman class made up almost entirely of Inuits had 33 kids in it. When the senior class graduated, there were only three students from the original 33 in the graduating class. Inuits did not see the sense of learning Shakespeare and other pre-college courses; and of course, English was not their chosen language.

In Tuk, (Toyakatuk) the hunter and his wife were sanguine about global warming. They did not see it affecting their way of life; at least not yet. They looked at the frozen ice.

"There may be many fish under that ice," the hunter said. "Some may be new to us and valuable. We will soon see."

Their four kids are all employed. The son works with his father. One daughter works in a museum in Yellowknife; she is in charge of public relations and also does the animal and bird displays. The other girl works for the telephone company.

Havana

Cuba

I have visited Cuba three times; once with an Elderhostel tour in Havana, then on a Road Scholar cruise around the island with a day's stop in Havana, and most recently on the final leg of a five-day Caribbean cruise—but that trip was not for me, but for Laura, my grandniece, who was determined to see Cuba and get some cigars for her partner's uncles.

The cruise ship offered tours of the city, with stops at historical places. I had done all that. So I hired a horse and buggy instead. That meant we hired the driver and interpreter. Both had to be paid, but it was less than half of the bus trip. Laura wanted to buy cigars and see a little of Havana. The man on our horse and buggy was a native of Havana and certainly knew where to take us, as did the driver. I think the horse knew too.

Our man was prepared to show us a number of churches and had a very big picture book about Catholicism. He had his trip all planned around religious symbols. I refused to pay him unless he took us to see a medical clinic, a hospital, and the city hall. He was disappointed but philosophic. Money was money, and there was always next time.

I did allow him one church which he said was the oldest in Havana. I doubted this, but not being religious, I wasn't sure that I hadn't seen it before. I did know, though, that tours show me too many churches and they all are just about the same. We then had a very nice trip around Havana, stopping at an inside shopping mall for cigars for Laura and rum for me, real bargains in Cuba.

I had several bottles of prescription pills which I was no longer using, so I wanted to visit a hospital or a medical clinic and donate the pills to the people of Cuba. The driver found a downtown clinic and I gave them my meds which were accepted eagerly. Cuba, because of the U.S. embargo, cannot get the amount of pharmaceuticals they need. In my first trip to Havana we were asked to bring two over-the-counter medications costing at least $15. We presented them to a hospital for alcoholics and AIDS patients. I brought along two large jars of aspirin.

I was unsure about whether I could bring my discarded pharmaceuticals, so I had decided to bring them and ask the people at customs when we entered Havana. I did this. Neither the Americans or the Cuban customs officials had any problem with me giving my excess pills to a clinic or a hospital.

Laura and I trotted around Havana for about four hours, stopping here and there, and then we were returned to our ship. I was tired and willing to call it a day. Not Laura. She started out on foot and wandered on her own around Havana returning at five. She said she went in to a coffee shop and found that she was the only white person there. She was greeted amiably, and the group sang a song to her.

She said she observed some probable prostitutes on one of the streets. She found an open market and bought some gifts. Laura had a good time roaming Havana and was delighted that the cruise stopped there, if only for a day.

Of course it is a dictatorship, and people *must* obey. Cuba has a sports and activities program in the summer which all children must attend. It is completely integrated as are the schools. Cuba spends ten percent of its central budget for education compared to five percent in the U.S. This is a lot of money for a poor country.

We visited a small country school in Cuba on my first trip. Elderhostel, which is now Road Scholar always asks its participants to bring gifts to the people of the country. In this case, virtually all of us brought school supplies. One woman made little aprons which the kids could slip into like small jackets, and also made them each a baseball cap. She did this for the first and second grade. She phoned Elderhostel to find out how many kids to sew for. This was very unusual.

Most people brought small gifts like pencils, notebook paper etc. I brought 12 colored pencils. Under Batista education for country people or poor people was not available, nor did they get adequate health care. Even now, poor people are the country people. But Cuba is providing good health care and education for those living in the country. Opportunities for work exist in the countryside and in the cities, but Cuba is poor.

The government is in control of the country and allows little private businesses. This is changing, and the change could be seen in our third trip. There are private bed and breakfasts, stalls in markets, restaurants, and for the first time in 50 years individuals can buy and sell private property. Aid from relatives living abroad helps a great deal particularly cash.

In 2014 a deep-water seaport was opened by Brazil at Mariel harbor in Cuba. This is a large foreign investment project.

Here are some interesting facts about Cuba, that I have picked up from the three trips and the lectures we got before each trip. Education is free in Cuba from kindergarten through graduate school. It is completely nationalized. Cubans are 100 percent literate and education under Castro was free to all Cubans and foreign residents of the island.

Before Castro only the middle, upper class, and rich were able to pay for an education. We visited two schools and they seemed to be very similar to USA schools as far as desks and materials. One difference: Cuban emphasize rhythm and teach classes in rhythm in elementary schools. They also believe in physical education and sports—in fact the right to partake in sports is written into the Cuban Constitution.

Students have six years of primary education and three years of middle school. Then they decide whether they wish to enter a vocational school or a college prep school. Cuba is one of the few countries where blacks do as well as whites in schools. This is something the USA has been unable to do and blacks constantly score lower in tests than white. We might learn from Cuba, for they are doing different things to achieve integration in their country.

This was one of our first field trips and I realized later that it was done to prove to us that people in the country do get an education. The school was made up of several double bungalows, two grades to a bungalow. I was

The school library

impressed with the school. The kids seemed relaxed, interested and eager to question. When they were doing their school work, all of them seemed to understand it. Of course, we were visitors and that was exciting. But it seemed more than that.

In the first and second grade class which was combined, two dogs lay quietly by their owners. The outside door was open so they could come and go, which one dog did for a toilet break. For some reason the Cuban guide thought I spoke Spanish so he asked me to speak to the kids. I tried English, and they knew a few words. Then I told them I had a gato (cat) and they got really excited. I asked how many had a gato at home and more than half of the kids raised their hands. We had a great time.

Then we toured the other class rooms and found between ten and twenty kids in every class except the sixth grade. It had only one student. It was too hard to integrate one grade into the other classes, so this student was given a television set with taped lessons and a tutor—a recent high school graduate from the school sitting by his side. We asked him if it was lonely to be the only student.

"Yes," he said, but he said he played with the other kids during recess and celebrations. The school went from grade one to eight. We then visited a school in a suburb of Havana. It operated from K through 12. Both schools were basically well equipped. They lacked supplements. Libraries needed more books. Classroom libraries had only a few books for those kids to read who finished work early.

A couple of elementary students—a boy and a girl sang a song for us. We were told about the free lunch every student got and visited the lunchroom, where a teen ager was eating lunch early because of a dental appointment. It should be noted that Cuba's educational system is far superior to any other in the Caribbean, at least in math. In a math test given to primary grade students in the Caribbean and some Central and South American countries by UNESCO to fourth graders, the lower half of the Cuban kids were superior to the others tested.

Much information is lacking about the makeup of the kids and the tests, but even so it appears that Cuba is educating its kids. Cuba's health care system is recognized worldwide for its excellence and efficiency. It is based on preventive medicine. WHO—the World Health Organization has repeatedly praised the Cuban Health system. Life expectancy is 80, which is higher than the U.S. (75.6). Cuba has more doctors per person than any other country in the world at 133 doctors per person. The next country is Monaco at 150.

On the average, Cubans live 30 years longer than their Haitian neighbors. Since 1963, Cuba has sent doctors and other health workers throughout the Third World to treat the poor. In 2016 nearly 30,000 Cuban medical staff were working in over 60 countries in the world. For example, Operation Miracle, a vision restoration program, was started in 2004 by Fidel Castro and Hugo Chavez. This program, with the help of the Bolivian Alliance for the Peoples of our America operates without charge on Latin American poor suffering from cataracts and other eye diseases. In 10 years nearly 35 million people have had their vision restored through Cuban doctors. Nearly 165 Cuban institutions participate in this operation. It maintains a network of 49 ophthalmological centers and 82 surgical units in 14 countries in Latin America.

In Africa in 2014 Cuba started a vaccination campaign against malaria in 15 West African nations. According to WHO this unusual virus, kills 630,000 people a year, most of them African children under five. Cuba also trains young physicians worldwide in its Latin American School for Medicine, ELAM. Since its start, in 1998, ELAM has graduated more than 20,000 doctors from over 123 countries. Currently, 11,000 students from over 120 nations are studying at this Cuban institution.

Ban Ki-moon, secretary general of the UN says ELAM is the "world's most advanced medical school." He also praised the Cuban doctors working

around the world: "They are always the first to arrive and the last to leave."

Cuba, because it does not have much besides sugar to trade, has sent thousands of doctors to countries in exchange for oil. It is an innovative country, and as WHO says, Cuba shows the world that much can be done to provide good health for a country even though the provider is poor.

In our first trip to Cuba we visited a hospital for alcoholics and AIDS patients, on the other two visits we saw clinics only. In the clinics we visited, the doctor was available 24 hours per day and had an apartment above the office. The nurses gave a brief talk about conditions in their area. They lived in a specific area and were assigned people who lived there.

Their office had a one room emergency room plus a waiting room, an examining room, and a room for the dentist and dental technician. The doctors had to work for Cuba but were given a choice of where to work. Diabetes and high blood pressure were most prevalent diseases in her area of Havana.

Cuba excels in the arts. Therefore, when we went there on the two Elderhostel trips arts were emphasized. We watched dancers. We tried

Opera rehearsal

dancing ourselves. We learned that dancers are paid for taking lessons, and that going to dancing school is a job. This is something that artists in the USA have been asking for ages. When I was in college at the University of Minnesota Theater, one of the goals of artists was to be paid for their training. As it is now in the states, and then too, the training is so expensive many talented artists do not have enough money to learn their trade.

An opera was performed for us the second time I went to Cuba. In costumes. It was a dress rehearsal. Then we went to a dancing studio and watched the teacher drill the students. Then she drilled us, and on film it is a sight to see. For recreation we danced. We danced with Cubans, most of them black. I thought that was Cuba's way of integrating the USA. We danced together about three or four times, not counting the times we danced with kids and teen agers. One of my greatest thrills was being asked to dance by an eight-year-old. We really rocked!

Food in Cuba for tourists is good. But the people do not get that food. However, they are not starving. They appear to be very health, trim. and no obesity to be seen.

I did enjoy my three visits to Cuba. It is no democracy. It has not paid the people who left Cuba for their property, nor have they paid the corporations for their equipment or property. To me the USA is being a little two faced with Cuba. We refuse to trade with Cuba or allow it to trade with us, because it is a socialist country. But we trade with Vietnam and China. They too are socialist. I have frozen fish from Vietnam in my freezer and have had many things from China.

We have southern states who are willing and able to trade with Cuba and anxious to do so. But when? Perhaps it is time to remember we are dealing with people, not just a form of government. People need care to live. We are not getting friendlier with a country just ninety miles from us by keeping an embargo going which causes people to suffer.

The thing is the USA has been trying to bankrupt Cuba for the last fifty years or more. They have not done it, and they will not be able to do it. Cuba is amazingly resilient. It is being hurt by the blockade, badly hurt, but it continues to progress.

Blair and the Rabbit

I set out one morning with Blair, the dog, just to enjoy the day. I walked five or six steps and saw the marigolds. I decided I would clean up the breakfast stuff then get at the marigolds. It was a great day to plant them. Sunny, light wind, felt like the middle 70s.

But what? What? There on the other side of the flat was a rabbit, chewing away at the marigolds. Medium sized, brown with big ears white tail up and perky.

"Shoo," I said. It raised its head, gave me a look, chewing all the time and continued munching away. I took the leash off Blair.

"Go get that rabbit! Sic 'em!" I ordered She wagged her tail and went over the grass to the rabbit and the flat of marigolds. She looked the rabbit over. The rabbit kept munching. She got closer and sniffed the rabbit stopping at its head. The rabbit let her do this, and then looked up, swallowed a stem, and wriggled its nose several times. Blair wagged her tail and sniffed the air. The rabbit ate quietly. For about two or three minutes the two just passed the day.

"Hey!" I said to the rabbit. "The marigolds…you can't eat the marigolds." It was like talking to the TV. It was as if I wasn't there. A friendship had started. I rescued the uneaten marigolds from the flat and promptly planted them. The rabbit promptly ate them all the next day, with Blair peacefully watching. And the friendship continued even after that.

About once or twice a week the rabbit would appear and Blair would wag her tail and go over to have a sniff. I mulled over their friendship to myself, for that was what it was. Why was my dog not chasing that rabbit, as all other dogs do? Easy, Rosie, you do not know what all other dogs do. You know some of the things Blair doesn't do. Anyway, one thing. Was it because Blair was old that she refused to chase the rabbit? Was it her breed? Bichons are bred to work with organ grinders, they are not working dogs or hunters. But they are dogs and a year ago she would have chased the rabbit. Not now.

I choose to believe she has a brain and she figured out that kindness and respect has a place in today's world and she would start the trend. Blair took the high road. Why hate or kill when a nice friendship is possible? I thought about that and smiled. She was a good dog, I said to myself.

A couple of weeks later my cousins Peter and Linda from Wisconsin came. I was glad to see them. I always enjoy Peter and Linda. They are fun to talk to and they like to do things. That morning we were eating our oatmeal and Cheerios by the kitchen window. Another perfect Florida day!

"Oh! Oh!' Peter said. "Look over by the garden. a red-shouldered hawk has got a rabbit. I'm going to get the camera."

The Hawk had the rabbit in its claws and was stripping its flesh from its body in strips. I gulped some coffee. That rabbit was Blair's pal!

I choked, and my eyes filled with tears. Linda looked at me.

"We're watching a life cycle, Rosie. Because of the rabbit, the hawk is able to live."

Peter came with his camera and stood at the window.

"It's a red shouldered hawk, a beauty," he said. "I got a good picture."

The Toad

I was out before bed
With my dog, Blair.
I got tired of waiting
For her to perform,
So I kicked a rock on the
driveway.
It wasn't a rock! It was a toad!
It sailed into the air,
Landed with a thump and
vanished.
I felt awful. I had kicked a
toad
Arbitrarily, for no reason.
It didn't come back for a week
Then one night, there it was.
"You talk to it!" I said to Blair
I just scare it.
So Blair sniffed the toad from
top to bottom.
She was about as
nice as any
Bichon could be.

Tried not to scare it
But the toad tightened
And became a rock.
I took Blair down the street.
And the rock was still there.
When I came back
I determined to make amends:
Bent down, and in a very
kindly
voice
With a smile on my face,
Said: Well, hello there!
The toad gave a great
start
And jumped into the
darkness.
I haven't seen it since.
It just goes to show.
It is hard to make friends
with something
If you kicked it in
The first place

HoHo Takes a Walk

When we lived by Prospect Park, we had a couple of places where we could go for a walk. There was the park itself, which the neighborhood committee had cleaned up and even built Olympic-sized tennis courts on it (you never know where talent is). They put some benches up by the Witches Tower so that people who wanted to just sit by the tower and look out at Minneapolis could do so.

The tower was a. brick thing about 40 to 50 feet high. It was used in olden days as a look out for Indians and other dangers. The top of the tower was shaped like a witch's hat, hence the name. They also put a nice meandering trail around the park so that it could be used as a place to sit, walk, lounge or play.

Our duplex was right across the street from the middle of the park. Pratt Elementary was at one edge; the recommendation from the neighborhood had been that instead of having Pratt across the street the city should fix a bridge or a walkway from Pratt. to the park. That way kids wouldn't have to risk their necks when they wanted to get to the park from the school.

This is still in the planning stage, but the rest of the park has been finished and people are using it all year long. Workers from those stores and businesses located on the side of the park opposite Pratt school sit on the benches and grass and eat their lunch. It was then, and still is a nice little city park.

The other place we could walk was around the block. This is not as simple as it sounds. The block was more than a square, a little more than a pentagon and has space besides a lot of big old-fashioned houses which were built in the late 1890s or early 1900s. They used to hold single families. Now they have been broken up into apartments, condos, duplexes and boarding houses. This is because it is within walking distance of the University of Minnesota and an easy bus trip to downtown Minneapolis or to Midway in St. Paul.

We chose to live there because Paul taught at the U of M and I was at Northeast Junior High—maybe 15 minutes away by car. I got HoHo a feisty orange kitten from Hope Kukielka, a clerk at Northeast. I brought her home in the only box we could find, a monster the kitty tumbled around in— it had originally held a TV or some such thing.

Home then was not Prospect Park, but Coon Rapids and the Mississippi River. HoHo grew to a big cat there and had many adventures. The point is we tired of Coon Rapids and the half hour or more ride every day to work and began looking for something else. Our friends Sy and Helen wanted to buy a big duplex opposite Prospect Park, but needed help paying for it. So we went in on the cost with them, and shared it. We had the upstairs, they the down. We lived there for about ten years. Rented it out when we went on sabbatical, which about covered the cost of the trip.

We named the cat after our island on Lake Vermilion, which we called HaHa Island. We went through a lot with that cat. She lived to be 22. When we went on our year's sabbatical we had Marian Fletcher look after her, which she did willingly and well. She liked HoHo, and said she had been a good cat.

At the time we moved down to the Prospect Park place she must have been 15 or 16. When we left Coon Rapids and the Mississippi we lost HoHo for a week. We thought we had seen the last of her. She vanished the day we arrived at the duplex. We had her locked in one of the bedrooms, but she got out and made a run for it. We had no idea where she had gone. We went around inside and outside the house for the next couple of days calling "HoHo!" which usually brought her running. But no luck.

We wondered if she had maybe gone back to Coon Rapids. But no— It was 30 miles away and did not seem likely. So we more or less gave up on HoHo and went about our business of settling in a new home. A week later a nice night around two or three a.m., we heard her meowing loudly. I got up and went to the window, and there in the driveway looking angrily up at us was HoHo our orange tabby cat. We ran down to the door and brought her up.

She seemed in good enough shape. Had no injuries, but where had she been? Wherever it was, she must have had a water source. Had she been caught in a garage? She had spider webs all over her face and ears. Paul thought for a while and remarked that many garages had sinks, so that may have been where she had been.

But where did she get food? Then we realized that a week without food wouldn't really injure a cat. And it was fall, and the mice were coming in. She probably ate a mouse or two.

Paul looked at her more carefully.

"She is an awful dusty cat—her face is really dirty," he remarked. And it was—around the ears and eyes especially. We gave her some water and some left-over chicken which she promptly demolished and then she sat down and began cleaning herself. We never did figure out where she had been for a week. Anyway, she was back, and we were glad to have her. She was an old cat then and all of us were used to each other.

HoHo lived happily with us in the duplex for about six years. She went out frequently and got back in via an entrance we made for her in the back door. She used it regularly even in 20 below weather. She also took walks with us around the block and in the park. She still had her claws and could get up a tree rapidly if an angry dog came around. She would come when she was called, and sometimes reminded us of a dog rather than a cat.

I will never forget one time when HoHo walked with us around Prospect Park. It was a hot, late summer night. There was a slight breeze going which helped the air and the night outside was comfortable and pleasant for the first time in ages. All of the neighborhood was out walking

We started down the hill toward Pratt School. We were on the sidewalk and HoHo followed along on people's lawns. We got down past the school and made our turn and we met some friends and stopped to talk for a minute. Just as we were leaving them a dog appeared—a Lab or German shepherd— a big dog. It caught sight of HoHo and started after her. She vanished into the night and into the trees. I was upset.

"That dog is going to get my cat!" I yelled. Paul reassured me and pointed to the trees.

"She'll get away!" he laughed. And she did. She joined us again half way around the block. She was panting, which is unusual for a cat. She had been running, no doubt about it. She looked silently at us and followed along. We came to another turn and started up a hill. Another dog appeared—a cocker spaniel who joyfully took after our cat. I yelled at this one and so did the cocker's owners. but it did no good. They were both gone.

"That poor cat!" I moaned. The dog's owners commiserated with me and apologized for their dog. Paul reassured them.

"She'll be OK, she wanted to come on the walk," he said.

I was not so sanguine.

"That poor cat! She's had nothing but hell all around the block!" I said.

We had about ten minutes left on our walk and we continued and got back peacefully. It was a lovely night and we had had a nice walk despite HoHo's troubles. The sky was soft, people were walking and biking, and kids were still playing. We got to the final little hill to our duplex and as we reached it, there in the middle of the street opposite our driveway stretched out and panting was our cat.

We stopped and looked at her. She looked up at us too, green eyes unblinking. She groaned slightly—kind of a uhhuhuuuuh! and lay her head on the pavement.

"HoHo" I said. "You can't stay here in the middle of the street! You've got to get up and come with us!" I gave her a nudge with my foot. She would not budge. She just lay there. Paul laughed.

"She's had a rough night," he said. "She's going to rest here, she can see any dog coming and get out of its way."

I looked at the tired old cat, and realized as far as she was concerned she had had it. Humans could just can it for a few minutes and leave her in peace.

But we could not do that. I bent down to pick her up. She growled at me! She didn't want to be picked up. She was in the middle of a street, which although a quiet street at night, was still a city street. Paul bent down to her.

"C'mon Kitty. I'll carry you upstairs."

She growled at him too. So we left her and went in the house. About 15 minutes later we looked out the window. HoHo was still there in the middle of the street. Paul went down to her. He stood over to her and talked to her. She looked at him impassively and finally got up, stretched, and followed him inside.

Camel of Egypt and Camel of India

I am going to discuss two camels. Dexter, the camel of the pyramids, and Vera, the camel of Egypt. I am sending around a picture of me on Dexter, and a picture of Dexter's driver, a very good-looking young man. That is one of my rules in picking out a good camel to ride. Make sure his driver is good-looking. That will make you feel better when you are on the top of the camel.

I also sent around a picture of me practicing riding a camel, which is very important. It gave me a great deal of self-confidence. I have no picture of me on Vera, because I gave my camera to a lady who said she was a professional photographer and told her to get a picture of me on Vera. She failed. For one thing her camel was frothing at the mouth and had digestive problems, and this did interfere with her picture taking. She succeeded in getting a picture of my foot and a leg. I am not even sure it was my leg...could have been anyone's.

In Egypt you can ride a camel for $20 for half an hour. They have them all lined up, ready for you to choose. I looked at the drivers, found a handsome one and then looked at the camel. You should check the camel's eyes. Are they kind, thoughtful? Is the mouth sensitive and knowing?

After that check for fleas, by simply looking at the hide of the camel carefully. If you really are worried about fleas, you may ask the driver but you should do this very diplomatically, for you do not want to offend him.. A sure fire way to determine if the camel has fleas is to run a comb through its hair. This is what my vet does to my cat, Bill. If there are fleas on the comb, the camel has fleas. If this happens, and it bothers you, you have to reach a decision. Either forget about the fleas—there are bugs all over—or leave the camel and choose another which means you will have to go through all of the steps again in choosing a camel.

At any rate, Dexter did not have fleas and he gave me a nice half hour walk, led by his driver. I found out his name by asking the driver He said said uijhnhgytrdehkter. So Dexter it was.

Like most people, I have dreams of things I want to do. Since a kid one of my dreams has been to ride a camel. This obsession came from the books I read as a kid and the movies I saw. *The Lost Patrol;* David Niven and Errol Flynn, the oases, the camels, the desert, the hardships. Oh, if I could only ride a camel.

Well, two or three years ago I did get to ride a camel, and while it was not like being with Errol Flynn, it sure was different! Now I am speaking about Vera, the intrepid camel of India whom I got to ride during my tour of India, with my old friend, Barb.

This happened at the Overseas Adventure Travel's Tent Camp, the tour we were on. Tent Camp is not the word I would use to describe these tents. They were all on platforms, air conditioned, had a private sink, toilet and shower in another room, and even had a porch. We ate in a luxurious dining tent, or in a circle around a campfire at night. It was beautiful and romantic, and it was then we found out that we were to visit a small Indian village the next day and that we were to get there on camels. I was very excited because one of my dreams was going to come true.

The next day the Indians had 14 camels for us. Some were sitting quietly, legs tucked under, and some were milling around. But in time, everybody got a camel. Barbara's camel looked old. It limped a lot at first but then got

over it—arthritis, thought. But Barb worried that the camel might have hurt himself. Her keeper assured her that her camel was one of the best camels in the group.

That caused us to check the rest of the camels. We saw a diverse bunch. Some were used to people riding them; others were pack camels that had never been ridden. The people on the pack camels got the treatment. Their camels circled round and round making noises from the front and the rear and some had upset stomachs from the rear. Barbara's camel keeper was right. Her camel was one of the better ones.

But Barbara had not chosen her camel carefully. Her dreams had not been about camels. So she paid the price. Not me. I had gone to look at the camels early. I knew immediately when I saw them that some were nicer than others. I stared at them carefully, up and down. I wanted the best. I wanted the full experience. I wanted to be on the lead camel, forging ahead into the desert storm looking for lost patrol members. So I went after the lead camel and through a little pushiness and politeness I became first camel rider on Vera. All it took was a little brass to get the best camel of the bunch.

Vera led the parade. I was determined to be her rider. Not because I wanted to be first. I'd given up being first years ago, it was not as wonderful as I expected. Being first always ended up being hard work. No, I wanted to be first for another reason. I wanted to be on the first camel because I was sure it would be a well-behaved, nice camel, would not misbehave but would give me a smooth ride. So when the rest of the group was crabbing among themselves about the morning coffee, and it was something to crab about, I went over to the Indians who were lining up and organizing the camels. In a friendly way, I asked the name of the first camel. They told me, and I couldn't understand them, but at the end it sounded like Vera, so Vera it was.

I then asked if I could ride Vera. I held my breath. Would I get away with it? I was pushing myself forward but really, in a nice way, I had a sudden thought; what if they expected me to be an experienced camel rider, one who knew how to lead other camel riders, and take charge. My eyes got very wide. Would it really be up to me? They would know just from looking at me that I was not an old hand camel rider.

I'm from Florida, for gosh sakes. Florida has alligators and manatees and Mickey Mouse, what do they expect of me? Nothing, it turned out. Sure, I could be the first one up on the first camel. It was fine with them. I mounted Vera with their help. In the first place, camels are very tall. I don't know about Lawrence of Arabia, but we all needed help to get on and we all were given a bench to stand on and two men to hold us so we wouldn't fall! It probably was the most dangerous time.

I have no photograph of me on Vera, which is unfortunate because it was an unusual first experience. I lent my camera to a lady who said she was a professional photographer and assured me she would get a picture of me riding Vera. She failed. For one thing her camel was frothing at the mouth, and moaning. She told me she was holding on for dear life and praying. She clutched the pommel of the saddle with one hand, and the camera with the other. Frankly I don't see what her praying had to do with not taking the picture. The camel's nervousness and circling made it hard to focus the camera, particularly with one hand. She did tell me afterward that if she had used both hands with the camera she was afraid she would have fallen off. I doubted that, but she believed it, so for her it was true.

I did agree with her that it must have been hard to get a good shot. She succeeded in getting a picture of my foot and a leg. I am not even sure it was my leg. But at least she tried her best. And, as it is, with all of us, her best sometimes was not very good.

So I led the camel parade to the village about a mile away. But not really. None of us were trusted to really ride the camels. Each camel was led on a leash by its driver, so really all we were doing was sitting carefully on a camel. It is quite true I may have overreacted about the importance of all of this. But as I have said, it was a new experience, and I believe in making the most of all new experiences. Forget that I was the head of a straggling group of tourists on mostly peaceful camels; except a few who were still having queasy bowels.

I began to fantasize. In my mind I was an Arabian wife, searching for her husband in a sand storm in the desert, intent on rescuing him from evil people. I was on Vera, my intrepid camel who, though struggling through the sand storm, knew just where to go. In the middle of that bit of concentration a little boy on the side of the road ran up to me

"What is your name?" he yelled.

"Rosemary," I replied. he smiled.

"What is your name?" he yelled.

"Rosemary," I replied. he smiled

This continued for about a quarter of a mile, until I began to lose patience.

"What is your name?" he yelled.

"Rosemary," I snarled. It was too much for Vera. She lifted her head, turned it upside down and brought it in a huge arc similar to MacDonald's arches, and placed her head upside down on the nape of her neck which happened to be about six inches from my belly button.

I was startled and thought mightily of something to say that would be calming.

"Well, hellooooo Vera," I cooed. Her huge kind eyes stared at me upside down...as was her sensitive mouth. She stayed in the position for several hours it seemed to me, but it probably was not that long. Suddenly she lifted h er head and was gone. She had examined Rosemary and was satisfied.

We reached the village and the villagers gathered around us. It was a small village with just a few bedraggled houses. They were a friendly, proud group, and I think they had had seen campers before because they seemed at ease.

I was upset at the poverty. The houses were not particularly well built. And I although I would declare definitely that my camel was in fine physical condition, I could not say this about all the villagers.

Another thing bothered me too. An older man. probably in his early sixties came to me proudly carrying a small boy in his arms. He held the child up to me and asked me to take the picture, which I did. As I was showing it to him, he told me proudly that it was his son. I had thought he was the grandfather. He then introduced me to his wife, the mother. She was young, very young. maybe 14 or 16. It was a child marriage. They still do this in some of the villages of India. Young girls are not wanted in the crowded family and are sold, or traded to old men to work for them and to reproduce.. The girls have no say in this at all, although they are given a very elaborate wedding.

The villagers gathered together and sang us a song which I did not understand a word of. Then, we decided that we should sing them a song in return and we argued a bit about the song to sing. *The Star-Spangled Banner* was too hard, and we needed a piano to be able to sing it on key, so that was out. *God Bless America* involved the word "bless" and India has so many religions and different Gods we wondered if that was wise. I was going for *I've Been Working on The Railroad*, but someone thought of *My Bonnie*. So we sang:

My Bonnie lies over the ocean
My Bonnie lies over the sea
My Bonnie lies over the ocean
Bring back my Bonnie to me

Well, so much for intercultural relations via music anyway. I looked for Vera to take me home, but she had left. We had only rented the camels one way. So we walked back to our camp. The air was lovely, the moon was coming out, the wind was gently rustling the grass as we went down the path. If was even nicer than riding on a camel.

Chou Chou Gets A Plant

It isn't often that dogs get a plant sent to them, but our Bichon Frise Chou Chou (chew chew) got a plant from Mrs. MacCready with a note. The note said that she was glad Cho Chou saved her life, and she thanked Paul too, because without him nothing would have happened. But both Mrs. MacCready and Paul said that Chou Chou was the true heroine because she was the one who discovered Mrs. MacCready and stuck by her.

It was a bleak, cold snowy day in March in Roseville, Minnesota when we pulled into our town house garage. It was the kind of day that killed any promise of spring that dared show its face. It was snowing slightly and the temperature was in the twenties. We always walked the dog when we came home, whether it was day or night and she looked forward to getting out. It was a pleasure for her to relieve her bladder, but what she enjoyed most after that was investigating some of the thirty town houses which made up Westwood Village Ill in Roseville.

Because of the light coating of snow, the walking was treacherous and slippery. The service road in front of all of the townhouses had splotches of ice and plenty of sand from the snow and ice crews. It was around five or six when we got home and we were glad to get off the icy streets and into a warm home. We lived in a town house in a suburb of St. Paul. We liked where we lived. The townhouses were well made, roomy, warm in winter and air conditioned in summer. They were on a pond that was full of ducks and geese and it had a pool many of us used. In winter it was grim.

But that was winter in Minnesota. We made up for it by having a great deal to do in wintertime. Concerts, political meetings, movies, our UU church, and lots of other activities. We were content in our townhouse and lived there for over 25 years.

However, for people there during the day it was quiet and could be quite lonesome. I remember Paul's mother, Charlotte, who lived with us when she had to leave her home in Connecticut, saying things like, "There's nobody around here. It's a lonesome place."

She was right. Out of the 30 townhomes there were only four or five who had people in them during the day. The rest of us worked. One day when Charlotte was out walking she couldn't find the keys to our house and really panicked. But she dumped everything out of her purse and found them. In winter being stuck outside without keys would have been a scary thing. A person would have to knock on many doors to find someone home. We were upset about what almost happened and brought Charlotte down immediately to our friends Nell and Lyle Sorum who were retired and almost always at home. So Charlotte knew where to go in an emergency.

Walking with Chou Chou

We could have taken her to Mrs. MacCready, but we didn't really know Mrs. MacCready, we had just met her once or twice. Mrs. MacCready's husband had died a year or so ago and she lived alone in the townhouse. However, she had a daughter who lived nearby with her family, so Mrs. MacCready was content where she was. She was alone during the day and no one near her was home.

Nell and Lyle were about a dozen houses from her and no one was near her on the other side. Way down at the end of all the townhouses, about two or three blocks away, there was a cluster of people who were there during the day. They were nowhere near her. This proved to be a real disadvantage. Tonight, I told Paul I wanted to change into more comfortable clothes before starting dinner. He went to the door with Chou Chou.

"I'll take her out for a minute," he said, "she won't need a leash."

I nodded Chou was well trained. I worried more about Paul.

"Be careful, don't slip." And I headed upstairs to change my clothes.

"This is going to be a short walk, Chou. Just a pitstop. I'll take you out longer later on," Paul said to the dog.

I laughed. It wasn't that Chou Chou didn't understand a lot of what we said, I was laughing at his belief that she would readily agree to a short walk. Lotsa luck! I was just putting a sweatshirt on over my head when the front door opened. Paul and the dog came racing in. Paul was agitated and excited.

"Rosie" he called "get some blankets and a big pillow, Mrs. MacCready has fallen."

I grabbed a couple of throws at the foot of our bed and a big pillow and ran downstairs. Paul was the phone and hung up as I got there.

"Ambulance?" "

No" he said. "She told me to call her daughter. She is calling an ambulance. I gave her my coat, but we need to get over there right away with some blankets. I think she's broken something. She slipped on the ice in her patio."

I gulped. Mrs. MacCready was in her late 80s and fairly frail.

"How long was she laying there?" I asked.

"I don't know," Paul answered as we hurried over to her house. "It was the darnedest thing. Chou Chou apparently heard her calling."

We reached Mrs. MacCready's house.

"I'll explain it later," he said as he opened Mrs. MacCready's patio door. She was laying in the middle of the patio with Paul's storm coat over her. I put a pillow under her head, and Paul carefully adjusted some blankets around her.

"Hi, Mrs. MacCready, how are you feeling?" I cooed. "Where do you hurt? Paul called your daughter and she called an ambulance, so you'll be out of here soon."

Mrs. MacCready looked at me and smiled and then looked very serious.

"That little dog, that sweet little dog saved my life," she said.

"She wouldn't get away from the door," Paul said. "No matter how much I yelled at her. I wanted to go home and was mad because she wouldn't obey."

"She heard me," Mrs. MaCready said. "No one else did."

I rearranged the pillow so it covered more of her back.

"Chou Has always been a curious dog, "I said. "And she has good ears. She hears everything."

"She heard me and saved my life, "Mrs. MacCready said.

Then her daughter arrived and right behind her came the ambulance. So we gathered our blankets and went back to our house. Chou Chou was ecstatic to see us and jumped up and down and all around us. I bent down and rubbed her head.

"Chou Chou, you are a good dog."

Her black eyes sparkled and she wagged her tail.

"Looks like she knows it." Paul smiled and offered her a dog treat, which she took happily. Paul went over the whole thing for me.

"I took her out and she did her business and headed down the service road. I called to her and she slowed down for a minute and I thought she was going to come to me, but I was wrong." He said. "She swung in to MacCready's and stopped at the patio door and stuck her head under it and wouldn't move. I didn't want to go way in there, so I called her again. You know how she gets. Pretended she didn't hear me. Just wiggled further under the door. So I finally gave up and went to the patio door and bent down to grab the dog when I heard Mrs MacCready call for help. And that is what Chou Chou heard too. It was a very faint voice, 'Help me, help me... Oh please help me!'"

"She has a very light voice," I said. "It would never reach up to the service road. She was lucky Chou Chou was there."

"You said it," Paul continued. "The patio door was locked, so I had to break in and there she was on the ice." I shook my head.

"You know," I said, "we both yell at that dog all the time to obey us, and get really mad when she doesn't. Thank God she's a bad dog sometimes!" I sat on the couch and Chou Chou jumped up by me. I gave her a hug.

"You are a good dog, Chou Chou. You've got more sense than either of us."

The next night the doorbell rang. Chou Chou barked excitedly and came running.

"Chou Chou!" I yelled. "Stop that!"

Paul opened the door and there was a man in a uniform from Flo's Flowers. He looked at the name on his list.

"Is there a Chou Chou Hagen living here?" he asked.

"Huh?" Paul said.

"I've got a plant here for a Chou Chou Hagen," the delivery man "Can you get that dog to stop barking so I can be heard?"

Black Snake

This snake, all six feet of it
Had been around the last
couple of months
We had seen its discarded
skin
And been impressed. Most
of us hoped
It wasn't pregnant.
Chet, my neighbor, told me it
went into my garage.
I got the broom to
sweep it out.
The more I swept it
The more it slithered
To the kitchen door.
Finally! I got it out.
Alice had it the next day.
Their dog brought it in and
Alice, like me, took her
broom to it.
Black snakes are good. They
eat rats and mice.
But they belong outside. We
Don't want them as house guests.
Esther, down the road was sick.
The phone rang, but Harry had gone
to pick up medicine.
Esther forced herself up to answer.
Afterward, she saw the coverlet
she had been under
Moving. Moving. She pulled it back.
There was the black snake.
It had come in from the cold January day
Seeking a warm place to sleep.
SHUDDERING, Esther called 911.
"There's a snake in my bed!"
Silence. Then 911 spoke:
"Can you give us

his name, lady? Or
Is it really a snake?
The Department of Natural Resources
sent two men,
And a long pole which they
poked at the snake.
The snake coiled around it
And they put the pole on
their shoulders
And carried it far into the woods.
They found a good place
Laid the pole down into
the leaves and
After a while the snake uncoiled,
took a look around
And slinked into his new
damp, dirty home.
It had to go back to being
a black snake
It could not change, even
By crawling out of its skin.
For it, the fine life was gone
The warmth, fresh linen, cupboards
of food…Gone.
Just cold, mold, wet dirt and leaves.
It had attempted the impossible
and failed.
It believed in the American Dream
like many of us
And like many of us, the Dream
passed it by.
It had to remain a black snake
no matter what..
Like Ahab, Quixote, Hillary Clinton
It had to give up what it
Tried so had to get and
had achieved
For one brief, shining moment.
It must give it all up, and
Crawl back into reality instead.
Cold wet dirt, mold and dead leaves.

My childhood menagerie; Herculena, Blaze and Skippy

Cats

In my life I have. had many cats. The most recent is a huge tomcat I named Kim Chee because his green eyes slant. We always had cats to catch mice when we were up at the lake.We kept cats in Minneapolis too, because our big old house was not mouse proof. We had dogs too, and even rabbits. Once we had a bird but Herculena, my cat, killed it and tried to eat it through the bird's cage.

I never wanted Kim Chee. I never asked for him and was genuinely startled when he appeared at my house. My good friend, Roslyn, had to move to Arizona to take care of her daughter's dog. Jose, which is what they called the cat, could not go with her, and I was the logical one to take Jose. I changed his name and took him and I will say he takes some getting used to. He is a scaredy-cat. He runs under the bed when I go by him, when the landscapers appear with the chain saws, or when people ring the doorbell. He is a mess.

In other ways he is an ideal cat. He does not jump on the table. When my cat, Bill, was alive I could not set the table until about five minutes before my guest came, or Bill was all over it—smelling napkins licking the water

Kim Chee

dishes, sniffing forks, eating olives if I dared to set them out early. What a pain!

Kim Chee could care less. He also is not interested in people food, only his cat food. He will not go outside at all. He runs under the bed if you even open the door for him. He has never jumped on my bed, or on my chair when I am in it. He loves to be petted and stands by the left arm of the easy chair and wants me to reach down and pet him constantly. He has never complained about the food I feed him, and my left arm has new muscles in it.

Recently he had to have two teeth out. He is scared of his crate, and I cannot get him into it without help. Chuck Johnson came over the morning of his appointment and caught him and helped me shove him in. He howled bitterly on the 10-minute ride to the vet. She took out the teeth. Told me to give him antibiotics and to squirt some pain killer into his mouth. What a dreamer. I couldn't get near that mouth.

I had to take him into her a couple of days later for a recheck because he

Bill

refused his meds. Actually, I couldn't get the meds near him. Gloria came this time to help me get him in the crate. We succeeded. On the way over he had diarrhea all over himself and the crate. He had to have a bath, an injection and a new examination—$90 more. The whole thing cost me over $600, more than I would pay for my own teeth, maybe!

Now he is back and as friendly as he ever is. Eating well and rubbing against my legs. I assume he is feeling better too, the poor thing. He is a good cat for my old age, as long as his teeth hold out.

Arlene Starkweather and me.

Papyrus Plant

I had no opinion about the papyrus plant at all. It just occupied a space in the yard a corner and did a good job. Also, it was given to me by Arlene Starkweather, a friend of mine. She had given me other plants too.

I did not realize until sometime later (when she told me accidentally) that all of the plants she gave me were ones the Landscaping Committee had told her to remove from her yard because she had not gotten permission to plant them and they didn't fit into Foxwood's master plan of Landscaping (whatever that was). I was her way of objecting.

She knew I was such a tightwad that I would plant anything anyone gave me. For three reasons: I was Swiss and they are a very thrifty people; it was living, why should I end its life?; and I had a big yard. I got by with several plants from Arlene because of our big yard.

The mowers simply didn't notice them. Once or twice I was called on it by the head of the landscape committee. He or she (who remembers, for they changed at every yearly election) went around with the head of the commercial company doing our lawns that year. (They changed often because of mass irritation from the people of Foxwood who are different from the committees of Foxwood or the Board of Foxwood).

Anyway this person was doing a more thorough job than most of the

others— notice I don't say better. He/she was commenting on the various plants I had which did not agree with his/her master sheet of plants of the landscape committee. I had various excuses which were either ignored or rejected.

In some cases though he/she liked Arlene's plants in my yard. (Of course I did not tell them they were Arlene's or that would have disqualified them immediately).

I remember one looking at the variegated hibiscus. and saying "I like it! What is it?" I replied that it was a variegated hibiscus. He had never heard of it. That was no surprise to ne because generally the landscapers only remembered the name of a few plants and according to my two friends who are master gardeners it was not a variegated hibiscus. It was something with a Latin name. But Arlene said it was, so I went by her.

They came to the next plant though, and they both had a fit about it. It was the papyrus. It turns out it is impossible to trim a papyrus with a chain saw and it has to be done with clippers. This takes valuable time and costs money. That is why the Foxwood landscape chair did not like it.

The other landscaper thought it did not look good where it was, and that it would eventually grow too large. I asked him to define "eventually." He gave me a hard look.

"About 15 years."

I told him I was 80 and in 15 years I would be 95 and would probably not miss it then—although I am 94 now and I think I would.

Anyway he laughed at me, so I had to think of a better reason or they would for sure take the papyrus down and then I would have to find another plant, and I liked the papyrus.

So I told them the truth: and it stunned them both and they looked at me solemnly and with a certain amount of respect mixed in with fear. I told them it was an ancient plant. In biblical times the Baby Moses slept in a papyrus bush and escaped being slaughtered!

They walked away from me and from the whole yard. (whoopee!). I could hear them faintly, "...religious nut, leave her alone." Now that was really silly because I am a humanist and an atheist. I do belong to the Unitarian Universalist Congregation of Venice which respects all faiths, and philosophies such as Buddhism and atheism who do not believe in God. Humanists on the whole do not believe in God, they believe in humans.

I let it go. Explaining my philosophy was not worth losing a living plant. Especially not a papyrus given to me by my good friend, Arlene, who died three years ago. They were right about one thing though—it did grow too large. It became so big it was taking up the whole side of the house.

I conferred with my friends the two master gardeners and they recommended digging it up and putting in a hibiscus. This disturbed me, because the papyrus was really just doing its job—living and growing.

To check on my experts I asked Henry, a member of the UU congregation in Venice, who is also a leader in the Sarasota Democratic Party. He told me once he was a master gardener, so i thought another opinion on the papyrus was easy enough to get, free and might be illuminating, especially from a Democrat.

Alas, it was not. He agreed with the other two. So I had the papyrus removed and replaced with a shocking pink hibiscus. This time I even took it through the landscaping committee. The chair was next door arguing with my neighbor about her bromeliads and saw the men removing the papyrus.

"Good" she exclaimed. "And what are you putting in?" taking out her notebook. I told her. So the hibiscus got approved.